1992

The Real Estate Investor's Q & A Book

Hugh Holbert
as told to
Ron Tepper

John Wiley & Sons, Inc.

New York   Chichester   Brisbane   Toronto   Singapore

Library of Congress Cataloging-in-Publication Data

Holbert, Hugh, 1939–
    The real estate investor's Q & A book / by Hugh Holbert as told to
Ron Tepper.
        p. cm.
    Includes index.
    ISBN 0-471-54032-3 (cloth). — ISBN 0-471-54031-5 (paper)
    1. Real estate investment. I. Tepper, Ron, 1937– . II. Title.
III. Title: The real estate investor's Q and A book.
HD1382.5.H65   1991
332.63'24—dc20   91-3564

Contents

Introduction

Ever since the first cave dwellers posted nameplates in front of their new hillside homes, real estate has been one of the few universal commodities that civilization has always prized and desired.

But prizing a commodity and making the right investment decision are two different things. Where do you buy? How do you buy? How can you determine the value of two homes adjacent to each other? How can you determine whether the house down the street is worth more than the one around the corner? How do you know what to look for when inspecting a home, strip center, minimall, office building, or industrial site?

Real estate investment can be extremely profitable if buyers know that they must not only kick the tires but see what is inside them.

In this book you learn exactly how to evaluate those "tires" and, at the same time, how to determine the type of air with which they are filled.

Investors do not need a license to be successful at real estate investing. They do, however, have to know what to ask, what to look for, and how to evaluate investments—in other words, some common sense, observation, and knowledge.

The Real Estate Investor's Q & A Book specifies exactly how to master those steps . . . and it is the first book that details how to evaluate and judge investments in a practical, how to manner. It is a book that can be read by the layman or the professional. The step-by-step suggestions and advice are all based on more than 30 years of my practical experience in law and real estate.

It is also based on solid evidence that real estate is the best investment any person can make. Every so often, an economic pundit comes along who predicts a great real estate crash . . . the end of the industry . . . or a drying up of demand. Yet, throughout the centuries, through wars, famine, depression, and recession, the Great Dream—the Great American Dream—continues to be home ownership. Certainly, there are times when real estate appreciation slows, when the market slumps and when nothing moves. But, in the long run, there is no better investment—for investors who know what they are doing.

In my years in the business, I have found that real estate is like a game . . . it can be fun and rewarding. But, like any game, you must know the rules, practice, and study before you play. For the prepared players, real estate investment will not only be rewarding, but it can also be the road to financial independence.

1

The Questions Buyers
Should Ask

How can anyone lose—especially when it comes to buying real
estate in a part of the country where there is demand?

That question went through Harry Arnold's mind as he carefully eyed the beginning construction of a large, two-story office
building alongside a busy intersection. The office complex was
the first of its size to be constructed in the location, and Harry
rubbed his hands together in anticipation as he thought about the
return on his potential investment.

The location was a relatively new suburban community. It
was located about 40 miles from a bustling, growing downtown
area, and had developed quickly. In less than 10 years, the suburban community had gone from a sleepy village of a few thousand
residents to a fully incorporated city of more than 23,000. With

the population explosion had come a dramatic growth in the number of new, local businesses. Although a good percentage of the community's residents commuted daily to the downtown area, a growing number were finding employment in the suburban area through a burgeoning service sector. Within the city was a rapidly expanding light manufacturing base, as well.

Harry was ready to invest in a building that was next to one of the busiest thoroughfares in the state. The building would be in the first major office complex—so how could he miss?

There are pitfalls that are seldom thought about when an investor sees the prospects of a substantial return for an investment. Before any investor succumbs to the temptation to back the first commercial venture in an area, there are questions that should be asked and answered.

Q: What might be wrong with being the first investor to build in an area?

The builder or investor who pioneers an area is taking a risk because there is no scientific way to determine whether people are willing to rent or buy in the community.

Q: Do large companies have any advantages over single investors or small builders when it comes to determining whether an area is suited for building and/or investment?

Large companies have the benefit of market research. They usually conduct thorough market studies, and they know if there are tenants and/or buyers for the project. In addition, they usually have the capital to sustain themselves if business is slow. Small builders or investors do not usually have this luxury. They have to be more careful, especially when they are the first to invest in an area.

Q: Can an individual or small group of investors check on the validity of a project if nothing has previously been built in the area?

Not really. As a rule, it is best for first time investors to shy away from "pioneering" an area. The risk is too high.

Q: Are there other ways that small investors can make money in areas that are being pioneered?

Yes, there is one way. If you, the investor, find an area you believe will be excellent for investment, hold back; do not invest. Let someone else develop the first building and/or complex. Watch the results. If the property is rented or sold with little trouble, that is a sign that the area is good for investment. In other words, let someone else do the pioneering. Be the second or third in the market. The return may not be as great, but then neither will the risk. This fact is illustrated in the fast-food industry. Most of the time, fast-food restaurants will wait for a leader—usually McDonald's—to choose a location. McDonald's is the pioneer, and it is a good one because it has the market research and other resources necessary to determine if an area is viable. Once McDonald's opens, and the traffic becomes evident, other fast-food restaurants will locate nearby. This principle is true in real estate investment, as well. Let the major companies make the major financial commitments.

Q: Are there physical barriers that can hinder the success of a real estate project?

Yes, and at times they are not obvious. A builder may have selected a location that is appealing to customers and that appears to have an ample flow of traffic, yet there can be physical barriers that may interfere with the profitability of the project. For instance, there may be a median that blocks access to the project from one side of the street. If a shopping center is being built, the investors may suddenly find that tenants balk at leasing space because half of their customer base cannot find easy access. This does not mean that the entire half will go somewhere else, but an investor who has funds in a highly competitive venture, such as a shopping center, wants to make sure that nothing can hinder people from physically entering.

Q: Are there psychological barriers that can hinder a project?

Definitely. If an investor has built a project in a part of town that people are not accustomed to frequenting, the development may not lease or sell simply because people are not used to traveling to it. For instance, an office building may have all the amenities a tenant could want, however, it may attract few tenants because it is in a part of town where people are not used to seeing an office building.

Q: During the past few years, there has been an increasing trend for similar businesses to locate close to one another. What does this mean to the commercial investor?

This trend presents an important lesson for investors, best illustrated by automobile dealers and their showrooms. In the past, dealers preferred to be away from direct competitors. They felt that if their dealership were the only one in the area, they would have a captive buyer once the consumer entered. Although this proved to be true in some cases, for the most part, dealers discovered that consumers wanted a choice. They also found that when the consumer had more choices, they were more willing to buy. Hence the emergence of the auto malls, a block-long, or even mile-long, strip where consumers can visit a variety of automotive showrooms. When consumers emerge from shopping, they often believe they have seen everything, and are ready to buy.

Notice this same phenomenon in the fast-food industry, which is developing fast-food malls. Even enclosed malls now increasingly locate all food in the same area. The lesson is obvious. Investors who see two or three car dealerships near a parcel of land they want to develop should build a structure that would suit another auto dealer.

Q: Is there any problem with investing in commercial (or other) ventures located in familiar areas?

There can be. Because an investor knows a section of town and believes it is good for investment, does not mean it is. The fact that investors know the area may cause them to lose their objectivity. Always research thoroughly. Check traffic patterns and other similar businesses or complexes in the area. Are they doing well? Just being familiar with an area does not indicate whether it is viable for your investment.

Q: Do consumer laws protect the commercial investor as well as they do the residential investor?

No, definitely not. When it comes to commercial properties, consumer protection laws, which are so prevalent in the residential arena, are virtually nonexistent in the commercial field. The law views the commercial investor as someone who is more sophisticated, and consequently not in need of consumer protection laws. In fact, in many states there are few, if any, disclosure requirements made on the seller and broker when it comes to commercial real estate. Unfortunately, many investors do not realize this caveat and, to their chagrin, find out first-hand.

Q: What does the vacancy rate tell you about a commercial building?

A high vacancy rate can indicate a number of problems. For instance, perhaps the location is undesirable. It may be an extraordinary appearing building, but it may not be convenient or located where people want to rent office space. Compare it to other similar properties in the area. If they all have a high vacancy rate, it may simply be economics and the fact that business in general is slow.

Q: Many builders offer you the opportunity to invest in a commercial property without visiting it. Is there a problem with this approach?

Yes, there can be. As a rule, investors should not put money into any development they cannot see or inspect. If it is worth putting hard earned cash into, then it is certainly worth taking the time to personally visit the property. Visit it. See the surroundings. You may be surprised at what you find.

Q: In a shopping center, what is an anchor tenant, and how important are they to the center?

Anchor tenants are the major stores that occupy the center. Usually, these tenants are chains or members of a well-known franchise, and they will occupy one end of the development or the other. They are the stores that are usually responsible for drawing customers to the center. Anchor tenants usually do heavy advertising and can benefit all the other establishments in the center. If they are good, reputable businesses with excellent reputations, they are going to attract similar clientele. A quality enterprise as an anchor tenant becomes a selling point when it comes time to try and convince other, well-known businesses to locate to the center.

Q: What part does an anchor tenant play in the value of a mall investment?

A quality enterprise—if it is an anchor tenant—becomes a selling point when it comes time to market the center. Investors find they will have an easier time marketing (selling) a mall with a well-known, quality, anchor tenant in place. A good example is a store such as Nordstrom's. Known for its quality merchandise and superb service, a Nordstrom's would significantly increase the value of a mall should the investors decide to sell it. At the same time, investors can consider centers with quality tenants as investments that will be more expensive compared to those surrounding it.

Q: Do smaller, so-called strip centers or minimalls (usually anywhere from 4 to 10 or 12 retail outlets), have certain tenants that are more desirable than others?

Aside from quality, traffic-drawing anchor tenants (i.e., convenience stores), investors in minimalls should be aware that there are certain establishments that may seem desirable but actually leave a lasting, negative impression on the mall. For example, pizza and submarine shops. These retail outlets cook, and the smell from the ovens is virtually impossible to get out of the walls if the owners ever close shop or move. There is nothing wrong with having a well-known pizza shop or other type restaurant in a minimall. However, investors should be aware of what could happen if the store should close and another restaurant is not waiting to locate in the center.

Q: How should investors weigh ingress and egress in a minimall or other similar commercial investment?

This is critically important. Obviously, if a customer has to struggle to get in the driveway, or finds it almost impossible to exit the center because of traffic conditions, the center may not be a good investment. Convenience is of prime concern to consumers, especially those who frequent many of the minimalls or strip centers. If they have problems entering or exiting they are not going to shop in the center and, of course, if they do not shop there, stores will not be profitable.

Q: What do prospective anchor tenants in a mall look for before leasing space?

Aside from the obvious ingress and egress, some stores perceive other stores to be beneath them and will not locate in the same mall. A Neiman-Marcus or Marshall Fields may not blend with a K-Mart or Sears. Astute mall owners know it is critically important to attract good anchors, because they set the standard for customers as well as other stores.

Q: How can investors check parking and its impact on a commercial investment?

Investors should never assume that just because the structure has been built according to building codes, sufficient parking has been provided. Many cities are lenient, and as long as there is sufficient space for the businessperson who is leasing, and a secretary, they may not care about space for the visitor or client. Or they may allow an insufficient number of visitor spaces. Investors should check the parking lot themselves. In the case of an office building, it is best to do this in the middle of the week (a Wednesday or Thursday) during late morning. Usually, at this time of the day, everyone is in their office and you can get a good idea of the parking situation. Is it jammed? If so, you may have a serious parking problem that would impact other, potential tenants, and cause them to decline a lease. In the case of a strip center or minimall, parking is best evaluated during the early evening, when traffic is at a peak for convenience stores, restaurants, and other similar establishments that may be in the center.

Q: How can different parking needs impact the tenant mix in a commercial building or strip shopping center?

Certain tenants will require more parking than others. A restaurant, for example, is going to need more spaces per square foot than a furniture store. Although there may be a dozen or so people shopping in the latter, there can be several hundred in the former. More than one center has lost tenants because of poor planning when it came to parking.

Q: How can an investor use rent rates to help determine the worth of an investment?

If an investor is contemplating buying a center or commercial building, rents of nearby properties should be checked and compared. Ideally, the rent of the building an investor is thinking of purchasing should be lower than surrounding, competitive structures. This gives the new owner/investor a competitive advantage when going after renters.

However, the investor should analyze why the rents in the proposed building are lower. An investor may be told that one building is $1.50 per square foot per month, and another is $2. At first, the investor may assume that the less expensive building— let us say it is the one you are thinking of purchasing—has the advantage when it comes to competing for tenants because of the lower rent. It may not. The building with the higher rent may include janitorial service and maintenance. To make a valid comparison, investors need all the details. Make sure you get them.

When evaluating rents, make sure you do more than determine how much they are. Why are they higher or lower? Is it just a case of the landlord not keeping up with the times, or has the owner purposely kept the rates low to maintain a low vacancy rate and make the property more appealing when it came to selling? If the rents are low, can they be raised? Will you be able to retain tenants if you raise them?

Q: If a potential investor is thinking about putting money into a center, and he discovers a major tenant is about to leave, what things should be checked before the investor goes ahead with his commitment?

Obviously, the reason for the forthcoming vacancy should be checked. This can be critically important to the viability of an investment. For example, assume the major tenant is a nationally recognized fast-food chain. If this tenant leaves, it is not likely that another fast-food operation will be interested in the location. If the large, nationally recognized store cannot be profitable, others will shy away from the site.

If the vacating major tenant is a recognized grocery store or supermarket, you will have difficulty persuading another major market to accept the location as viable. Supermarkets are anchor tenants and vitally important to the profitability of a center that has them. Lose one and it can be disastrous.

Q: Is it possible for office buildings to have anchor tenants and, if so, what importance do they have to the investment value of the building?

Anchor tenants in malls are well-known stores that project a good image, draw traffic, and cause other retailers to locate in the mall. Office buildings have anchor tenants just as shopping centers and malls do. A major bank would be an example of an excellent anchor tenant. Finance companies prefer locating with major banks to pick up potential borrowers who may not be able to meet the tough lending criteria of a bank. Professionals such as CPAs and attorneys also prefer locating in proximity to a reputable, prestigious bank. And once these tenants are in place, insurance agents, architects, and others will jump in and lease space.

Anchor tenants are more than just banks and well-known department stores. In a small community, an anchor might be a store owner who is actively involved in the community (i.e., chamber of commerce, service clubs, church, city council, etc.) and who has an excellent reputation for being fair and honest. Others will want to locate close to this type of tenant.

Q: How can the length of a lease help an investor determine the viability of a property?

Before buying, investors should carefully evaluate tenants and determine how long the leases have to run. If possible—and this can be ascertained—talk to the management of some of these anchors. Find out if they plan to move. If not, try signing them to a new, long-term lease as part of the purchase. If the old tenants are offered new leases with favorable rates and decline, the purchaser should do some careful reevaluation of the property and determine the exact reason for the anchor rejecting the new lease.

Q: What is a short-term versus a long-term lease?

Generally, a short-term lease is 2 years or less. Medium will run 2 to 10 years, and long-term over 10 years.

Q: When investing, should all available funds be put into a project to get the maximum amount of building and return, or should investors seek to have a cushion?

Never sink every available dollar into any commercial investment. A good rule is that it is better to have four or five moderately priced investments than one very large one. Four or five enables you to spread your risk in different areas. If something goes wrong with the one investment, you are stuck. If, however, you have spread the risk over four or five projects, perhaps, one or two can be sold if something goes wrong and if there is a cash shortage.

Q: What role can tax play in dictating why investors should put their money into more than one project?

Assume, for example, you purchase a property for $300,000. Years later, the property has appreciated to $400,000, and you want to sell it. When you sell (assuming a cash sale), you will have a minimum capital gain of $100,000, and the federal tax will be due and payable. You would be taxed in the highest bracket because your gain occurred in one year.

Now, suppose you had invested in four different properties at $75,000 apiece, and each appreciated to $100,000. The gain would be the same ($100,000 or 4 × $25,000), but you would have an advantage because you could sell the property as needed. In other words, you could space the sales. This potentially lowers your tax liability ($25,000 for one building versus $100,000). Another benefit that accrues to investors who spread their funds is that they will usually find it easier to locate a buyer for a $100,000 than for a $400,000 property.

Q: Although there are many different variables to weigh when it comes to commercial investing, is there any one element that counts more than any other when it comes to putting money into a property?

Location, location, location. A strip center away from the traffic flow may not be a sound place to put your money. An isolated office building that is blocks away from other similar complexes may not be either. Where is the property? Is it close to the customers who will use it?

Q: When examining a commercial structure, what are some of the physical characteristics every investor should scrutinize carefully?

Investors should examine the roof, windows, construction materials, heating and air-conditioning, electrical, and sewage systems of any prospective property (or have an expert do it for them). Take, for instance, air conditioning. Is it an air conditioning or a heat pump system? Both systems cool air, however, the heat pump can also heat. A heat pump takes outside air and either cools or heats it as needed. An air conditioner takes humidity out of the air; the heat pump does not. Thus, if you have a potential investment in an area with high humidity, and it has a heat pump, your tenants may still be uncomfortable. Perhaps that may even be the reason why the building has a consistently lower occupancy rate than a similar structure across the street. Determine the age of the air-conditioning unit or heat pump system, and inquire about the manufacturer or distributor. What is the life expectancy of the unit? Ask to see repair bills, and call the manufacturer's service representative for an opinion.

Q: How does glass impact the cost of a commercial and/or apartment building?

Glass can add significantly to the cost of a building. Basically, there are two types, tempered or regular glass. Regular glass comes in various thicknesses ranging from one-sixteenth of an inch to one-quarter inch *plate glass*. The major difference is the way both break and shatter.

If you throw a baseball at tempered glass, it will probably bounce back. If tempered glass does break, it will not shatter but will break into sharp one-quarter-inch chunks that will not normally cause any serious injury. On the other hand, regular glass can shatter into dangerous, pointed, sharp shards. As a result, many states require all new buildings to have tempered glass, and many states are beginning to look at older buildings and pass laws requiring the replacement of regular glass. Glass shower enclosures in apartments also should be carefully checked. Obviously, if a building has regular glass, there is a chance the investor may have to replace it. And, because of the dangers, insurance rates may be higher as well.

13

Q: Why is a new building generally a safer investment than an old one?

Generally, a newer building will be a safer investment when it comes to building codes and requirements. Obviously, a structure that is only 4 or 5 years old has been constructed under recent codes, and features such as tempered versus regular glass will usually not be an issue. However, if you are looking at a 20-, 30-, or 40-year-old structure, there may be significant hidden additional cost. In addition, newer buildings are better insulated resulting in lower cost for heating and cooling.

Q: What pitfalls do investors sometimes fail to consider when it comes to older buildings?

If you purchase a building and decide to remodel a portion of it, the government agencies may require that the entire building—and not just a portion—be brought up to code. Investors will also find that older buildings usually have inadequate parking because when they were built the codes may not have been as strict.

Q: What are "as built" plans and why are they important to investors in commercial property?

Before purchasing a commercial property, investors want to make sure they obtain a set of "as built" plans from the seller. When a building is constructed, the contractor obviously follows a set of plans; however, during this period there may be obstacles the builder encounters that make it necessary to run a line or pipe in an area that is not indicated on the plans. Some cities require that the contractor submit a set of plans as modified, whereas others do not. Usually, the city—or owner—has a copy of these plans. "As built" plans reflect any modifications made during the course of construction that deviate from the original construction plans. They are a must, especially if the structure needs repairs, and can save thousands of dollars in repairs. For example, if plans have been modified and a water line breaks in the wall, the owner may be faced with tearing out an entire wall if updated ("as built") plans showing the exact location of the water line are not available.

Q: How do exterior materials impact an investment?

Exterior materials can make a significant difference in maintenance. Some are built with low-maintenance materials, whereas others require constant attention. Check the building and compare the exterior. One of the most common differences is stucco versus rock sheathing. Rock sheathing is cement mixed with aggregate and sand and cut in sections. It requires virtually zero maintenance throughout its lifetime, compared to stucco, which needs constant maintenance. Wood, of course, is a material that requires constant maintenance. It may be cheaper in the construction phase, but is much more expensive in the long run. When building or buying, the investor should weigh these considerations.

Q: Why don't commercial buildings have the construction problems that might be found in a single-family residence?

When commercial plans are approved, the agencies involved know that the building may have to hold large numbers of people and support excessive amounts of weight. Therefore, the structure is built to different standards. Generally, it is "beefier" and more solid than the single-family structure. Still, there can be problems. There is no better example than the hotel that collapsed a few years ago in the midwest because of faulty engineering and/or construction. Thus, the reliability, past experience, and reputation of an engineer and/or contractor are important. If it is a new center, determine who the architect is and who the contractor is. How long have they been in business? What is their reputation? What other similar structures have they built?

15

Q: How should investors utilize a "contractor's licensing board" to help them when it comes to developing the land in which they have an investment?

Many states have a "contractor's licensing board," and they will inform you of any complaints that have been filed against a contractor. Make sure you hire a contractor who has a reputation for completing projects on schedule. Even if an investor is not in a hurry to complete the project, for each month over schedule you are losing income from the building while paying interest on the construction loan.

Q: How can investors try to protect funds that they are about to put into a building?

Hire an inspector to examine the structural factors in a building. (To find one you can check the telephone book under engineers, with a subheading "structural"). That is a good idea, but astute investors do not completely rely on an outsider. Remember, an inspector is searching for deficiencies, and not necessarily comparing structural materials. For example, the use of stucco is not a deficiency, and therefore would not be listed as one by the inspector. Yet, the astute investor would immediately realize that a building with rock sheathing could command a higher price, and might be a better investment than one with stucco.

Q: How should an investor use a real estate broker to determine the viability of an investment?

Talk to real estate brokers who have nothing to gain by the buying or selling of the property. There are many who are tuned into the market, and may know something about the structure that may not be obvious. Question them about the neighborhood and about businesses that may be moving in or out.

Q: What value is the local chamber of commerce in evaluating an investment?

The local chamber is an excellent source to determine movement in the area. For instance, the chamber director will usually know if any major employers are planning to enter or leave the area. The chamber can also supply you with growth trends of the community, and many have a forecast as to the area's economic development. The chamber people will also know about upcoming legislation that could make investing in a structure risky or more costly.

Q: What can help wanted ads tell you about a potential commercial investment?

Few help wanted ads indicate that not many employers are looking for help. A low demand for help means there are few jobs in the area. Few jobs could indicate an employment problem. Take this one step farther: an employment problem, indicated by a lack of jobs, means that consumers in the area do not have excess funds. Thus, if an investor is thinking about buying or building a minimall, strip center, or any commercial development, there may not be the demand.

Q: What should investors be wary of when it comes to schools that are in close proximity to a residence they are thinking about buying?

They need to determine that the school and the residence are in the same district. A home might be a block or two away from a school, but because of how district boundaries are drawn the children may be attending a school two miles away.

Q: Although most residential homes are more expensive when they are next to a school, under what conditions might investors find that the school is a minus?

17

Not everyone wants the school (and kids) next door to their house. This feature is usually a plus when selling to a family, but it can diminish the potential market for a property if you decide to sell later and the majority of the buyers are older couples or singles without children. When investors buy in a residential area, they should keep this in mind—especially if they intend to sell within a short period of time.

Q: What should investors examine before settling on a residence in an area with wide streets?

Although wide streets in a residential development offer better turning and parking convenience, they frequently turn out to be places where people step on the accelerator simply because the street is wide. Before buying, it would be wise for investors to monitor the traffic flow. Are people driving excessively fast? Speeders detract from the value of any residential investment.

Q: What should investors determine before buying in a residential area that is close to a main thoroughfare or highway?

Is there commercial activity nearby that ends up generating trucks and larger vehicles through the tract? If so, this is going to detract from the value of the area. Before investing, determine the traffic patterns. If the tract is impacted by commercial traffic, it should be priced less than other nearby tracts that are not affected. Investors should also remember that commercial traffic will have a negative impact on the residence's value should they decide to sell.

Q: What should investors determine if a residence is next to a vacant parcel of land?

Find out who owns it, and for what the parcel is zoned. There is, however, no guarantee that the owner of a piece of land will not get a zone change. Suppose the owner of a piece of land zoned for residential development passes a petition around to have the zoning changed so that a convenience store can be built. The neighbors may love the idea and sign, because the store is not next to them, but it could prove a disaster for the owner of the adjoining residential property.

Always check with the local government to see what is planned for the area. Nearly every community has a master plan, and it can be a valuable resource tool for investors who want to see which way the area is going. Even if the plan indicates a parcel of land is marked for one thing, that is no guarantee that the zoning will not be changed. Someone who invests in a piece of land with an acre of vacant land next to it could end up with a church, park, convenience store, or gas station next door. There are no guarantees.

Even if you buy a home with a beautiful hillside behind it, there are no guarantees it will stay that way. A developer could come along, obtain the proper zoning, and end up cutting into the hill and constructing improvements. This has happened more than once to the dismay of the owners.

Always try to picture the property fully developed. If you are next to a commercially zoned parcel, imagine how a convenience store would impact the investment.

Q: Should an investor purchase a home in an area in which there is vacant land, what precautionary steps should be taken to ensure knowledge about any proposed zoning or planning changes?

Call the local planning and zoning department. Request that your name be put on the mailing list for all proposed zoning and/or planning changes. Thus, if someone decides to ask for an unusual zone change or seeks to amend a plan, the investor will know, and will have a chance to express an opposing view before any regulations are changed.

Q: Can homes differ in appreciation, even though they are in the same tract?

As a guide, you can assume that homes on primary ingress and egress streets will appreciate more slowly than those within the tract, and not on primary streets.

Q: What are the positives—and negatives—of cul-de-sacs?

Cul-de-sac streets have definite advantages. An abundance within a tract usually means that the area will not get much drive-through traffic. Cul-de-sacs are like a maze and they discourage drive-throughs, which is, of course, a definite benefit to owners.

Every positive, however, usually has a negative—as do cul-de-sacs. Remember, in a cul-de-sac the homes at the end of the street have less curb space and, therefore, fewer spaces for guests to park their vehicles. Parking can be a problem for residents who live outside cul-de-sacs. This is especially true of developments that are close to the ocean. Although the investor may see the property during the week, it is best to visit it on the weekend (preferably a warm one), so the full impact of beachgoers is evident.

Q: What is the difference between homes that are 10 years old (or less), and those over 10 years?

First, homes that are 10 years old or less are generally better insulated, or have dual glazed windows or thermal panes, which means lower heating and cooling bills. And, in today's rising energy cost environment, those costs can be significant. The all-electric home is a thing of the past. In all-electric homes the heating payment in winter often exceeds the mortgage payment.

Q: How should an investor inspect the interior of a home?

There are several ways. One of the best—and most thorough—is the "right wall" inspection. No matter what you do, when you enter the residence, stay to the right and keep to the right. If you continue along that path, you will end up inspecting every wall. (If there is a second floor, repeat the technique upstairs.) Inspection consists of opening and closing every door and window, checking all electrical sockets and switches, looking at the ceiling for wet spots or stains, and checking the wallpaper or wallcovering for crinkling or gathering.

Q: What should an investor do if something is found to be wrong when inspecting a home that is for sale?

Make a written inquiry of the seller, and expect a written response. Do not assume that the stain on the ceiling is from a leaking roof. It could be a water system failure. As of this writing, not all states have full-disclosure laws. In fact, fewer than 10 do.

Q: What do receipts for home repairs tell an investor who is planning to purchase a home?

Receipts for repairs can reveal a great deal about the condition of the home and the qualifications of the person who made the repairs, for example, was the repair made by a contractor or the homeowner. If the home has natural gas, and the owner replaced a hot water heater without a contractor, an incorrect repair could be life-threatening. Usually, most hot water heaters are in the garage and they are on an elevated platform. Hot water heaters on the ground in the garage are dangerous. If the owner works on cars, the fumes from the fuel from the automobile can be ignited from the pilot light on the heater, and set off an explosion and fire. Heaters are elevated so the fumes dissipate before they reach the pilot and burners in the heater.

21

Q: Which is generally better, copper or galvanized pipe?

Copper has a significant advantage. It lasts longer and will not corrode as fast.

Q: Why should a professional roofer be used in an inspection?

Hire a professional roofer to inspect the roof if it is more than seven or eight years old. In some cases, it is possible to obtain a written certification for the roof from the roofer. It represents the roofer's opinion as to the remaining "life" in years. This is only an opinion, but it does come from a professional.

Does it have shake, light wood, heavy wood, or spanish tile, or one of the new, synthetic roofs. On a continuum, shake would be the least desirable and synthetic the most. Shake would also be the least costly, and synthetic the most. The prime difference, aside from the material's life, is fire resistance.

Synthetic roofs may look like tile or wood, but they are usually made from a fire-resistant material and will last longer than wood or shake. Shake, of course, has been the subject of many articles, and, in newer tracts, builders try to avoid using the material because of the fire hazard. Tile along with some of the synthetics offers the ultimate fire protection. Some states are considering passing building codes that will preclude the use of wood as a roofing material.

A homeowner who replaces one of these hazardous roofing materials with a fire-retardant material can spend in excess of $10,000, depending on location and size of the roof. In areas in which there is not a high fire danger, this may seem to be a moot point. However, fire is always a factor. Even areas with an abundance of rainfall have Fourth of July firework's problems.

Q: When should investors definitely check the condition of a roof on a residence?

As a rule, if a roof is relatively new (i.e., a year or less) there is little chance of anything being wrong. But if the home is seven or eight years old, hire someone to check it.

Q: What can the condition of a fence tell you about the home?

If the fence is pulled away from the wall/house, find out which is pulling away from which. Is the house pulling away from the fence, or vice versa? If the fence is pulling away from the building, it can generally be easily repaired. If the house is settling or moving from the fence, this could result in a considerable sum of money to correct.

Q: What are double-pane windows, and why are they important?

For those investing in residences that are located in very hot or very cold climates, an excellent feature in a home is the double-pane window. The window has two panes instead of one, with an air gap in between. In the summer, the glass facing the outside will be hot, while the pane inside will be cool. The air space in between absorbs the heat and keeps it out of the house. In winter, the double pane helps prevent loss of heat. Recently windows have been developed that have a rating of R-19, the equivalent of an insulated wall! These windows are still in the development stage and are not available, as yet.

Q: What should investors look for when examining walls in a residence?

You can examine almost any wall and find it is not square or flat. Most wall surfaces are irregular, and investors should not expect them to be totally flat. The supporting timbers (i.e., the 4 × 4s and 2 × 4s) almost always cause a bulge because of the curing process, and they can warp slightly; that is normal. However, if the wallpaper is wrinkled or gathered, it may mean there is stress somewhere and something is either sinking or moving.

Q: How should water pressure be checked before investing in a residence, and what can it tell an investor about the home?

Check the water supply by turning on the taps. Examine the pressure. Does the water come out forcefully, or does it lack pressure? Diminished pressure could indicate everything from a broken or leaking pipe to pipes that are clogged and corroded. Or, it could mean that a valve under the sink is not opened properly.

Q: How should the electricity be checked in a home?

Check the electricity by turning on the light switches, and move plugs from one socket to another to make sure they all work. If one does not, ask why? Try all the sockets and all the switches.

Q: What is a mechanic's lien and how can it impact the investment?

A mechanic's lien is a lien put on a property by a supplier of materials or a worker or company that has done work on it and was not paid. The investor can lose the residence if the lien is followed by a lawsuit to foreclose against the property by the supplier or contractor who did work on the home and did not get paid. As protection the purchaser should require the title company to supply a "mechanic's lien" endorsement. If you obtain an endorsement, and if there was unpaid work, and a lien is subsequently recorded, the title insurance company will be obligated to defend your interest in the property. In the event the title insurance company is required to settle such a claim, it will normally have recourse against the seller—who obviously did not reveal everything.

24

Q: Because full disclosure (on the part of the seller) is not required in every state, are there guidelines that investors should keep in mind when questioning sellers?

Yes. Always ask about anything that bothers you. Sometimes investors shy away from asking questions because they think their questions may offend the owners (they won't). If you have this fear, you can always joke about it. For example, why not say something like "I remember my grandpa when he bought a home . . . He climbed to the attic, looked in the closets, and did all those weird things. We all laughed about it. I hope you don't mind, but some of those weird habits have stuck with me."

Q: What qualities usually create the most problem for investors?

Greed and trust are the human frailties that create the most problems for investors.

Greed causes us to jump at a deal that "is too good to pass up." Astute investors know that you do not get something for nothing. They know that the higher the return, the greater the risk. When motivated by greed, the investor's concerns are overriden by the thought of a high return.

Greed runs hand in hand with trust. Before someone can tempt you with a "great return" on your investment, the investor will generally "trust" the person making the proposal. He has usually done something to gain the trust and confidence of the investor.

Trust is the other edge of the sword. To believe someone without fully reading the paperwork, and having an attorney check things out, is foolish. Both residential and commercial investors find themselves guilty of this practice. Recently, a reputable group that had been putting together reliable real estate limited partnerships for a decade called a friend of mine about a new project. They described the project, and told him there would be two kinds of investors. The first would provide funds for a 120-

day period until second trust deed funds were obtained. At the end of the 120 days, the investors would have the option to invest their monies in a two-year plan that would secure the second trust deed.

A few days later, the paperwork arrived, and without reading anything the investor signed. A month later he received his first interest check; another month went by and he received a second. When the third month came and went without a check, he called. He was told the company was suspending interest payments because of a cash shortage. He asked when he would receive the money back that he (thought) he had invested for four months. At that point he learned that he had signed papers for two years and that the interest payments for two-year investors were suspended.

Three weeks later the investor received another letter. This told of the deeper financial problems of the company and cautioned that investors could lose all their money. The concerned investor called his attorney and (for the first time) had him go through the paperwork. Later that afternoon the attorney called and gave the investor the bad news—there was nothing he could do. The papers he had signed were for two years.

Trust and greed. To some they may appear to be two terms that are far apart, but when it comes to real estate investment, they are the investor's worst enemy.

A popular joke says it best. Trust should be left for the adage on the dollar bill: "In God we trust." All others should pay cash.

2

How to Analyze Residential Properties

In the last quarter of 1990, the National Association of Realtors (NAR), the trade association to which more than 800,000 real estate brokers and sales associates belong, reported the lowest sales figures in a decade, and a decline in the value of the average-priced home. Commercial real estate (i.e., shopping center development, office complexes) also showed a significant drop, and in many areas of the country vacancy rates were at a 10-year high.

Publications ranging from the *Wall Street Journal* to *Newsweek Magazine* proclaimed the demise of the industry and the disappearance of real estate as a viable investment. With these dire reports, why would anyone buy or invest in real estate? Associated Press writer John Cunniff supplied part of the answer in a late October column:

When housing prices are falling and investment analysts are frothing about a collapse of the real estate market, there still is no safer place for your money than the home in which you live. . . . The truth of the statement lies in the historical evidence. It shows that while price declines do occur they are rare and relatively short-lived, and that housing prices recover with the economy and often grow faster than it.

Q: What does real estate tell the investor about economic cycles?

Ray Chappell, the broker/owner of one of the 10 largest independent real estate companies in the country, put it this way:

Traditionally, real estate leads the down cycle and stays ahead of the up cycle. Real estate actually started its demise in late 1988 and early 1989. The cycle usually runs about two years, and that means we should have seen an end to the downturn by late 1990. That's exactly what happened. In October, 1990, for the first time, the number of homes for sale (in one five-state market area) dipped, and the number of sales rose. When that happens, recovery is on the way, and the entire economy should recover shortly thereafter.

Q: How does real estate differ from other investments such as stocks and bonds?

The interesting factor about real estate investment is that like stocks and bonds, it is a national industry with customers in every market. But, unlike buying shares of stock in industries such as banking, automobiles, energy, or electronics, real estate is said to be driven by local conditions. For example, while Los Angeles and Orange County, two communities located in Southern California, were going through a decline in both residential and commercial sales, San Diego—a community less than 100 miles away—was going through a boom period. And, Bakersfield, another community about 100 miles north of Los Angeles, was booming as well. So was Seattle, parts of Florida, and Texas,

28

which was rebounding from lean energy years. At the same time, in the midwest real estate continued a steady 5–6% increase per year.

The reason for the variation is that in real estate each market has its own cycle, and the cycle depends on local economic conditions. When the automobile industry dips, it shows a decline nationally. The same is true of bank or electronic stocks. But that is not the case with real estate. It will be low in one area and high in another. Obviously, the key to successful investing is to buy low and sell high. But how do you know when low is reached in real estate? There are ways for investors to narrow the guesswork by tracking the up-and-down trends of prices in an area.

Q: What technique can investors use to track price trends?

One of the best techniques is to select a tract of homes that has been around for about 20 years. Create a chart and divide it into five-year cycles. For a tract built in 1970, the cycles would be

1970

1975

1980

1985

1990

The first entry would be the average price of the home during those periods. If the home cost $100,000, and it appreciated at 5% for the first five years, the 1975 figure would be $127,630. But if the 1975 figure came in at $130,000 or $120,000, that means the cycle either reached a low (or high) at some point. If investors map the cycle of the tract for 20 years, they may find periods of abnormally high (or low) appreciation.

If the low appreciation occurs at regular intervals, the investor begins to see the shape and length of the cycle. For example, if every three years, appreciation in the tract dropped to 1% (or even 0%) for that particular year, you can surmise that there are some factors that come into play during that period that cause the cycle to hit a trough. If there is a consistency in the troughs, the investor begins to see when the best time for buying occurs.

Q: Is there any sure way that investors can determine real estate trends, and reach a decision as to when is the best time to buy?

This is difficult to determine. Some investors rely on the media. They read the daily newspaper or watch television, and hear about the trends. All the reporters do, however, is gather information and often the data they compile are either too little, too late, or too inaccurate. For instance, the media is always quoting the NAR, but NAR statistics are not always good barometers of where things are going. Like most statistics they tell you where you have been.

Q: What do residential real estate cycles reveal to the investor?

Becoming familiar with the length and economic conditions surrounding a cycle enables the investor to forecast when real estate will slow (an excellent time to buy), and when it is heading up. If, for example, a community depends on defense spending, and there is a government cutback in the industry, that cutback is going to be reflected in the cycle. Perhaps the community does not have a major defense contractor, but it may have sufficient suppliers who depend on a nearby contractor. And when the major contractor suffers, so do the suppliers.

Q: What is meant by the "ripple effect" in real estate?

The so-called "ripple effect," the impact one industry has on other businesses in the area when it cuts back, can be significant. Even diversified communities that may not depend on any one industry can find themselves in trouble if one major industry declines. It is not uncommon to see an industry that accounts for 20% of a community's economy impact 50% of the community because of cutbacks. Not only are industry suppliers hit, but those in unrelated industries who do business with the suppliers can be impacted as well.

Q: What effect does "fear" have when it comes to investing and residential real estate?

People hear about cutbacks and immediately cut discretionary purchases. Restaurant business declines, as well as the auto industry, and purchases in a dozen different industries in a local market.

Even those who may not be impacted by the layoff hold back. There may be many workers in other industries who see their friends lose jobs, and they hold back their purchases, including homebuying. Thus, a significant layoff in one industry is going to impact an entire community, slow real estate (because no one is buying), and start the area on a down cycle.

Compounding the impact of a down cycle is the media, which feasts on bad news. The more gloom and doom people see on television, hear on the radio, and read in the newspaper, the more they tend to believe it and hold back spending. The more people hold back spending, the worse conditions become. It is a self-fulfilling prophecy.

Q: What clues can investors look for to forecast down cycles in real estate in their communities?

It is possible to forecast spending decreases in certain industries. With the government's pressure to balance the budget, defense will continue to take a beating. One thing is clear: the more a community depends on one industry, the greater the chance it has for a down cycle. In areas in which there is economic diversity, no one industry will put the community into a downslide. But in areas in which the entire community depends on one industry—for example, oil in the southwest—an industry reversal or problem will impact the entire area.

Q: How do brokers and real estate agents influence price?

When prospective investors come into a broker's office searching for a certain type of investment, the broker is able to steer them to whatever tract or section they want. This is particularly evident in communities in which properties in one section sell for a significantly higher price than comparable properties in an adjacent section not more than a mile or two away. Yet both have the same amenities, schools, and shopping. Why? Because the broker has chosen (for whatever reason) to influence buyers to purchase in one section rather than the other. Perhaps it is only the broker's personal preference. However, if a host of brokers all feel the same way, they may all be directing buyers to the same area. In doing so, they are creating more demand, depleting supply, and, of course, raising prices more rapidly in one community than another.

Another technique that brokers utilize is one that revolves around inside information. A broker who hears about a new defense contract, or company locating in the area, knows that appreciation will accelerate because of new workers moving in; consequently demand increases. Many brokers buy-in at the beginning of these cycles. They may be selling homes in a tract, and they know the properties will appreciate rapidly, so they invest their own money. By doing so, they deplete the supply, and the prices rise.

In some cases brokers anticipate a rapid escalation in prices and they may put money on three, four, or even five properties.

Then, before the final down payment has to be made or escrow opens, they resell the properties. This technique earned some brokers thousands of extra dollars as a result of property appreciation as well as additional real estate commissions.

Q: Are there examples of real estate prices escalating because of broker activity, and not consumer demand?

There is no better example than Southern California during the mid- to late 1980s, and New England during the mid-1980s. Values literally exploded in each area. People lined up to obtain a lottery number to see if they would be entitled to buy a home. During a three- to five-year period appreciation was double-digit. There were few communities that did not jump 15 to 25% per year.

Two factors were driving the skyhigh prices: first, there were new contracts, a growth in defense, and new businesses moving in; many investors therefore saw this as their last chance to buy. Thus, they scraped, borrowed, and did everything possible to raise down payments to buy a home before it increased another 25% in value. The second factor was the broker influence. Although little has been written about the broker (and sales associate) impact, it had just as much to do with price escalation as other economic factors.

Brokers saw the influx of business and industry. Those who were particularly astute kept abreast of market conditions with chamber of commerce data and economic development information.

Economic development groups are usually part of local, city government and they have an endless amount of data on who might be moving in or out of a community. By putting the information from these two organizations together and adding it to whatever other local rumors and data they may have obtained from local bankers and other businesspeople, real estate brokers and salespeople were in a position to buy property before the demand peaked. They could purchase options on a piece of property, hold it for 60 to 90 days, sell it, and quickly make $5,000–$15,000 in additional profits.

Obviously, these techniques did wonders for the brokers and sales associates who were involved; however, the tactics did little for other investors who were faced with purchasing properties that had been inflated because of broker interference. This cycle of short supply slowed significantly in New England and in California during the late 1980s. Then, suddenly, it ended.

With the entry of the Bush administration, defense cutbacks began and the supply of buyers dwindled. In fact, the cycle headed down so rapidly that some brokers who did not keep abreast of economic developments found themselves holding options on properties that they could not sell. In essence, they had become victims of their own greed.

Q: How do move-up residential buyers impact values?

For the most part, they create additional demand for properties and help push prices up. For example, there was a core of move-up "gamblers" during the 1980s, especially in areas in which there was rapid appreciation. A buyer would come in and invest in a piece of property with a minimum down payment. Often the down payment was so low that the investor had to agree to a mortgage with a balloon that was due in five to seven years, sometimes sooner. At the same time, the investor would also finance the purchase with an adjustable rate mortgage (ARM), which could be obtained at a lower rate of interest, at least for the first year or two.

Some investors had a strategy in which they secured the property for as little as possible. The deposit and/or down payment was minimal as was the monthly holding costs. At other times, investors would put a $5,000 deposit on a home being constructed. Several months later, when the home was completed and had appreciated $40,000 to $50,000, the investor would assign their interest in the property to another person, thereby reaping a substantial profit on a minimum investment. Even brokers followed this strategy.

During the mid-1980s, it was not uncommon to see an investor buy a property in the $250,000–$300,000 range, move into a $600,000–$700,000 investment within two to three years (via the appreciation), hold the new property for another year or so, and then move into a $1 million home. The actual cash involved could be as low as $20,000–$25,000, and the investor owned a $1 million investment. This was a nice, profitable approach—as long as there were no changes in the local economy.

Q: When is a good time to buy residential real estate?

The adage is buy low and sell high. But how does the investor know when things are low? Obviously, many prospective buyers have backed off the real estate market because it has softened in most parts of the country, and they do not see the rapid appreciation. Additionally, the gloom and doom that has been painted by major media has scared the investors. For astute investors, however, this (the early 1990s) could be the best time to buy. Interest rates are low, and appreciation has slowed. There are many bargains in numerous areas.

Q: Are there any special concerns to investigate before buying real estate in the Midwest?

In the Midwest property has consistently appreciated at a steady, but slow pace. Unlike other parts of the country, the Midwest has been more stable and shows less fluctuation in prices and appreciation. The area's major industry, farming, nearly always has a market for its products.

Q: How does real estate in the Northeast compare in value and appreciation to the rest of the country?

The Northeast (New England) went through a boom in growth as a result of rapid growth in the electronics as well as other high tech industries. High tech industries started taking a beating from foreign competition in the mid- to late 1980s, and so did New England real estate. The 25–30% appreciation per year came to an abrupt halt. During this period of time, the Northeast grew in a similar manner to California, however, it has been in a decline since the late 1980s. Prices have stabilized, and homes are appreciating once again, but not in the double-digit range.

Q: Where are the best investment markets in this country and why?

As we head into the last decade of the twentieth century, there are a number of markets with excellent bargains and investment potential. Unquestionably, the single best real estate investment market in the country is California. Investors would do well to study the state and see what factors have made it such a hot market. Many of those same ingredients are present in other areas, although not to the extent of California.

First, there is the population factor. The state continues to grow rapidly, hence there is a continuous demand for housing. Spurring the growth are factors such as ideal climate, diverse economy, and an abundance of recreation areas. Thus, even in southern California, where appreciation has slowed because of a sluggish economy, real estate is still an excellent investment, because the population continues to grow at an abnormally high rate, companies continue to locate in the area because of its proximity to the Pacific Rim (an import/export trading center), and there is an abundant supply of labor.

Q: What are some obstacles to investment potential in the California real estate market?

There is a shortage of so-called affordable housing. Companies thinking of locating in the area view this as a problem, and unless the state can find some solution, affordable housing may be a serious problem in the future. The state has recognized the need for affordable housing to provide homes for the incoming work force but has not yet done much about increasing construction of these homes. If industry cannot find the labor market in California, companies will begin to leave the state and locate where housing is reasonable and the labor force is in place. With companies moving out, unemployment will grow, and there will be less people able to afford housing. A second obstacle could well be a water shortage.

Q: What financing difficulties will most investors encounter throughout the country?

Financing for projects is difficult in almost every market. With the huge losses and subsequent failure of so many S&Ls, this source of financing is drying up. The former practice of allowing a builder to obtain a construction loan based on the estimated retail value of the completed project allowed many developers to secure 100% "plus" financing. In other words, they were able to withdraw more funds than they had invested into the project. The end result was that only the financial institution was at risk. Of course, this was in the days when almost anything sold. That is not the case anymore.

Q: What new requirements are many lenders asking for when it comes to real estate construction and investment?

The financial institutions want builders/developers to have all their assets—including personal ones—at risk. Generally, this results in higher financing costs, which are added to the price of the housing. This impacts homes in every price bracket and makes affordable housing even more difficult to plan and build. The one affordable housing source that still remains is bond money (public financing). Although bond financing is relatively inexpensive in comparison to bank loans, it is controversial and whether voters approve these issues varies from election to election. In the meantime, states such as California and Massachusetts, and other areas of the country that have seen rapid appreciation, find themselves in a quandry. The higher priced homes bring in more tax dollars and, theoretically, more affluent (and higher paying) taxpayers. At the same time, the high prices are beginning to disturb companies that are either in these areas or thinking of relocating to them.

Q: What general criteria can investors apply when it comes to evaluating property along the coastline?

As a rule, the closer an investor gets to the coast, the more expensive the property—and more rapid the appreciation. Coastal areas usually represent an ideal living environment and are more desirable than any other areas of the country. Generally, property 15 miles or more from the water is going to cost less, and will not show the rapid appreciation of property near the coast.

Q: Where are the rapid coastal growth areas that show the most promise for investment?

Washington, and, in particular, the city of Seattle. It is a growth area with an expanding economic base. Although it does not have the ideal climate of California, it does have access to the Pacific Rim and the lucrative trade with nations in the Far East. It also has a strong aerospace industry that is being joined by other support industries related to defense/aerospace. There are, for example, a host of subcontractors that make parts for the defense/aerospace sector of the economy, and they follow the prime (i.e., the Boeings) contractors in the industry. If the prime contractors mass in the northwest, the subcontractors will not be far away—and neither will the rush on housing.

Another state that is growing rapidly is Florida. Much of it is coastal, and it has obvious advantages for companies wanting to do import/export business. Although it does not fall into the Pacific Rim theater, it is ideal for the coming growth in European trade. In fact, with the detente in Europe, and the opening of the common market, import/export could become a major growth industry in the next decade. Part of that growth could also come from South America.

Q: How might the aging population impact real estate investment opportunities?

Warm weather states beckon to retirees, a growing segment of our population. In fact, by the year 2000, the number of senior citizens, that is, those 60 years of age and above, will have increased faster than any other segment of the population. Although not all retirees are on fixed incomes, most are cognizant of the growing cost of energy, and they are looking to move to warm weather states for retirement. Aside from California and Florida, there is the sunbelt area—from Arizona to Georgia—which also hopes to lure this segment of the population.

Q: Why did long-term, fixed rate mortgages virtually disappear in the early 1980s?

The cause of the near disappearance of the fixed rate loan was the "due on sale clause." This clause was a valuable tool for lenders because it allowed them to demand that a loan be paid off or the interest rates modified on conveyance of the title to the property to the new owners. When the property sold, the terms changed. Each state was formerly allowed to determine whether the lender could enforce such clauses, and there was a variety of decisions. Finally, a federal law was enacted to permit lenders to enforce the clause. But, before the law was changed, banks, S&Ls, and other lenders were in a bind. If the bid to enforce the

39

clause was defeated, the lenders might be stuck with thousands of loans that were granted at a time when inflation (and interest rates) were relatively low. They would be lending mortgage money to new owners at a rate they could not afford. For instance, if a due on sale clause was determined to be unenforceable, then a homeowner who sold a residence could pass on the lower interest rate to the buyer. If the seller lived in the property for 20 years, the rate could be as low as 6%. To finance the new loan, the lending institution would be losing money, because it could not possibly obtain the funds in the late 1970s and early 1980s for as little as 6%.

Q: Why are ARMs so popular with lenders?

During the 1980s—a period of uncertainty and fluctuating interest rates—lenders came up with the ARM, which would allow them to lend money and offer a loan with an interest rate that rose as the cost of living went up. ARMs became extremely popular in the early 1980s when interest rates approached 20%. They were one of the few types of loans that were being offered to buyers, and they had the distinct advantage of starting at a lower rate. Eventually, of course, the interest on the ARM would rise, but for the first few years the buyer had the advantage of a rate he could afford. The availability of ARMs kept the residential real estate market from complete collapse during this high inflationary period.

Q: What causes higher interest rates for homes?

Typically, higher interest rates are caused by the same factor that causes anything else to go up in price—a shortage. One of the few exceptions was the extremely high rates that plagued the industry in the early 1980s. There was no shortage of money. It was simply a case of the government manipulating rates and driving interest rates higher in an attempt to artificially manipulate the economy and to control inflation. The "experiment" was a disaster and brought on one of the worst recessions in our history, especially in the building industry. The government (hopefully) learned from this disastrous experience, and we will not see excessive manipulation of the money supply and interest rates in the future.

This period was certainly a buyer's market, and for those who were able to purchase and afford the initially high interest rates, there were many good investments available. Those same buyers were able to refinance at lower rates when interest started to come down in 1984–1985.

Q: Is the building of new housing an accurate measure of present consumer demand?

No. Typically, when interest rates are down and there is a demand for housing, builders enter the market. They are, of course, following the demand. But houses are not built in a day— or a year. It can take two or three years before a project is underway, due to government approvals and regulations. Thus, the 100 new housing starts that got underway yesterday in a community are not a reflection of today's demand, but of demand that was generated two years ago.

Q: What data and statistics should investors look into before putting their funds into a project?

On a daily basis, investors can find everything from employment/unemployment statistics to the balance of trade to countless interviews with economists who often do not agree. Investors should not ignore these surveys and interviews, but if a sound investment decision is going to be made the focus should be on local issues and the economics in the area in which you intend to invest.

At the same time, investors should never forget the media. It has the power to influence, and generally it does so in a negative manner. And, negativity is going to impact local conditions.

Q: How can title company statistics help someone with their investment decision?

By watching title company statistics, an investor can obtain more information than by reading all the magazines in the country. Title companies record the number of open escrows, which means the transactions (sales) that are being put together. These are not "closed" transactions, which actually refer to the number of homes sold, which is the most important statistic.

Still, open transactions give an investor a point of reference. It is relatively easy to compare open transactions for this quarter with the comparable quarter from last year. (When making comparisons and gathering data in the industry, it is important to match equivalent quarters from one year to another, since real estate is generally a seasonal business. Traditionally, the business is slow during the first quarter, picks up steam in the second, hits a peak in the third, and slows again at year end.)

Q: How can investors determine when the industry slows, and when it turns from buyer's to seller's market?

By watching the openings closely, an investor can determine when the industry slows, and when it turns from a buyer's into a seller's market and vice versa. The fewer openings, the more the market is leaning toward buyers.

Q: How can a realty board help with an investment decision?

Every market has a board that posts information on open transactions, or the number of "deals" that are in progress. Usually, communities with populations of one million or less have one board. Those with more than one million will have multiple boards, with each covering a smaller, geographic area.

Real estate brokers belong to these boards and, as members, obtain information from them. The board is also the keeper of the multiple listing service (MLS). The MLS is a listing of all properties for sale from all brokers who belong to the board. Most of the brokers have computerized access to the MLS system, thus giving the broker (and the investor) rapid access to important investment information. The MLS information also gives the investor a chance to compare the number of listings, that is, properties for sale, this year compared to last. More listings (the supply) this year may reflect a downturn in demand. By developing a relationship with a real estate broker, investors can obtain much of this information.

Q: How can the real estate broker benefit the prospective investor?

They have access to important information, and they may share it with investors. To ensure the sharing, investors should develop a relationship with a broker. Find a broker with whom you have rapport. Let them know you are interested in investing, but before you do you want to know all the facts. The broker who wants to make a sale will share information. It is a good idea to remain loyal to the broker who assists you in your search for information. The broker has demonstrated service and an interest, qualities that are difficult to find in many professionals today.

Q: How can investors use the daily newspapers in making investment decisions?

Investors should be perusing the real estate and financial sections. Most daily newspapers carry a weekly real estate section, however, different newspapers have different approaches. There is, first, the traditional real estate section. This is one in which the news is all good, and the companies that take advertisements get editorial space (within the section) in return. Thus, you may see an ad for the XYZ development, and on the next page there is a story about Sally Smith, a salesperson for XYZ. These sections provide little in-depth news or analysis on which the investor can rely. In essence, the entire section is a paid advertisement.

The second approach is becoming more common, especially when it comes to major metropolitan dailies. These real estate sections still carry the usual "executive appointments," however, they are filled with stories and analyses on the industry. Because a builder, developer, or real estate broker takes an ad does not mean they will get editorial space.

Q: How might real estate and business editors of newspapers be of help to prospective investors?

Getting to know the editor and/or writer(s) in the section can be important. They may be able to supply investors with additional insight. Although many would shy away from calling an editor for information, most are receptive to consumers who have questions. All an investor has to do is call, ask for the editor/writer, and pose a question such as "I was thinking about buying in X development and wonder what you thought about it." Most of us are flattered when someone asks for advice, and reporters are no different. They frequently will go out of their way to accommodate callers, and supply them with information on a project they may not have otherwise been able to get.

Q: How should the financial section be utilized by investors?

Financial sections may not contain real estate news on a daily basis, but most of the time the news you find on the page will impact real estate. One thing to keep in mind when reading these sections is that they may be slanted. Reporters have viewpoints, and sometimes these views come through in the story. Thus, it is not only important to read what is going on but to investigate the actual statistics as well. Check with brokers, salespeople, and others in the industry and verify what you read.

Q: How does the sale of new homes versus existing homes impact the industry and investors?

Investors should closely examine statistics on the sale of "new homes" being built versus the sale of older "existing homes." Because there are fewer new homes than existing homes, new home sales in this country are only a fraction of the total homes sold. Statistics quoted by the media in regards to new home sales pale in number when compared to sales of existing homes. Investors should be aware of this and understand that a drop in home construction may not have much of an impact on the industry.

Q: Do existing home sales fall into categories? If they do, what is the significance of each?

Existing home sales fall into two categories: the homeowner who wants to sell and the homeowner who must sell. The latter, of course, is going to provide the better buy for investors since they must get out because of job change or some other factor. The former is going to be tougher because they do not have to sell. Thus investors should try to determine if the seller "wants" or "needs" to sell. The difference can mean tens of thousands of dollars saved when the purchase is made.

Q: Why are there price variations in a new tract of homes?

Builders rarely construct an entire development at one time because of financing restrictions. For example, suppose a builder has a 100 home project. The builder constructs the first portion—

it may be 10 homes—and attempts to sell them as they are being built. If he succeeds, he goes back to the lender for additional financing for a second section of homes. If the homes go rapidly, the builder may try to convince the lender to let the remaining (all 90) or a good portion of the homes be built. The lender may or may not go along with the plan. Regardless of what the lender provides, the second segment of the tract is going to be more expensive than the first. And if there is significant demand for the first segment, the price rise on the second will be substantial.

Q: What is the best time to buy for an investor who decides to purchase a home in a new tract?

If an investor has examined a proposed new tract and decides it is worthy of an investment, the best time to buy would be during the first phase. By the time the third or fourth phase in a project is developed, the initial purchasers may have already seen the value of their investment increase by 10–25%.

Q: How long should an investor plan to hold a residential property?

Five years is the benchmark figure. When investing in a residential property, plan to hold it for at least that period of time. Although some brokers and speculators took risks and made profits by gambling on residential real estate in the short term, that does not happen frequently. California's and New England's rapid appreciation are not everyday occurrences, and astute investors will realize that to make a relatively safe real estate buy, it should be with the thought of keeping the property for five years.

Q: What amount of appreciation should investors expect?

Conservatively, historical trends show that real estate appreciates about 5% a year. To verify that figure, an investor can track any area (as suggested earlier in this chapter) and divide it into five-year cycles. There are few residential real estate areas that have not doubled in value during the past 10 years, and there are many instances in which properties have tripled and quadrupled during the past two decades. The rise in real estate values is not surprising, particularly when one considers how costs of other goods have soared. Remember when a Volkswagen sold for $1,675—new. That was in the early 1960s. Today, a comparable automobile is in the $10,000 range, an increase of more than 500%.

Q: How does the appreciation of real estate compare to inflation?

Real estate will generally keep pace with inflation, and usually rises more rapidly. Thus, it is not surprising to see a home that sold for $25,000 in 1970 now valued at more than $100,000. Or, in several areas of the country, that same property is in the $200,000 range.

Q: When investing, what is the relationship between the cost of the structure and the return on the dollars invested? How should investors calculate and evaluate these figures?

When investing in real estate, the consideration should not be the overall cost of the building but the return in relationship to the dollars that are put into it. Take, for instance, the following scenario. An investor is going to purchase a $100,000 home, put down $20,000 (20%, which is the standard required for 30-year fixed mortgages), and is going to have an $80,000 mortgage.

When calculating the monthly payment (assuming an interest rate of approximately 10%), the buyer will be making a payment of somewhere around $800, excluding taxes. Now, say the property is being bought as a rental, and the going rate in the area is $825 per month for a similar structure.

Many investors would assume that yearly gross income is $825 × 12 = $9,900. In reality, every investor should allow a 5% vacancy allowance because the owner never knows when and if a tenant is going to leave. If the tenant leaves there is going to be some "down time." The new tenant cannot immediately move in because of cleanup and other similar considerations. Timing like that would be nice, but it will rarely occur.

Allowing for a 5% vacancy factor brings the gross rental receipt down to $9,405, or $783 per month. That means the buyer (investor) has a potential loss of $17 per month on his $20,000 (the actual cash) investment, plus maintenance and repairs.

Wouldn't the investor have been better off putting the $20,000 into a certificate of deposit and collecting from $1,600 to $2,000 per year with no risk? In this case, the return would have been anywhere from 8–10% a year.

Compounding—that is, assuming the investor is going to reinvest the yearly proceeds and collect a similar 8–10% each year for the next five years, the CD investment would look like this:

Year	Amount	8%	10%
1	$20,000		
2	21,600–22,000	$1,600	$2,000
3	23,328–24,200	1,728	2,200
4	25,194–26,620	1,866	2,420
5	27,209–29,282	2,015	2,662
Gross Profit		7,209	9,282

With a relatively safe investment and no maintenance problems, the investor would have anywhere from $27,209 to $29,282 at the end of five years. From this, however, would have to come any taxes, and assuming the investor is in the 30% bracket, the payout to the government would be anywhere from $2,100 to $2,750. This would reduce his profit to $5,100–6,530.

What would have happened to the investor who had bought and was renting the property? Assume a 5% appreciation, with a loss of $17 per month on the property.

If the investor utilized a broker to sell the home, there would be an additional 6–7% deduction to allow for commission and closing costs. This would reduce the profit on the investment further:

Broker's commission $121,550 × 6% = $7,293

Broker's commission $121,550 × 7% = $8,508

Net profit on investment: $13,237 (6%)

Net profit on investment: $12,022 (7%)

This figure, incidentally, would not include the potential tax benefits that might save the investor money on his other income. It does show that even in a conservative (5%) appreciation market, real estate is an investment that is difficult to beat. Of course, the investor has potential maintenance problems during the five-year period.

Year	Value of home	Appreciation at 5%
1	$100,000	$5,000
2	105,000	5,250
3	110,250	5,512
4	115,762	5,788
5	121,550	6,077

Total appreciation: $21,550
Less rent loss: (1,020)

Profit (assuming the property is sold for $121,550): $20,530

Suppose the same property is taken and is rented for $900 rather than $825 per month. Assume the 95% occupancy as before, or a gross rental of $855 per month. This gives the investor a $55 per month ($660 per year) profit per year or $3,300 additional profit during the 5-year span.

Examining the three scenarios, it is easy to see that the real estate investment (when figuring the actual cash return on investment) pales when compared to the CD. In fact, the $660 per year comes to just over 3% return (on the $20,000 investment). But when other factors are taken into consideration, real estate becomes a much more viable investment.

The case shows how the real value in real estate for investors is riding the cycles. For those who do, the previous case illustrates that the astute investor—instead of looking at an 8–10% return on funds—may be looking at more than 50%, as illustrated by the final example.

But before investors can ride the cycles, they have to be able to spot them. Buying high and selling low is a problem numerous real estate investors have encountered. Don't jump at the first piece of property that is put on the table.

For the astute investor who studies the market, talks to the people in it, spends time evaluating previous cycles, and examines what is happening today—and tries to project events tomorrow—real estate can be one of the most profitable investments ever made.

3

Analyzing Commercial Investments

Although she had spent more than 15 years as a CPA with a well-known accounting firm, Alison McKenzie was determined not to rely entirely on the company's pension for her retirement. For several years she had been saving her money and studying the commercial investment field. She was convinced that there was money to be made in it. She had looked at industrial developments and office complexes, however, she was intrigued by "strip centers" and the potential for profit in them. Alison did not have enough money to purchase a strip center of her own, but she knew there were ways of getting involved in the strip center investment. The most common was through a limited partnership.

Q: What type of commercial investment is a "strip center?"

Strip centers were a phenomena that developed shortly after the initial gas crisis in the early 1970s. By the time the crunch was over, many gas stations were in dire straits. The market had consolidated and numerous independents could no longer compete. With the demise of the stations, property owners were faced with small parcels of land that would no longer be viable as a location for a gas station. The sites were, however, ideal for housing mini-shopping centers, that is, so-called "strip centers" that were usually identifiable because they almost always contained a convenience store in addition to three to five other retail shops.

Q: How has the consumer desire to save time impacted the value of strip centers?

Since the early 1970s, Americans have become obsessed with saving time and making their trips to the store as convenient as possible. As a result, everything from drive-in fast-food outlets to drive-in cleaners, and even a drive-in clinic where motorists could be inoculated with the latest flu vaccine, have blossomed. At each one of these outlets consumers usually pay a premium for the rapid in-and-out service. The increasing number of retail or service outlets willing to locate in strip centers as well as the increasing willingness of consumers to pay more for time saving and convenience have increased the demand for strip centers and, consequently, the value of the center.

Q: Does the strip center with a convenience store in it have an advantage?

The convenience store creates traffic, which lures a host of other retail establishments—everything from Chinese fast-food restaurants and donut shops to video arcades—into the center. With a convenience store, a center is virtually guaranteed traffic, which provides the other merchants with a steady flow of customers.

Q: What are the advantages to real estate limited partnerships?

They offer two advantages: (1) the ability to pool funds from a number of investors and purchase more real estate as a group than an individual could and (2) limited liability. That is, the limited partner investors usually can lose only the amount of money they put into the investment.

Q: What are the drawbacks to real estate limited partnerships?

Those advantages have drawbacks. Although the investors were able to pool funds for the purpose of investing, as limited partners they seldom have any voice in the decisions that are made. For the frustrated limited partner who loses his patience with the general partners—the individual or group that runs the investment—there is often little recourse. What is sometimes particularly unnerving is the fact that general partners run the investment and often have little, if any, of their own funds invested. General partners are usually paid on the basis of a percentage of rents they receive from the investment and a cut of the profits when the property is sold.

Q: What advantages do the general partners have in a real estate investment?

Many limited partnership agreements allow the general partner to change the rules if the project warrants it. If, for instance, the plan was for the partnership to hold the property for three years and sell it, the general partners could decide to hold it for "another year" if the lengthened time would, in their opinion, benefit the partnership. The general partner can make mistakes and the limited partners may have to pay for them—in the form of delayed sale or additional funds required for the project.

Q: Once you invest funds in a limited partnership, can the general partners come back and seek more money?

Additional investment is not mandatory unless the Limited Partnership Agreement so states. However, if the partnership is in financial trouble the investor may consider the request for additional funds to protect their original investment. The latter possibility could be a problem. Those partners who augmented their initial investment could be given a priority payout if their additional advance is characterized as a loan. In other words, they would get their money first. Once again, the general partners could manipulate the partnership.

Q: What organization supervises the operation of a limited partnership?

Today, in most states, if a partnership remains at 35 (or less) participants, the partnership is subject to the scrutiny of only the state's corporation or real estate commission. Although it would appear that 35 partners would not involve an extensive amount of capital (i.e., typical limited partnerships ask anywhere from $1,000 to about $25,000 per share per partner), it can involve millions. General partners often solicit funds from investment groups, and if the manager of a fund decided to invest, they could invest $300,000 in the name of the fund and it would still be considered only *one* limited partner.

In most states, if the partnership has more than 35 persons or entities, the partnership comes under the aegis of the Securities and Exchange Commission (SEC). (Partnerships with fewer than 35 member persons or entities are generally considered "private offerings" and are exempt from SEC regulation. All others are "public offerings" and are subject to the SEC regulations and must be qualified.) Once under the SEC, the partnership usually has to issue a formal prospectus, which will spell out the risk to investors in clearer detail.

Q: What is the advantage of having the SEC involved in a limited partnership?

The SEC, with its severe penalties, usually provides more protection for investors. It also means the limited partners have recourse in the event they were dissatisfied with the general partners.

Q: What is the drawback to having the SEC involved when a limited partnership goes over 35 partners?

The drawback to the partnership in this arrangement is cost. SEC filings are costly, and they have to be done on a regular basis. This usually means more of the funds generated from limited partners would be going to administration, and not to investment in the property. It makes the partnership slightly less attractive to investors who want to gamble, but safer for those who want some strict rules and regulations behind their investment.

Q: Are there disadvantages to investors when a corporation commission regulates a real estate limited partnership?

From the standpoint of the general partners, the rules could not be more beneficial. Being regulated by a corporation commission virtually guarantees there will not be any scrutiny of the project or the general partners. Although most corporation commissions do a fine job of issuing the guidelines for corporations, they have little experience when it comes to real estate, investment, and the potential problems that can crop up.

There has, however, been a growing movement in many states to put real estate partnerships under the real estate commissioner's office. The argument in favor of this change is obvious: the real estate commissioner's office is more familiar with real estate investments and could be a more effective watchdog over the entrepreneurs who put the partnerships together.

Q: What does the prospectus for a limited partnership tell investors?

It can be deceptive. For example, the following actually happened. A prospectus supplied to a group of investors where the total number of limited partners would be less than 35 said the estimated construction time would be 15 months. During that time, the general partners mentioned—in a cover letter—that they had already had conversations with a major tenant who was "anxious about the location." The partners even named the tenant: K-Mart. (If a prospectus had mentioned K-Mart or any other tenant, it would also have had to qualify the statement and say something like "there is no guarantee that the proposed tenant will take the space.") With a partnership agreement that does not fall under SEC scrutiny, there is usually no such requirement. Thus, the general partners can make numerous statements about the viability of the center without qualifying them.

Q: What is the standard management fee that general partners get for handling a real estate investment?

This can vary significantly. The general partners could receive a management fee of 5–10% of the monthly income, plus costs. This is standard in the real estate investment field. When it was fully leased, it would be sold and the investors (limited and general partners) would divide the proceeds according to the agreement.

Q: Is there usually a time frame indicated in a limited partnership agreement? That is, does the agreement say how long the project would be kept?

Sometimes yes; sometimes no. The important thing to remember is that if the general partners have a difficult time with the project, they may decide to hold it longer. If this decision is made, it is difficult for the limited partners to protest because to sell it beforehand could decrease the profitability of the project and even endanger it. Thus, the limited partners are practically bound by what the general partners decide to do, regardless of what the limited partnership agreement says.

Q: What does the limited partnership agreement generally indicate?

Typically, most limited partnership agreements indicate the duration of the life of the partnership and outline what kind of return the partnership seeks. For example, for every one dollar invested, the partners might seek a return of an additional fifty cents at the time of sale. In other words, an investor who puts in $10,000 would be returned $15,000 on the sale of the property. There are tax advantages, but with the laws changing so frequently, the exact benefit an investor would receive is difficult to pinpoint.

Q: How have the tax benefits changed for limited partnerships?

Several years ago, one of the prime selling points of the limited partnerships revolved around tax benefits. The general partners could allocate depreciation for the entire building or center to the limited partners. Thus, aside from the obvious appreciation benefits, the partners had a significant write-off.

If, however, the two certainties are death and taxes, a third may well be that tax laws always change—and they have for partnerships. Although the government has been careful not to remove the tax benefits of home ownership, it has been harsher with commercial investors. Some more recent tax changes have taken away the deductibility of depreciation or any other tax benefits if the investor was "passive." That is, investors who did not actually put in time maintaining the building could not deduct expenses that were incurred beyond their actual investment. If, however, investors spent time on the site, took part in maintenance, and invested time as well as funds, they could deduct depreciation and other expenses.

This tax law change removed one of the more appealing aspects for investors. No longer could they just put up money and wait for a return coupled with tax benefits. The tax laws that were passed in the mid- to late 1980s ended that advantage. Changes of this type also made it more difficult for partnerships to generate investors since they no longer could tout the unrestricted tax benefits.

Q: To what extent can general partners alter the agreement?

Almost to any extent. For example, the following letter came from a general partner (to a limited partner) and revolved around an investment that guaranteed the limited partner a monthly interest payment.

> Due to unforeseen costs and delays in construction, we have decided to suspend interest payments to investors for the time being.
> We are doing this in the belief that all of the limited partners would rather our project stay financially viable in the long run, than drain it of funds in the short term.
> If you have any questions, please call.
>
> Sincerely, Leroy Robinson

Despite the objection of the limited partner, there was nothing that could be done from a practical point of view.

Q: Can limited partners remove the general partners? If so, what happens?

The general partners are in control unless the limited partners elect to have them removed. The problem is that should the limited partners be able to remove the general partners, the limited partnership may then take control. Are they qualified? Can they complete the project? Or is the project in more danger of failing because of the limited partners' lack of expertise?

Q: What is a "lis pendens" and how can it impact a limited partnership?

A lis pendens is a legal notice recorded to give constructive notice that there is pending litigation relating to the property (i.e., someone is claiming an interest in the property). It also gives notice to anyone who acquires an interest in the property after the date of the recording that they may be bound by the outcome of the suit. In other words, several of the limited partners could be suing the general partners.

Q: Why do partners sometimes sue other partners in limited partnerships?

There are usually a variety of reasons. Perhaps, the general partners were paying excessive fees to themselves or paying personal obligations with partnership funds. Or perhaps the general partners were also general partners of another partnership and were comingling funds—robbing Peter to pay Paul.

Q: Why do some creditors file mechanic's liens and what are they?

The mechanic's lien is usually recorded by a contractor or supplier for the purpose of securing payment for work performed or materials supplied to the project. The work is in the form of some kind of improvement to the land. If the contractor or material man is not paid they can sue for breach of contract. By recording a mechanic's lien, they can foreclose the lien rather quickly. Without the lien, a simple breach of contract lawsuit may take years until a judgment is obtained.

Q: What is a secured creditor?

A secured creditor is one who has a lien on the title to the property. For example, those who hold trust deeds (to the property) are secured creditors. But the first trust deed takes precedence over the second, and no monies are returned to the second holders until the first trust deed holders are satisfied.

Q: What is the difference in the position of the holder of the first trust deed and the second trust deed?

In essence, a holder of second deed of trust is in a position of greater risk. They generally react to the legal manuevers of the holder of the first, in this case the bank that provided the initial financing.

Q: What are the advantages and disadvantages of different types of foreclosure?

Upon default, the owner of the deed of trust can elect to foreclose. If the owner chooses to do so, there would be two options: judicial or nonjudicial foreclosure. The judicial foreclosure would have to go through the courts, and that could mean additional expense. If the partnership is in serious trouble, and the partners are dissatisfied, the holder of the deed of trust could opt for nonjudicial foreclosure, which is the most common.

Nonjudicial foreclosure involves having the trustee named in the deed of trust record or publish, according to certain procedures, a "Notice of Default," which simply means that the borrower (the partnership) is delinquent in fulfilling their obligations. Once published, there is a time limit, about 3 months in most states, to reinstate the loan. If the default is not corrected within the 3 month period, the secured creditor (the bank) may direct the trustee to proceed with the sale by recording and publishing a Notice of Trustee's Sale once per week for three weeks. If corrective actions are not taken during that period, the trustee can, on direction from the bank, hold the Trustee's Sale, thereby foreclosing on the property.

Q: Why do banks hesitate when it comes to initiating foreclosure proceedings?

As a rule, banks do not want to foreclose on property. They are in the business of lending funds, not owning land. The institution would much rather have the borrowers remedy the problem.

Q: What should investors be wary of when they hear the words "high return?"

High return means high(er) risk. Many high-risk returns pay off quite well during periods of high inflation and are the first to hit the skids during a downturn in the economy.

Q: How can investors ensure the competence of the general partners in a limited partnership?

The answer to that question is not always obvious. There are no special requirements for someone to become a general partner. All it takes is the idea for the project, an attorney to draw up the paperwork, and the raising of the required funds. There is no one to question the qualifications of the general partners. That burden rests on the prospective investors, who seldom question the background and capabilities of those with whom they are about to enter business. Once again, the "trust syndrome" is at work.

Q: What steps should be taken to check on general partners of a limited partnership?

What prospective investors should be doing is scrutinizing the general partners and their track record. How many projects have they built? Have the projects been on time? Have there been problems? If so, what kind? Investors should also be talking to local bankers, accountants, and attorneys. Bankers, of course, are an excellent source of information. They not only know what is happening financially in their own community, they talk to other bankers who are familiar with horror stories in other areas. Prospective investors who have a rapport with their banker should be able to pose a question about a local company and generate some information.

Another source of information is the local newspaper. Aside from talking to real estate writers and reporters, newspapers maintain a "morgue," or library of past clippings. Some of the clippings are stored and others have been microfilmed. The newspaper generally files previous news under "names," thus Land Ranch or the name of any of the general partners, particularly if they were involved in lawsuits or difficulties, can be found. It takes legwork and time, but it is better than losing thousands of investment dollars.

Q: How do "priority payouts" impact limited partners when it comes to an investment?

If a partnership gets into trouble and the general partners solicit additional funds from existing partners, the general partners could effectively alter the agreement and give priority (first) payouts to those limited partners who paid the added monies perhaps as loans to the partnership. That is, as soon as the project was completed and sold, per the original agreement, those limited partners who had put up extra money would be paid first. The amount of leeway the general partners have, however, would be limited by the original partnership agreement. That is why it is important for investors to scrutinize agreements, give the agreements to attorneys, and determine what happens if the project does get in trouble. Find out if there can be priority payouts.

Q: How complex is the typical limited partnership agreement?

Very. For example, the following is from an actual limited partnership agreement:

Instructions to Investors
for Completing Closing Documents for Purchase
of Limited Partnership Units

After you have carefully reviewed the confidential private placement memorandum and have decided to subscribe for and purchase one or more units, please observe the following instructions:

All information is to be typed or printed in ink. All completed documents must be returned to Long Ranch, Inc. (address).

If purchaser is a corporation, trust or partnership, special documentation is necessary.

Unit amount (dollar figure). Minimum purchase is (number) units or (dollar amount).

Enclosed you will find my check for $15,000 representing the purchase of 15 units as a capital contribution to (name of project), a California limited partnership.

Make check payable to Long Ranch, Inc., trust account. (signature) (address)

This was followed by an investor questionnaire, which asked for the name, address, social security number, and banking information of the proposed investor. Another page followed, which asked how the investor wished to hold title to the property. This was followed by the following statement:

> Please note: By signing this you are entering into a limited partnership agreement and agree to invest money. No person shall be offered the opportunity to become or be admitted as a limited partner to the partnership who does not meet the suitability requirements for a non-public offering. Whether or not any person meets such requirements shall be at the sole discretion of the general partner.

> Therefore, I (we) agree to all of the foregoing and agree to become a limited partner in the Partnership and contribute money as set forth hereinabove. Each party whose name will appear on the Partnership records must sign below.

Q: What should investors watch for with limited partnership agreements similar to the one above?

Check the partnership document itself to determine whether any rules are indicated as to what would happen if the project needed additional funds and to determine whether there is anything to prevent the general partners from reallocating payments and giving other investors a priority return on their money. Nowhere in the above document was either of these points covered. In the body of the partnership agreement you will discover that the general partner usually has the power to borrow additional funds in the name of the partnership.

Q: What is the attitude of the banks and other lending institutions when it comes to limited partnerships?

Banks have gone through a difficult decade, and they have become increasingly sensitive to the viability of any investment.

At the first sign of trouble with a project, a bank will unload the investment, if possible.

Q: How have bank attitudes changed when it comes to lending and foreclosing on limited partnerships?

The bank has to answer to depositors, shareholders, and regulators, and in today's environment, with bankers increasingly becoming targets of politicians as well as regulators, the amount of risk an institution will take has diminished considerably. In good times, of course, the bank could hold on and extend credit. Even if it was forced to foreclose, it could hold out for a price above the amount of money it had invested and possibly return funds to those holding the second deed of trust.

Q: What general steps should investors take before investing in a limited partnership?

Before investing in a commercial project, examine the real estate industry and economy. In the long-term, real estate will prove out, but when times are difficult, money is tight, and there is an abundance of vacant commercial space, the investor should be cautious.

Q: How can investors limit risk in a commercial real estate investment?

In real estate, as is the case with all investments, the risk is proportional to the reward. When an investor puts funds in a project that has the potential to yield a return three times the rate of inflation, the investor must expect high risk.

Risk in commercial real estate can never be completely eliminated but it can be minimized if investors keep the following in mind:

The Real Estate Investor's Q and A Book

1. Be aware of demand. Every area has its ups and downs depending on local conditions. The strip center is no different than any other investment. Is there a demand for one? Are there other nearby centers? If not, why? Did other developers examine the area previously and decide it was not worth the investment?

2. Find a local real estate firm that has a commercial/investment department. Let them know you are a serious investor; however, before you put any money in a project you want to know what's happening locally. By talking to a firm much can be learned. The firm usually knows the history of a piece of vacant land and will know of previous development efforts.

3. Keep abreast of changing demographics and how they can impact developments. The most obvious is the aging of the population. As the baby boomers (those born from 1945 through the late 1950s) age, and their children move out, they no longer need larger, single family residences. Many sell these and then buy condominiums or smaller units. This aging trend will continue through 2000, and investors should keep this in mind when evaluating potential housing projects.

Q: In general, what is the impact of downtown areas on most commercial investments?

Most downtown areas declined in population when suburbs developed. Retail centers died because the population did its shopping at neighborhood suburban centers and malls. Although this caused most downtown retail centers to collapse, it opened the door for office complexes.

Many downtown areas came under redevelopment (which may provide the developers a special tax break if they decide to build in the area). The development of an office building will

66

bring a work force to the area. The work force will spend a portion of its earnings near its place of employment, thereby bolstering the economy.

With the emergence of the so-called "Yuppie" who preferred to live downtown and closer to work—or where the action was—many inner cities revived and old buildings were torn down to make way for new, high-rise apartments. Many of these younger executives and workers invested in old, downtown properties and homes, and restored them. In a number of cities, such as Washington, D.C. and Los Angeles, a revitalization took place.

Q: How can—and do—demographics impact real estate investment?

Demographics have changed radically. Recently, many areas have seen an influx of immigrants, from Vietnamese and Chinese to Latin and South Americans. These changes impact communities—and investors—extensively. They will dictate changes in both housing and shopping patterns. The immigrant does not necessarily frequent the same shops or retail stores as the native American. Consequently, investors and developers in centers should keep this in mind as they build and lease new centers.

Q: Is it a good idea to talk to local government officials before making a commercial investment?

It is a good idea to check with the local planning commission staff members, especially if you are planning to invest in a project that requires building, a variance, or zone change. Much can be gleaned by outlining plans and getting a reaction from the staff. If the staff seems opposed to elements in the development, it is almost a certainty the commission will be as well.

(In most communities, the planning commission is a four- to six-member board that votes approval on all plans before developers are allowed to build. Commission members frequently do not have the time to visit each project and investigate it thoroughly. Thus, they rely on staff members to investigate the project and make recommendations as to approval and changes. Although not all commission members go strictly by staff reports, in most cases they will rely on staff and go along with the recommendations. Investors should also keep in mind that in many smaller and medium-sized communities, the commission members and staff are not necessarily trained in land use. Many are volunteers, and in most cases the commission members are political appointees.)

Q: Can investors get definite opinions from city and county personnel in regard to a proposed project?

Staff members will never commit and say whether a plan will be passed; however, they will give an indication of what they think. By getting their opinion, investors and developers will be able to anticipate a commission's action, and can make modifications to plans before they finalize their construction loans. Most projects are modified by the commissions, and developers know this will happen. In fact, many know their plans will be scaled back, consequently they may ask for more (i.e., more square footage to lease) than they know they will get. The most likely modifications involve scaling back of rentable space to allow for more parking space and shrubbery.

If parking problems have plagued the area, investors can expect an impact on allocated parking spaces within a development. The commission may require the developer to add more spaces because of surrounding or changing conditions. The same can be true of office buildings or industrial developments. Codes may say one thing, but when it comes down to approval, most commissions will evaluate present conditions and problems and they may require changes in plans because of them. That could mean there will be less retail, office, or industrial space to rent.

Therefore, there will be less revenue and the return on investment may not be as expected.

Q: How do zoning boards impact projects?

Commercial land may be zoned in a variety of different ways. It may be zoned for agriculture, manufacturing, commercial (retail), or some variation of it. Before any building commences, zoning has to match the type of proposed development. Developers who are working with general partners must first go before a commission and request a zone change if the project requires it.

Q: What zoning is the most difficult to obtain?

If zoning must be changed to build, the most difficult designation for a project to obtain is manufacturing, followed by commercial, residential, and then agriculture. In many areas, particularly those in which farming was a prime occupation of the population, a developer frequently finds his project is earmarked for land zoned agricultural. Commissions do not enjoy changing agricultural designations because the land is perceived as serving an important function, feeding people. Generally, agricultural zoned land is worth slightly less than residential, residential less than commercial, and commercial less than manufacturing. Thus, if a commission allows a land owner to upgrade—that is, go from agricultural to manufacturing, for instance—it is enhancing the value of the land.

Q: What does a "land's best use" mean to developers and investors?

Wherever there is enormous residential development, investors and builders constantly find themselves in front of zoning commissions in an effort to convince them of the necessity for the zone change. Commissions generally try to decide "which zoning will provide for the land's best use consistent with the surrounding area." Obviously, zone changes can mean millions of dollars to land owners; thus in recent years "land consultant" has been an emerging occupation. Consultants work for builders, developers, and investors and they lay the groundwork with commissions for zone changes and other property modifications. Effective land consultants know the zoning laws, and they know the zoning and planning commission staffs, too. Many are former planning and/or zoning commission staff members, and they have the ability to present informal plans and get a reaction to them before they are finalized.

Q: How can an investor find a good consultant to help with a development, and the city and county officials involved?

Finding good land consultants is not difficult. Developers travel in similar circles and are willing to share information. For the newcomer to the field, all it takes is a visit to a planning or zoning commission staff office. Although staff members will be reluctant to recommend some specific person, they can usually be convinced to give you two or three names from which you may choose.

If staff members are willing to mention two or three names, they are, in effect, giving you a recommendation.

Q: Is it advisable for investors to retain a land consultant when planning to build and/or develop a property?

In most cases, yes. The emergence of land consultants and the solicitation of staff opinions before any plans are submitted are results of the increasingly difficult time builders are having when it comes to investing and developing projects. Twenty to 30 years ago, it was not difficult to obtain zone changes. Commissions were cognizant of how important it was to allow for the burgeoning population, and they often went with the development plans without requiring any modifications. In many cases, they also granted planning exceptions and allowed builders to squeeze in more units instead of having the required amount of parking space or greenbelt.

Q: What impact has zoning and planning exceptions had on development and the plans investors have had?

Zoning and planning exceptions caused local consumer revolutions. A typical example was one that took place nearly 20 years ago. It was during the heyday of residential development in Los Angeles County, and on a daily basis developers were submitting plans to change agricultural land into zoning for single family and/or apartments. During this period, a developer went before the zoning board and was able to get a 30-acre parcel of agricultural land changed so that it could be developed as apartments. The request was not unusual, and the commission granted it.

When the plans were submitted, the developer asked for a number of zoning exceptions that would enable him to build the project with less parking and greenbelt than required. The planning commission approved the plans despite the growing objections of a number of homeowners in the area. The developer knew of the objections, but he was confident of approval and ignored the opposition. Within days after he received his approval from the planning commission, a lawsuit was filed by the local homeowners. It was one of the first environmental suits filed in the county, and it not only delayed the project but ended up costing the developer and the partners involved hundreds of thousands of dollars.

Today, however, zoning commissions no longer ignore local groups. They frequently solicit opinions, and notification of any proposed change goes out to the surrounding community. Those in the area have the opportunity to address the commission before any change is granted. (The same is true at the planning commission level.)

Q: Which zoning changes elicit the strongest objections and from where is the opposition most likely to come?

Typically, the strongest objections occur when developer/investors propose zoning changes in agricultural land. Agriculture is characterized by seemingly endless acres of flat, open fields with corn, strawberries, alfalfa, and other similar crops. Imagine this transposed into a bustling urban community consisting of tract homes, shopping centers, and office complexes. That hustling, busy image is alien to most and tends to stir up emotions and vehement objections from those living in the area.

Those protests are especially loud in today's environmentally oriented communities, and many stem from past abuses at the hands of builders, investors, and local officials. The community activist is no longer the oddball, but commonplace. The presence of potential protests and objections means investors and developers should not only design projects according to zoning/planning laws and regulations, but they should also solicit opinions from surrounding property owners, homeowners, and environmental groups.

Q: What is the best approach to alleviating the concerns of groups that oppose an investor's development?

An evening or two spent with these groups prior to any formal presentation to city/government officials can often head off potential protests. Although some local groups may make unreasonable demands of the project, in most cases a few minor changes in a development enable a builder and investors to obtain the support of an entire community.

Government officials are sensitive to protest and community opinion. Just a few voices of protest can defeat a multimillion dollar project with little effort. Today's consumer groups are, of course, more astute when it comes to attracting media attention and increasing pressure. This is another area in which previously mentioned land consultants have developed a niche. Many are astute in dealing with homeowner and other groups, and they know how to present plans and win approval locally from non-governmental groups and organizations.

Q: What is meant by return on the investment, and how is it evaluated?

How much can you make, and is the return worth the risk. There are, for instance, numerous investments that will pay 3–4% more than the rate of inflation, and they are virtually risk free. For example, there are government-insured certificates of deposits. There are also municipal bonds, and a good number of tax advantages.

Q: How should return on the real estate investment be calculated?

Returns can be calculated in a number of simple ways. For example, assume an investor takes $20,000 and puts it into a property. After the down payment, his monthly payment is $800 per month. If he rents the property for $900 a month, his profit will be $1,200 per year. The return is $1,200 (return per year) divided by $20,000 (initial investment), which gives the investor a return of 6%. With a certificate of deposit for the same length of time, an investor could probably earn 8%—risk free. So why go for the real estate venture? Obviously, there are benefits in this investment other than a 6% return. The property is going to appreciate (on the average, 5% a year) and there will be tax benefits. So even though the return is slightly lower than a certificate of deposit, the investor has to weigh the other factors, such as tax considerations and appreciation.

73

Q: What type of contingencies should investors allow for when calculating the return on their real estate investment?

In the previous example, we assumed that the property was rented a full 12 months, without any vacancy factor. That is not always true. Although a tenant may arrive who stays for two or three years, investors should always allow, at a minimum, a 5% vacancy rate. This would change the $20,000 investment significantly. The return would drop to $855 per month (95% occupancy) and the yearly profit to $660. This means the return on the $20,000 would be just over 3% instead of 6%. The question is whether this project is still worth the risk when the investor can earn 5% more, per year, in a safe certificate of deposit? Once again, this is only a question the investor can answer. Obviously, the investor has the advantage of appreciating property (5% a year), plus the tax write-off. If the investor wants to hold the building for only two or three years, the answer is obvious— the certificate is going to be the better buy. But when you go beyond the four- or five-year period, real estate begins to look better.

Q: What factors, other than the amount of the immediate financial investment, should investors consider when trying to calculate their return on investment?

They should consider the condition of the building, center, mall, or home. Is it in need of repairs? What will the repairs cost and how will that impact the investment?

With apartments, investors should look into the tenants and see if there have been any problems. One outspoken tenant can rile an entire building. Before sinking funds into an apartment, office building, strip center, or industrial complex, the wise investor will go around and talk to each of the tenants. Find out how they feel about the owners and structure. Are they happy or unhappy? If they are unhappy, why? Can the problem be remedied or is it going to take an enormous expenditure?

Q: Are professional property managers worth considering?

Definitely. This is particularly true if the investor does not have the ability to be a good property manager. Handling tenants and properties requires good, sound, objective judgment. For example, consider the following situation.

An apartment and/or unit is rented to a young newlywed couple. The tenants put up first and last month's rent along with a security deposit. The owner, who manages his own building, hits it off with the pair, and they invite him to dinner. Several months go buy, the friendship blossoms . . . and then trouble. The couple has a fight, one leaves, and the other loses his or her job. A week later, they reunite and move back together. Because only one is working, they fall behind in rent. Since they are friends with the owner, they know he will understand why they have to make their car and credit card payments before they pay rent. Three more months go by, and now they owe two months in back rent. The owner has repairs he must make to the building, but he is short of cash because several other renters—including the newlywed couple—are all behind. He has come to know all his tenants, and is sure they will all make payments as soon as their income stream increases. In the meantime, the needed repairs are not made. Consequently, the heating system breaks down, winter arrives, and the remaining tenants, who normally pay on time, hold back their rent because they have no heat. Now the owner has no income stream and the bank is pressing him because he has fallen behind in his payments. Two months later, he receives a letter from the bank cautioning him that if his mortgage payments are not brought current within 30 days, the bank will start foreclosure proceedings. The owner looks at his building, studies his tenants, and realizes his investment is in trouble.

Far-fetched? Not really. That scenario is not only possible, but it actually happened to an investor/owner in the midwest. The problems could have been avoided had the investor (1) realized he was not a good businessperson and (2) hired a professional property management firm to handle the building.

Q: What type of fees do professional property management firms charge?

Professional firms may charge anywhere from 5%–10% of the gross rentals to handle a building, but they offer significant advantages to owners who are not versed in management. For example, the professional property manager may become acquainted with the new tenants but they also make sure the renters understand the importance of making timely payments. In fact, one well-known firm in the west has one of its property managers state the following when leasing any space:

> On behalf of (name of property management firm) we're extremely happy to have you as one of our tenants. We're going to do everything to make sure your stay in this building is pleasant, and that everything in the building works perfectly. We're going to avoid any and every inconvenience to you. At the same time, we expect timely rent payments from you folks. This is a business transaction, and I would impress upon you the importance of paying your rent on the day it is due. We do not accept late payments or excuses for them. If your rent is not in our hands the day it is due, we will start eviction proceedings the following day. I know this sounds harsh, but those conditions are critical if we are going to maintain this as a first class building. I realize you have other bills and obligations, but from our standpoint the rent in this building should be your number one priority.

Harsh? Of course, but this property management firm does the job. In the years it has been in business, it has never failed to collect rents in a timely manner, and it has never lost more than one month's income from a renter. If the owner/investor of a building can establish the same business relationship with renters as this property management firm does, then there may not be a need for a company to handle the management. Remember, though, that in addition to collecting rents, property management firms maintain the building, see that everything is running properly, and handle needed repairs immediately.

Q: How do you select a professional property management firm?

Selecting one is relatively easy. Simply look around the community at buildings that appear to be extremely well maintained. Inspect the buildings thoroughly. Are the halls clean, is the structure in good condition, and are there a minimal amount of vacancies? Good property management firms not only keep excellent tenants, but they generate new ones. A sign of a good property management firm is not only a well-kept structure, but a structure that has a vacancy rate lower than similar buildings in the surrounding areas. Investors should talk to the managers of these buildings, find out the names of the management firms, interview the firms, and compare them. For the investor who has a difficult time facing tenants and maintaining a building, property management may be the answer.

4

Location, Leverage, and Lenders

Ocean View Estates was a prestigious development in the hills overlooking the glittering lights of the rapidly growing city nestled in the northwest section of the U.S. When the first 12 residents purchased their $750,000 homes, they felt they were moving into a model, gated community with all the amenities a homeowner would ever want.

Unfortunately, that is not the way it worked out. The slumping economy derailed the builder—and his project. The Fortune 500 company that was planning to locate in the community delayed its plans, and with the postponement a number of executives who were planning to move into the community were no longer prospects. The builder, who had sunk everything he had into the development, was unable to complete it. The 12 owners found themselves in the midst of a ghost town. In contrast to their well-manicured lawns and impeccable homes, the remaining two dozen homes in the tract were vacant, and the yards rapidly became community eyesores.

Q: What is the most significant element when selecting a site for investment?

Location remains the most important criteria when selecting a site for investment. However, investors should be wary of properties that appear to be above suspicion as investment opportunities. The pitfalls—as in the case above—are not always obvious.

Q: In developments, what is the so-called "common area" and what is the significance in a project of common areas?

Common areas are areas within a development that are owned in common by all the property owners. Common areas, which are owned by all the buyers (when the project is completed), are most frequently found in condominium or townhouse projects. It is up to the builder to finish (landscape) the common areas before the development is completed and prior to all the buyers moving in. Occasionally, a builder who runs short of capital may not complete the common area. If the buyers do not insist on these areas being completed before they move into the development, they may find themselves putting in common areas afterward.

Q: Is there protection for the investor against developers who do not finish the common areas of a community?

In the past, when a builder failed in the middle of a project, the streets, curbs, gutters, and common area improvements in the tract often remained unfinished. Homeowners who had purchased property there would be left helpless, and more than one tract built by an overextended developer was put on the auction block or disposed of in bankruptcy court. But in today's highly regulated real estate environment, that outcome is highly unlikely. Investors will find that virtually every development tract has a bond in place with local government guaranteeing that homeowners—such as those in Ocean View—will not be left without recourse should the builder fail to complete the project. The local government will complete the development and demand payment from the bonding company. Bonds do not normally include improvements to individual lots.

Q: What are some of the factors that can negatively impact the value of residential developments?

For homeowners interested in seeing their properties appreciate, one of the worst pieces of news is that a strip center is going to be located contiguous to their residences. Strip centers seldom contribute anything to the enhancement of property values. In fact, the mixture of stores they frequently attract can have an opposite effect on homes—that is, they can, at times, cause values of nearby homes not to rise as rapidly as values of surrounding tracts.

Q: What is the purpose of a master plan as it relates to communities?

Generally, most communities have a master plan. The plan is usually drawn up by planners within the city or county and approved by the local planning commission. Years ago, there were few areas that were master planned, but the emergence of consumer groups and a growing interest in environmental issues caused government planners to pay more attention to how land in their communities was developed.

As a result, most planners sought the optimum configuration. Ideally, this would be a plan in which the property within a community was divided into the best, proposed usage. Planners would examine an area, and lay out exactly what portion of the area should be used for residential, commercial, and industrial purposes. Anyone thinking of buying a home in the community need only visit the local government agency and inspect the master plan to determine what was going to be built around them.

Q: How do government planners develop a master plan for a community?

Typically, the planners prefer to start with a main street or boulevard and work outward. The boulevard or main street would be designated commercial (i.e., retail stores, strip centers, minimalls). Behind or adjacent to it planners would place zoning for apartments, and behind the apartments there would be condominiums or townhomes. The area farthest from the commercial section would be single-family residences. In turn, builders would further divide these single family areas and put the moderately priced homes next to the townhomes and condominiums, and the higher-priced properties farther away.

In most cases, where single family residences are adjacent to commercial land because of zoning exception, homeowners suffer. The value of their properties appreciate at a slower rate, and the homes become difficult to sell.

Q: What "inside" investment information can the master plan provide for the developer and/or the investor?

Studying master plans gives the developer a clue as to what will be built in the surrounding area, and how it will impact (financially) his residential development.

Q: What is the value of master-planned communities?

The value of these master-planned communities can be illustrated by many master-planned areas throughout the country. For example, take the Irvine section of Orange County, California. The entire area, which is home today to close to one million people, was master planned. Commercial areas were restricted to boulevards, townhouses and condominiums were grouped together, moderate tract homes were developed in the same areas, and high-priced properties shared the same quality construction and location. Parks and recreation areas were well-placed, and although industrial sections are prominent, none adjoin any expensive housing.

Q: What advantages do master-planned communities offer investors?

The advantages are rapid appreciation and high demand. The Irvine section of Orange County has appreciated more rapidly than virtually any other area of the country. For example, the first, planned area (Mission Viejo), which was put on sale in the late 1960s with an average home price of $28,000, is today valued at more than $300,000. Certainly, there are many areas of Southern California that have appreciated rapidly, but there are few that can match the broad, rapid appreciation that has occurred in virtually every tract and project in Irvine.

In 1989 and 1990, when real estate throughout southern California suffered, and most developers were unable to move inventory, the Irvine section still attracted huge crowds for openings of new tracts, and in some cases there were still lotteries conducted to see who would be able to buy. It is an excellent example of the value and marketability of a master-planned area.

Q: Should investors stay away from areas that are not master planned?

Not necessarily. Investors and developers need not shy away from communities that are not master planned, nor should they avoid building new tracts next to old projects. On the contrary, there are numerous old tracts that have been well-maintained. A developer who is going to embark on a project next to an old tract should make sure the older homes are not rundown, the streets are maintained, and the lawns and yards are neat, well-groomed, and handsomely landscaped. A classic, old community of this type will not harm a new development.

Q: What should investors do if there is no master plan for the community in which they intend to buy?

If a master plan does not exist or has not been completed, the developer should visit city (or whatever government agency is involved) planners and staff members. He should outline his project and express his concerns. Every city would like to have a high-priced residential project, and the city/county staff can be of enormous help by making the builder aware of the possible commercial and other similar developments that could pose problems. Experienced builders have an understanding of zoning and what could be built on it.

Q: What is a "bad front door" in a development?

A bad front door refers to the access or entrance to a development. Before entering any tract, you must go through a perimeter or surrounding community. The condition of the encircling area impacts the desirability of the new tract. If it appears to be dumpy and ignored, prospects will shy away from the new area. If it is neat and well-manicured, it helps in marketing the area.

A bad front door, that is, an old, rundown, undesirable neighborhood adjacent to a new community, discourages buyers, regardless of the quality of the new development. Builders are aware of this impact, and if their project is next to a bad front door, they will go to almost any length to ensure access to their new development that is away from the less desirable community. They do not want prospects discouraged before they even have a chance to explore the new properties. Bad front doors can do exactly that.

Gated communities can be beautiful and filled with amenities, but if the surrounding area suffers it can be disastrous for the developer. Astute homebuyers do not purchase properties next to neighborhoods that are in poor condition and have old homes that are worth significantly less money. Their purchase will appreciate more slowly and their return will be substantially less than a home that is built among tracts of similar stature.

Q: What are some of the problems that might be encountered by inexperienced developers or builders when constructing their first tract?

There is a big difference between building one property and building a tract. Most developers get started with one and two homes, where the investment is significantly less than a tract. Ultimately, they get into larger tracts—when they are more experienced. The inexperienced developer or builder may not know the intricacies of planning and scheduling when it comes to building more than one structure at a time. For example, a builder has to be able to schedule painters, electricians, plumbers, plasterers, and a host of other expensive trade people without making them wait. Working this schedule for one or two homes is quite different than trying to coordinate an entire tract, in which the construction of some homes is ahead of others. A mistake in scheduling a tract can be a financial disaster. That's why experience—on the part of the builder—is an important consideration for investors.

Aside from scheduling of tradespeople, there can be location mistakes. When builders start out and only purchase one or two lots, they are usually buying in the middle of established residential neighborhoods. They could always determine how much the house would sell for by investigating the selling prices of surrounding properties. He never overbuilt. All the custom, single family homes he constructed were similar to others in the area. He never tried to put a five-bedroom, four-bath, two-story contemporary home in the midst of one-story, two- and three-bedroom houses. He recognized that would be overbuilding and he might never get the money out of the house that was required. His custom homes were always within the price range of the surrounding properties. If he built a home for someone who owned the land, he always constructed it to the owner's specifications. His marketing risk was nonexistent. That may change when the builder gets into a large tract and constructs homes that are not surrounded by similar structures.

Q: What problems do builders face if they decide to get involved in the selling as well as the building of the properties?

Building a project is one thing; selling is another. A builder has to worry about quality construction, adherring to codes, and dealing with government agencies. A builder who sells properties, however, has to deal with a far more complex entity—the consumer. Today's consumer is not only more sophisticated, but is ready to complain to an agency at the slightest provocation. And investors who intend to build and sell should keep in mind that there are countless government agencies waiting in the wings to aid consumers who run afoul of real estate developers.

Q: How long should it take a builder to construct one, single family residence?

It should not take longer than six months from the time ground is broken to construct one, single family residence. With three dozen homes, the same time is involved because an experienced builder would be using the same construction techniques, only there would be more people working on the project. Naturally, there is winter and adverse weather in some areas, so the builder strives to get the exterior work completed before inclement weather hits. Once the outside is completed, the interior can be finished regardless of weather conditions.

Q: What relationship does a construction loan—for investors—have to a line of credit?

The lender provides a construction loan—which is similar to a line of credit—and the builder draws money from the fund as needed. Interest payments start as soon as funds are drawn.

Q: Why is it so important to stay on schedule if you have a construction loan?

Obviously, the cost (interest) goes up if the project goes beyond the planned building schedule. Building schedules can easily get extended if the developer has little experience in scheduling skilled craftsmen and monitoring the progress on the project. Usually, the builder portions out work to subcontractors such as electricians, plumbers, and roofers. If they all arrive at the same time, they will be stepping on each other and standing around. It takes an experienced builder to avoid the confusion.

Q: At times, it appears that lenders are anxious to take over projects that fall in arrears with payments. Do lenders look for those opportunities so they can own property, and should investors be wary of this attitude?

Contrary to many popular notions, the lenders do not want to own property. They are in the business of making money by lending money, not by foreclosing on properties. When a lender runs into a developer who is less qualified than others, the builder will either be turned down or given a loan at an interest rate higher than the norm. The lender is evaluating the risk and charging for it.

Q: What criteria should be used when selecting locations?

Selecting the correct location for a development or invest-ment is a problem that is faced by everyone in the real estate field. It takes time, patience, investigation, and common sense.

With residential property, you do not want to pioneer a new area. That is, you do not want to be the first to build. Even though the community may be master planned, zoning and plans can be changed. On more than one occasion, investors found them-selves putting funds into a proposed master-planned residential community that was soon changed.

Q: What is the importance of demographics when investing?

Whether the development is new or old, investors must con-sider demographics—is the population moving, shifting, or aging. An investment in a tract of homes with a school nearby may cost more than one in which the school is a mile away, but suppose the population of the community is shifting; suppose it is aging and the number of school age children is rapidly shrinking. In many communities throughout the United States that is exactly what is happening. Communities that were once built and devel-oped for families are now housing "empty nesters," that is, par-ents whose kids have grown and moved out.

It is unlikely that these people are suddenly going to start raising kids again. If the empty nesters remain, what happens to the schools? Will they continue? Close down? What will happen if the school board decides to consolidate, close one or two schools, and send the remaining children to a third location? What hap-pens to the closed locations? Does the school retain and lease them? Or suppose the school district is short of funds and needs to sell the property. What happens if a developer purchases it, decides there is no market for single family residences, and in-stead builds apartments—in the midst of the residential area? Will the planning and zoning commissions oppose this? Will the city council (or other governing body) approve it? What does that do to the investor who has just purchased a piece of property a few doors away from the one-time school?

Q: Is it safer for investors to put their money in completely developed areas, where they can see what has been built, and they can evaluate the condition of the neighborhood?

Not necessarily. Things change—and so do communities. The following case involving Don Yaeger, an engineer, and his wife, a computer programmer, is a good example.

The Yaeger's saved diligently so they could invest in a community that was about 15 miles away from where they worked. Both were reasonably knowledgeable investors. They had studied the area, looked at the surrounding industry, and were careful to investigate the vacant land in the community. There was none in Inglegate, an upper, middle-class suburban city that had been incorporated for more than a half-century.

Inglegate was less than five miles from the ocean, and with its proximity to the downtown metropolitan area where the Yaeger's worked, it had grown rapidly. Originally a farming community, a good portion of its strawberry and bean fields were owned by Japanese who had come to this country in the early 1900s. The ties they had to the Far East remained, and following WW II, a number of Asian businesspeople used it as a base to develop trade relationships. Within a few years, the entire community started to boom, benefitting from the growing trade with the Far East.

Although it had not been master planned, Inglegate had significant commercial and industrial land set aside for development. By the early 1980s, all of it was developed because of the community's ability to attract companies searching for areas to relocate, and foreigners looking for communities in which to locate home offices.

During the 35 years following WW II, there was rapid growth. By 1980, Inglegate had a population of 250,000, its schools were filled to capacity, and vacant land was nonexistent. Housing in the area was desirable, but expensive. The average price for a single family residence was in excess of $200,000, and most of the homes were 2,000 square feet or more, designed for the growing family.

But as the decade came to a close, the population began to age. Children grew up and moved out. Empty nesters became a growing segment. The Yaeger's decided it would be an ideal community in which to raise a family. Aside from convenient location, it had a good school system, property that appreciated more rapidly than the norm, and a quality of life that was unmatched by many areas. They saved and purchased a $225,000, three-bedroom, two-bath, 20-year-old tract home that was within three blocks of a grammar school. Everything was ideal—and then it happened.

In 1990, faced with a declining enrollment, the school board voted to close two sites; one was the school in the Yaeger's area. At first, the Yaeger's were not concerned, but within weeks after the announcement they had cause to be. The board announced it had decided to sell the site to a local developer. Naturally, as homeowners and residents of the community, the Yaeger's were extremely anxious about the plans that the developer would unveil before the zoning commission.

The school occupied 12 acres and the developer proposed a combination townhouse/condominium project. In it would be a swimming pool and clubhouse. The Yaegers were concerned as they listened. The development would, of course, bring in more people, however, the Yaegers realized it would also bring in more children. With the demise of the school, that would put more pressure on the nearby school, which would absorb the children from the Yaeger's tract as well as the new development.

The Yaegers and other members of the tract banded together and decided to oppose the high density of the proposed development when it came before the planning commission for a vote. Although they would have preferred single family residences in lieu of the townhouse/condominium project, they knew that would not happen. With the average cost of housing as high as it was in the Yaeger's area, it was not feasible for developers to construct anything other than condominiums and townhomes. All they could hope for was a reduction in density—the city would allow the construction of fewer family units than the builder had requested.

Q: What political realities of putting money into projects should investors know about?

Revenue is one major one. More units mean more residents and more residents mean greater tax revenues. Few cities can turn that down, especially in today's environment of flat or decreasing tax revenues that many municipalities are facing.

Q: How do the revenue needs of cities impact investors?

With the increased revenues that some industries will bring to an area, the local governments are frequently bending the old rules to bring in a company and/or facility that will generate revenues.

Q: How do demographic shifts impact strip centers, malls, and industrial developments?

Demographic shifts in a community may mean investments in strip centers, malls, or industrial developments may not offer the hoped for return. With an aging population certain businesses that usually find success in a strip center are no longer viable. The video arcade, video rental facility, and convenience store have a difficult time generating a solid customer base from an older buying audience. Obviously, the arcade is a place that attracts kids, and although video rental stores find customers in virtually every age bracket, the bulk of its support comes from a younger audience, primarily 18 to 30 years old. Convenience stores, too, are primarily supported by a younger group of buyers, usually too impatient to shop in the supermarket and wait in lines. Strip centers that have tenants of this type, but a customer base that is aging, can be an abnormally high risk.

Q: What problems can an investor run into by putting monies into an industrial center that is located in an area with an aging population?

Industrial centers rely on the surrounding population for labor. In many cases, the wages are not as high as those paid in the service sector, and the prime employee is the younger, entry level worker. Owners of these small manufacturing concerns know that much of their work force depends on public transportation, as many young workers do not have automobiles. Unless an area has an abundance of young workers, many potential tenants will not locate in an area.

Q: What one phenomenon is every area subject to whether you are buying or investing?

The key in buying or investing in any residential area is to realize that it is subject to change. The school can become a condominium project, the industrial manufacturing park a property with few tenants, and the strip center a retail project that has leases with the wrong tenants.

Q: What is the first step investors should take before deciding on a location?

Before deciding on a location for residential, commercial, or industrial investments, the area should be carefully examined and divided geographically. Communities—which are essentially the same as areas—have one commonality that aids the investor in making a decision: an address, zip code, or name. Every mailing address (that is, the city) is determined by the post office in the area.

For example, every residence that is served by the Beverly Hills post office has a Beverly Hills mailing address. Every resident/business that is served by the Los Angeles post office has a Los Angeles address. Typically, all the residences and businesses that are within one city will be served by the post office in that city. City officials do not like to have their residents carry an address that reflects another city, even if the residents can be served more conveniently by the post office in that second city.

Q: How do communities sometimes end up with a more (or less) desirable mailing address?

It is possible for one community to be served by another's post office. This crossover generally occurs between nonincorporated areas. If the post office, for instance, is located in community X (a nonincorporated area), and it also serves community Y, both residents and businesses in X and Y will carry the X name. This procedure frequently results in a community carrying a more (or less) desirable mailing address.

More than one investor has made a buying mistake by assuming that the mailing address of the property reflects the city in which the home (or business) is located. Consequently, they may buy a home in an area and discover that they are nowhere near the school district or city that is reflected in the property's address.

Q: Can properties on one side of a street be worth more than the same properties on the other side?

Obviously, certain communities—because of their name— are more prestigious than others. Beverly Hills, of course, is one.

It is known worldwide for its high-end shopping, expensive housing, and impeccable name. Property in Beverly Hills is going to cost more than comparable property in another area that lacks the magic and allure of the Beverly Hills name.

This can be illustrated by the difference in property values on either side of Robertson Boulevard, a street that divides the city of Los Angeles from Beverly Hills. Properties on the Beverly Hills, or west side of the street, command a higher rental (and sales price) than properties on the east side, which carry a Los Angeles name. The prestige of the address carries credibility with it. For instance, mailorder is a multibillion dollar a year industry, yet despite its enormous sales the industry has always had an image problem. Years ago, nearly every mailorder firm that operated used a post office box as a return address because there was no need for a street address. Mailorder enterprises can be run out of someone's home, and merchandise can be shipped from a warehouse.

As consumers became more sophisticated, they also became suspicious and began to suspect the reliability of a business that "operated" with a post office box as an address. Astute mailorder firms realized the credibility (and sales) they lost by using a post office box address and they began renting commercial locations. As time went on, many mailorder marketers began to realize the value in not only renting a storefront, but in leasing a prestigious address—such as one in Beverly Hills.

Today, there is an inordinate amount of mailorder firms that are willing to pay premium rent if they can lease an office in Beverly Hills. In fact, one well-known mailorder jewelry firm paid almost 30% more rent to locate on the Beverly Hills' side instead of the east side (Los Angeles) of Robertson Boulevard. Almost every city has an example of this phenomena.

Q: What importance does address have for investment property?

A good (prestigious) address will always generate more rental income than one without the prestige. For example, the importance of an address has not escaped businesspeople. In the entertainment industry, for instance, attorneys, accountants, personal managers, and talent agencies are willing to pay premium rents for offices that reflect that "they are in the heart of the entertainment business." Many of these addresses are more prestigious than others. There may be excellent entertainment law firms, talent agents, accountants, or personal managers in west Los Angeles, but they do not have the prestige of firms located in Beverly Hills.

Q: What makes a property prestigious?

Virtually every city has locations that are prestigious, usually because of what people expect they will find on those streets. The value of a commercial office building is predicated on the same principles as a residential area. If everyone perceives the location as prestigious and a desirable place to live, it will be worth more than the surrounding area. When commercial real estate agents discover a prospect is in the entertainment business, and is an attorney, accountant, or personal manager, the agent will steer them to the commercial building where others of the same type lease space. And if all the leasing agents in an area direct clients to the same building(s), it becomes obvious what will happen. Within a short amount of time those buildings become more desirable than others, and the rent goes higher. Once the rents are higher, and the leasing terms more favorable to the landlord (owner), the property's price escalates as well.

Q: What is the prime determinant of the value of a property?

The value of a commercial building, strip center, industrial park, or residence is based on how strong is the demand and how limited is the supply. If everyone is clamoring for the same location, it is going to be worth more. Regardless of supply and demand, there are bargains for the investor who is willing to be patient, and carefully look for and evaluate properties.

Q: How does an investor determine the worth of a property?

The ideal scenario is one in which the investor has the building (or property) carry itself. In other words, the rents from the property cover the principal, interest and taxes—and there is something left over for the return on investment (ROI). This is, of course, the ideal investment. In real life, these are seldom found.

Q: What are some of the unrealistic expectations that investors may have when it comes to property?

Most want to put down the least amount of money and generate the greatest return. That does not happen. In fact, properties that have little invested and are leveraged to the maximum (i.e., buying the most property with the least amount of cash) can be dangerous.

Q: What dangers are involved in trying to buy the most property for the least money?

The danger comes from several areas. First, if an investor is examining a $1 million property, and is able to purchase it with $100,000 down, and finance the remainder, it is highly leveraged. The loan ($900,000) to value ($1 million)—that is, the 90% loan— means the buyer is faced with several problems. The buyer/ investor who wants to sell finds it is not easy to unload the property because there is little room for negotiating or maneuvering. In contrast, a property that has a 50% loan to value ($500,000 down and $500,000 mortgage) provides the owner with more options. The equity in the property gives the owner room to drop the price. The buyer also knows that with 50% equity, the seller has the option to sell, to refinance, or to borrow additional funds. But with a 90% loan, a seller has few options and the buyer knows it. There is little chance a bank is going to lend additional funds on a structure that is already 90% financed.

Q: What impact does a highly leveraged (buying the most property with the least money) property have on a loan?

Financing a highly leveraged structure usually results in a less favorable loan. Banks charge interest based on the loan/value ratio, and the higher the ratio the higher the interest rate and/or loan fees. It is also difficult for an investor to obtain financing on highly leveraged properties. Despite the difficulties of the savings and loan institutions, and the recent problems some banks have had with real estate loans, most bankers are astute and understand the danger of lending funds on a highly leveraged property. Bankers are not in the business of being landlords—which is what can happen with highly leveraged properties.

Q: How has lending criteria for real estate changed?

In today's environment, lending criteria have become tougher. The era of junk bonds and banks taking flyers with nearly every high roller and crapshooter who came along is gone. When an investor walks in the door of a lending institution, opens an account, deposits $200,000, and then asks for a 90% loan on a property, the reply of the banker differs today from a few years ago. Instead of opening their checkbooks, the banker will suggest the investor put the $200,000 in the property as well. Of course, there are exceptions. If the bank president or loan officer knows the investor, there is a chance they will bend. But, in general, the days of the high rates of return, the commissions, and the kickbacks are gone. Investors need cash, and equity in a property.

Q: What penalties may an investor encounter when trying to finance a highly leveraged property?

The investor who succeeds in obtaining highly leveraged financing may be signing away certain rights. For instance, the bank may ask the investor to assign all leases on the property to the bank. The moment there is a problem and the investor falls behind or defaults on a month's rent, the banker may contact the tenants and instruct them to make payments directly to the bank. Of course, this clause is a death knell to an investor who is highly leveraged and needs rental monies for both the bank payment and income. Investing in a property and leaving little margin has other problems aside from finding a lender. There is little room for error. For example, if the property suddenly has a significant maintenance problem, the owner may not be able to afford the entire repair at one time. The owner of a highly leveraged property also has difficulty asking bankers for additional funds to repair the plumbing or electrical circuits. Consequently, the owner may be unable to make the repairs. Once this happens, tenants become unhappy (rightfully so) because the plumbing and electricity do not properly work. Their employees complain, and finally they hear grumbling from clients who might be visiting. Obviously, there is only one step left: the tenant breaks the lease and moves. The owner is not only stuck with a vacancy, but decreased rental income and a building that is even more leveraged than before.

Q: What is meant by "working backward" when trying to evaluate an investment?

To evaluate an investment and determine if it is the correct one, investors should actually work backward from the desired percent of the rate of return to determine the purchase price of the investment. At this point, investors have to determine how much they want to leverage their investment. Maximum leverage—that is, buying the most property with the least output of cash—is certainly possible, but there are penalties in the form of higher interest (on the loan) or more collateral (investors have to put up their homes and other personal belongings).

Q: What determines the rate of return on an investment?

The rate of return on investment should be determined by the risk involved and what other investments with similar risk will pay. Investors should also examine how long they want to hold a real estate investment.

Q: How does property differ from other investments?

Unlike stocks, real estate is not liquid and cannot always be sold exactly when the investor decides it is time. In fact, real estate investors most often get "burned" when they buy for the short term (under three years) and hope to make most of their money as the property appreciates.

Q: What is wrong with buying real estate during a high appreciation frenzy?

The investor who gets hooked and loses is the one who buys in the midst of a high appreciation frenzy, in other words, when properties are increasing in value every year in double digits. Sooner or later this rapid appreciation will slow or end. Eventually, the market runs out of buyers who can afford the high-priced properties, or investors decide to wait for a slowdown. When this happens the sales and prices drop almost overnight. A classic case is New England. For more than two years, New England real estate soared in value, exceeding 20% appreciation per year. Suddenly, there was some negative economic news in the northeast, and almost instantly properties in the area stopped selling. Those that did sell sold at drastically reduced prices.

Q: How long should investors hold real estate before selling?

If the idea is to buy and sell in under five years and make a profit, real estate may be the wrong investment. Of course, if everything went well, it could be the investor would be able to sell a property without problem in under two years. But if there were any economic slowdown or change, anything to impact the confidence of investors, the short-term scenario is going to fail.

Q: What method can be used to evaluate the return on an office building investment?

There are definite ways the property and return for an office building should be evaluated.

Let us say, for example, that the net profit from rents (per year) in the office building is $30,000, and the investor is after a 10% return. Dividing the net profit by the desired rate of return gives the maximum amount of money the investor should put down on the property. A greater figure would return less than the 10%.

Consider starting from the amount of money one has to invest. Let us say, for example, that an investor has $300,000 to invest. The investor knows that the money can be invested in T-Bills, CDs, and money market accounts with little risk and still earn 5%–8%.

If an 8% spendable return on the $300,000 investment is sought, a property should be selected for which the estimated net rental income will be $24,000 per year. If the investor wants a 10% spendable return, the estimated net rental income should be $30,000.

$$\frac{\text{Estimated net profit}}{\text{Amount of desired return}} \quad \frac{\$30,000}{.10} = \$300,000$$

Estimated net profit $\quad\quad \dfrac{\$30,000}{.08} = \$375,000$
Amount of desired return

In other words, the investor can generate a 10% return, but cannot put in more than $300,000 in cash. To generate an 8% return, the amount of cash that can be invested is $375,000.

The key is for the investor to first determine the desired return, normally expressed as a percentage. If the building is in great demand, for example, a commercial office complex that is nearly filled to capacity, has long-term leases, is in an excellent area, is well-known, and is well-maintained, the investor may decide on a lower spendable rate of return on the investment; because of the demand for the property, the investor knows that it will appreciate more rapidly than other similar structures. Although real estate is not the most liquid investment, it has the unique advantage of appreciating. Thus, in addition to rents (cash flow) and depreciation (tax deduction), a real estate investment has the added benefit of being worth more than when the buyer purchased it.

Q: What can an average 5% appreciation per year mean to a real estate investor?

An average 5% appreciation means investors not only can earn their desired spendable rate of return on their investment, but they have a structure that is worth nearly 30% more in five years:

Purchase price = *$1 million*

End of year one value of building at 5% appreciation = $1,050,000

End of year two value of building at 5% appreciation = $1,102,000

End of year three value of building at 5% appreciation = $1,157,100

End of year four value of building at 5% appreciation = $1,214,955

End of year five value of building at 5% appreciation = $1,275,703

Q: What does net rental income mean to the investor?

If an owner is asking, for instance, $1.2 million for an office complex, the first thing for investors to examine is the net rental income (this is what remains after property taxes, principal, interest, and maintenance are deducted). If the net return is $80,000 per year, investors must determine how much they are willing to be indebted to get that $80,000. If they want the $80,000 to represent an 8% spendable return on their investment, they would divide the percent into the net return and get $1 million—the maximum amount they should invest to achieve their desired rate of return.

Net profit from rents (after taxes, interest, principal, and maintenance) = $80,000 ÷ .08 (8% desired annual return) = $1 million

Assume the investor had $1 million to invest and wanted an 8% return or $80,000 per year. Assuming the investor receives the $80,000 spendable return on the investment each year, the following analysis will reflect the average annual return.

Net rental income $80,000 × 5 years = $400,000
Five-year appreciation   +   255,703
Gross pretax return on investment   = $655,703

Gross return on investment

Holding period

$$\frac{\$655{,}703}{\text{Five years}} = \$131{,}140 \text{ per year}$$

Average annual return

Capital investment

$$\frac{\$131{,}140}{\$1 \text{ million}} = 13.1$$

The average return for this illustration is 13.1%.

This example would represent a conservative approach to investing, which yields a conservative return. Had the appreciation been 8 or 9%, as it can be, the return would have been greater.

Q: How does the average return on investment aid the investor in determining what price should be paid for a property?

If the investor wants the $80,000 to represent an 8% spendable return, the price of the property cannot be $1.2 million; it has to be $1 million. Otherwise, if the investor was willing to pay $1.2 million for the $80,000 profit per year, the percentage of spendable return would be less than 8%. In fact, it would be 6.67%. The investor's goal—for an 8% return—is to get the seller to drop the price.

Calculating the spendable rate of return in this manner is "forcing the investment" backward—but the forcing does not stop at this point. Next the investor should determine the loan, and the loan that the present owner has on the property to get a clearer picture of how much the property is worth.

Suppose the present owner purchased the property for cash. Now, the owner does not owe any principal or interest, but does have taxes and maintenance. Even though the owner does not have principal and interest payments, the net is only $80,000. Now, a buyer who comes along and pays $1.2 million for the property will not have a net of $80,000. On the contrary, the net will be far less since principal and interest payments, something the present owner does not have, have to be factored in. That means the new buyer will neither be making 8% nor generating a 6.67% return, either. Profits will be significantly less because of those principal and interest payments on the loan.

On the other hand, the owner who had to pay principal, interest, taxes, and maintenance, and was still generating $80,000 on the $1 million structure, would have an 8% return. But if the owner insists on selling it for $1.2 million, the return would drop to 6.67%.

However, the invested cash will also be less. Therefore, the rate of return must be recalculated. Assume that the investor wishes to obtain a 70% or a $700,000 loan. Assume further that the payment of principal and interest is $7,000 per month or $84,000 per year. Using the earlier example, the owner would have a loss of $4,000 per year (net income, $80,000 less payments of $84,000) on the investment.

This is deceiving because we have not yet factored in the appreciation of the property. The previous example assumed a 5% per year increase in the value of the building. At the end of five years, the building would have increased by $275,703. The following analysis shows that the rate of return on the investment is much higher.

Five-year negative cash flow at $4,000 per year	($ 20,000)
Five-year appreciation	275,703
Gross pretax return on investment	$255,703

$$\frac{\text{Return on investment}}{\text{Holding period of five years}} \quad \frac{\$255,703}{5} = \$51,140$$

$$\frac{\text{Average annual return}}{\text{Capital investment}} \quad \frac{\$ 51,140}{\$300,000} = 17\%$$

Seventeen percent is the average annual return on the investment. This illustrates why some investors will leverage their investments. In this situation the investor could purchase three separate properties with a down payment on each of $300,000, and a $700,000 loan on each. The investor would have had $100,000 left in the bank to handle a portion of the annual negative cash flow for each unit of $20,000 or a total of $60,000 for the first year.

Q: What problems may be encountered by an investor who has low cash reserves?

If a major, unexpected repair becomes necessary on the property, the investor (owner) may not have the funds to fix it.

Q: Why are maintenance records and maintenance critically important when it comes to office buildings?

An office building is similar to an automobile, and there are many property owners who treat buildings the same way they do their car. There is, of course, no question as to how important maintenance is when it comes to automobiles. Automobile owners who skimp on maintenance and put it off in hopes of saving a few dollars usually invite disaster. A simple maintenance problem turns into a major repair.

Some property owners feel that because their building is stationary, there is no need to constantly check the plumbing, heating, air conditioning, wiring, roof, and elevators. They often put off routine maintenance, and as a result what was once an inexpensive repair turns into a major expenditure. Most owners, however, realize the importance of building maintenance. They know that failure to remove one unattractive spot on the carpet may lead tenants (and visitors) to believe that no one cares about the carpet or looks of the building. Consequently, they can drop trash on the carpet and put cigarettes out on the floor.

Q: What can investors surmise when they see a building with poor maintenance records?

Poor maintenance records indicate something about the owner. Owners who are cognizant of the importance of maintenance are usually those who have invested significant funds in the property. They want to protect their investment. On the other hand, investors who are highly leveraged and in debt are more likely to put off routine maintenance because they cannot afford it. Even when the building begins to suffer, maintenance is put off.

Infrequent or poor maintenance is a sign to investors that a building has not been cared for properly. It is also a warning to check the structure carefully before making any financial commitment.

Q: What are the high-cost items when it comes to repair in a commercial structure?

Investors walking through a poorly kept building (or for that matter a well-kept structure) should make sure to check the roof, wiring, plumbing, foyer/entry, elevators, and carpeting. These are the high-cost items, the backbreakers. For example, it is relatively easy to get an elevator inspector to check on the condition of the elevator. If the elevator is out of alignment, the repair cost could be monumental. If the elevator surges, it could be a sign of other problems. It is usually one of these items that investors will have problems with if they purchase a poorly maintained structure.

Check the maintenance records of the building. Determine how often routine service was conducted. Is this standard in the industry? Is the maintenance infrequent? If so, why? Does the owner fear the cost of repairs (when they are found to be needed) will be too high, and thus puts off routine checks?

Q: In evaluating a building, is it advisable to utilize a property management firm?

In checking a building, property management firms can be of significant aid. They know what can go wrong and what the symptoms may be. It does not take much effort for a potential investor to visit a property management firm, talk to one of the managers, let them know you are planning to purchase the building down the street, and ask if they could give you some guidelines on what the maintenance should be in the building.

Most property managers will be happy to oblige. Although they are not managing the building, they know if they provide service and help an investor answer questions, they could be selected to manage the building. They are an excellent resource for the investor who is contemplating a property. Aside from guidelines, most property management firms that are near the building you are thinking of buying usually know the history (and problems) of the structure. They know if the property is in demand, and they know if the tenants are long-term or transient.

Q: What other factors—aside from the condition of the building and return on investment—should be checked by investors before making a purchase?

Among the other factors to be checked before entering into an agreement to purchase a complex are the tenants and the written conditions within the leases.

For example, suppose an investor decides to buy an office building that is priced at $1 million. Our investor puts down $300,000, and therefore is not highly leveraged, and borrows $700,000 from a local bank. Based on lease income and mortgage expense, calculations indicate that there will be a gross income of $9,000 per month from rents and an expenditure of $7,000 a month to service the debt, or mortgage.

The $2,000 gross profit retained each month translates to $24,000 a year, and based on our previous formula the return on investment will be 8%:

$$\frac{\$24,000 \text{ per year (gross profit)}}{\$300,000 \text{ total cash investment}} = 8\% \text{ return on investment}$$

Q: What is the relationship between the consumer price index (CPI) and rent increases?

Many investors anticipate or gamble that the CPI calculated annual rent increases will provide sufficient cash flow to reduce the negative return. The bottom line remains the same; the higher the projected return the greater the risk. Thus, the investor has a choice: to pay the $1.2 million and be satisfied with the 6.67% return or to try to negotiate the $200,000 difference between the present owner's price and what the investor calculates the building should be valued at if it is to generate an 8% return.

Q: How does the profit on a building and/or office complex relate to the CPI clause in the lease?

The CPI, which is an indicator that is published monthly by the U.S. government, reflects inflation and is not only a good indicator of how much rents should go up, but a fair one. It enables investors/owners to keep pace with rising costs, which will impact the running and maintaining of a property. For instance, a key component that impacts the CPI is the cost of fuel. Increased energy costs are not only reflected in the CPI, but the investor/owner experiences them firsthand through higher electric and gas bills. Any services provided to the owner (i.e., trash pickup) that are impacted by energy will also cost the investor/owner more. Without the CPI clause, investors would soon find their 8% return significantly diminished.

How much could an investor lose without a CPI clause? During the past four to five years, the CPI has risen an average of 4 to 5% per year. Therefore within two years, an investor's 8% return would be reduced to zero when considering the spending power of the investor's income within a few years if it were not for the CPI clause.

With the CPI clause, however, the value of an investment changes dramatically. Take, once again, our hypothetical $1 million building, with its $300,000 down payment, $9,000 a month income ($24,000 a year gross profit following mortgage expense), and $7,000 per month mortgage payment. Following the investor's first year of ownership, the CPI went up a nominal 5%. Raising a tenant's rent 5% will not be significant to most firms. But to the owner of the building it can have an incredible impact.

Once the rents are raised 5%, instead of a $24,000 per year gross profit, the investors/owners are looking at $29,400 (gross profit is profit before expenses, which vary because of maintenance, other repairs, etc.).

$9,000 per month × 5% CPI = $450 per month × 12 = $5,400
$5,400 plus the previous rental of $24,000 = $29,400 gross profit

Now, take the new gross profit and divide by the initial ($300,000) investment:

$$\frac{\$29{,}400}{\$300{,}000} = 9.8\% \text{ return on investment}$$

Investors/owners should not view this as increased profit—it primarily enables the return on the investment to keep up with the cost of living. The cash flow increases their gross return because their costs ($7,000 per month mortgage payment) have remained the same. It does not take long before that 8% return has nearly doubled.

$9,450 (gross rent per month) × 5% = $472.50 × 12 = $5,670

Now, $5,670 is added to the gross profit ($29,400) for a total of $35,070 (gross profit) per year.

$$\frac{\$35{,}070}{\$300{,}000} = 12\% \text{ return on investment during the second year}$$

Q: What does triple net mean when referring to rental properties?

The one way to calculate the net profit (profit after all expenses) at the time of investing is to invest in a property in which the rent is based on a so-called "triple net," which means the rent is net of taxes, net of insurance, and net of repairs. The tenants' leases state that they—the tenant—shall pay all of these expenses throughout the term of their lease. This is becoming an increasingly popular method of leasing. One drawback to the triple net is that a tenant may fail to do the repairs, therefore the landlord should estimate these expenses and collect them monthly and make the repairs, pay the taxes and make annual adjustments to the tenant's monthly payment for these items.

Q: What advantages does the CPI clause offer the investor or owner?

With the CPI, the owner does not have to separate utility bills and charge tenants individually for lights, heat, and water. Those increases will be reflected in the CPI when it is released by the government. Still, there are occasions when owners have to be careful about leaving the increased cost of utilities to the CPI. There may be, for instance, particular tenants that are energy intensive. They may use inordinate amounts of electricity, water, or gas. In cases such as these, it is a good idea to have a rider written into the lease that allows a higher proportion of these expenses to be passed on to the tenants who incur the cost or to have a separate meter installed.

Q: Can CPI clauses sometimes cause problems for manufacturers who lease space?

Suppose, for instance, a tenant is manufacturing or producing a part for the government. In many cases, the contract under which the tenant operates prohibits the tenant (manufacturer) from raising prices more than the CPI. Or it may have a ceiling of 5 or 6%. If the CPI goes up 7%, and the building owner has a lease that dictates an equivalent raise in rents, the manufacturer may be in a quandry. After all, the manufacturer's agreement restricts increases to 6%. In situations such as this tenants will often ask the owner to structure the lease so that the rent increase will not top the increase they can obtain from their customers.

Q: What benefit does every owner or investor in a building have regardless of the lease terms and presence of the CPI?

The one benefit every owner has is depreciation. Although the tax laws change almost every year, depreciation generally allows the owner to deduct the entire cost of the building over a period of years. In effect, depreciation is a tax deduction, and shelters the investor from taxes. In most cases, commercial real estate owners seldom pay taxes because of the depreciation factor. Imagine the cost of a $1 million building (not the cost of the ground) being deducted over a 20-year period. In other words, a $50,000 deduction is supplied to the owner each year for 20 years. Although the tax laws may not allow this specific scenario, the availability of depreciation to the investor is a benefit unmatched by other investments.

Q: What categories do industrial parks generally fall into?

Industrial parks generally fall into two categories: high-tech or high "schlock" (sloppy, rundown). As a rule, the schlock parks do not grow. They are usually frequented by noisy, sloppy, man-ufacturing-intensive companies. Although the rents may be lower than in the high-tech park, the tenant who is going to do high-tech business will stay away from the rundown facilities simply because of the image it will give his business.

Q: Why do high-tech parks offer the greatest incentive for investors?

The "four walls" that are the trademark of these parks are relatively inexpensive, but owners run into sizable expenditures when it comes to leasing space and building it out to suit the tenant. A portion of the cost of the interior improvement is absorbed by the landlord or owner. For this reason, the owner of the industrial building usually seeks a longer term lease and a stronger tenant than the owner of an office building.

The owner of an industrial building may approach a bank and borrow money over a 10-year period for interior improvements to meet the tenant's needs. To improve a 20,000 square foot building the owner may borrow $300,000 at 10% and amortize the expenditure over the terms of the lease. In other words, the cost of the improvement to the interior ($300,000) is built into the tenant's lease.

Q: How do you calculate rent on industrial properties?

The average, unimproved industrial property rents for about 30 cents a square foot. With the $300,000 improvement, the cost per square could nearly double, to 55 cents a square foot. This would be the base cost landlords/owners face. To profit, they would add the cost of the financed improvements to generate the return on investment they desire.

The lease the industrial owner will generally produce is one that binds the tenant to the property for at least 10 years. The goal of the owner is to make sure the tenant remains for the time it takes to pay off the improvement; in the case of the $300,000 loan (25 cents per square foot) that means a 10-year lease. Tenants who want the improvements have to be willing to commit to the time period.

The owner should be sure of other things in addition to the 10-year commitment. Is the tenant financially secure? Is the tenant a major company, or backed by a major company? Does the owner foresee any difficulty in the tenant living up to a 10-year lease?

Q: What is a "single purpose" tenant, and what impact can one have on an industrial park?

Suppose a tenant signs the lease, but through some unforeseen circumstances goes out of business and moves out? The owner must consider this possibility, and in doing so has to evaluate the usage of the improvements. How usable would the space be for another client? Would it have broad usage? Or would the design of the internal structure be such that only someone in the same line of business as the original tenant could rent it? For instance, suppose the interior was built out for a "single purpose" tenant, that is, a renter who asked for improvements that made the interior into tiny rooms. Obviously, if this tenant goes out of business, the owner is going to have a more difficult time finding a replacement tenant than if there were just four walls with standard offices inside. As a rule, the stronger the "single purpose" usage the space has, the longer (and stronger) the lease should be. If a tenant has special security, storage, or other needs that would be of little use to others, the owner must go after the stronger, longer lease.

Q: What are the hidden bonuses in having strong tenants with long-term leases in industrial-type buildings?

The tenant who asked for the $300,000 in improvements, which the owner amortizes over a 10-year period at 25 cents a square foot, is a plus for an owner. Once the 10 years is up, the $300,000 is paid off—and the owner has a 25 cent a square foot rent increase bonus. This is an excellent feature that investors should keep in mind when examining industrial parks and buildings.

Q: How does the strip center differ from the office and/or industrial park when it comes to location?

Although office buildings can be off the main street and still show a good return, location is critical when it comes to strip centers. Tenants and their clients may travel miles to get to an office building, and the same is true—although not to the same extent—of industrial parks. But when it comes to strip centers watch out—consumers will not travel or go out of their way to get to one (unless, of course, there is a unique retail location that is in high demand and cannot be found elsewhere). Strip centers require high traffic locations. As a rule, it is better for a strip center to be close to other strip centers. Isolation and exclusivity do not breed profit for the strip center owner. The strip center must be located (1) in a high traffic area and (2) preferably in a high traffic area that already is home to one or two other strip centers. The more strip centers around, the more proof that the area can support one. If there are none in the area, an investor who decides to build takes an inordinate risk. The investor becomes a pioneer.

Q: What is a main problem for the strip center investor?

One of the greatest obstacles the strip center owner runs into is the tenant. Unlike the office or industrial park tenants, which are usually service, high-tech, or manufacturing, the strip center is loaded with retailers. There is no higher failure rate among businesses than the retailer.

For many Americans, owning their own store is a dream they would love to fulfill. To most, owning their own restaurant is even a greater dream. To the strip center landlord, restaurants can be a plague and the naive retailer a problem. Restaurants, donut shops (nearly every strip center seems to have one), pizza parlors, and other similar food establishments bring an odor to the center that seldom leaves. This is particularly true when it comes to donut shops and the grease that is utilized. The pungent odor may not leave for years after the tenant has vacated, if ever.

Another business that is frequently found in the center is the neighborhood bar or tavern. To build trade, nearly every bar owner will start some pool or similar tournament. The end result is the bar's business builds and so does the noise.

Q: What type of tenant mix should be sought for strip centers?

Strip centers can be winners if the right elements are present. The convenience store provides an excellent anchor and will draw traffic for the rest of the tenants.

Complementing a 7-11 type business would be an ice cream store or an auto parts retail outlet. Although ice cream and 7-11s provide food, there is little cooking (mainly warming in a microwave at the 7-11) that is done on the premises.

Q: Are there parking pitfalls in strip centers?

Investors should also be aware that most strip centers do not have an abundance of parking. That means retailers (such as restaurants) that have tenants who make a half-hour to hour-long visit are going to clog the parking lot and make it difficult for other tenants. High-traffic convenience stores may stay away from centers that have a restaurant because of the parking problem that will be created. This problem was quite evident in a strip center that opened in the southeast. Of the seven stores, there was a restaurant, a fast-food outlet, a dress shop, a convenience store, a donut shop, a beauty parlor, and a travel agent. The parking situation created by the restaurant paralyzed business for the other store owners. About the only time there was enough parking was early in the morning, before the restaurant opened.

The convenience store complained and threatened to break its lease. The investors/owners gathered together and tried to work out a solution, but before they could a center across the street opened with twice the number of parking spaces. Within three months, three of the stores in the first center had broken leases and moved across the street. The investors were left with a center that had enormous potential but suffered because of a poor mix of tenants and inadequate parking.

Every commercial property has opportunity—and offers a return. The key to making the correct investment is to carefully examine the area, the customers, and the desirability of the location. Carefully look at the return and match it with your goals. Factor in contingencies. Make sure the location is correct, and not nearly correct. Talk to real estate people, bankers, and accountants. Although none will have the entire story, each can contribute important advice and history on a community before an investment is made.

Remember, too, objectivity. There is no room for emotion with an investment, save one—your gut instinct.

If it says pass, do so.

5
Financing and Negotiating

He was one of the best-known speakers in the country. In fact, in the real estate industry and to consumers who were looking for ways to take advantage of the skyrocketing commercial and home values in the mid-1980s, he was regarded as one of the shrewdest negotiators and financing geniuses in the country. To some, he became a legend and guru, and his techniques for buying a property with no money down were written about, chronicled, taped, and sold to millions of hopeful investors.

During his heyday, some 1,500 to 2,000 people jammed seminars to hear him speak. His notoriety came to the attention of a major west coast newspaper, which challenged him to buy a home without any money down. The newspaper spent several days traveling with him, and at the end of the time he did, indeed, purchase a property without any down payment. There was, however, a slight catch. As it turned out, the purchase was made because he was able to utilize another piece of property that he owned as security. Still, the newspaper could not deny it; he delivered what he promised and bought property with no money down.

Investors throughout the country eyed his techniques with envy. They saw property appreciating in double digits, and if they could duplicate the guru's approach, hold the property for just a few months and then sell, they might make 20%–30% on their investment.

It was during this time that 31-year-old Don Winston, a draftsman who lived in an apartment on the outskirts of downtown San Francisco, came to one of the guru's seminars. He listened intently as two people in the audience stood and attested to the fact that they did buy property without any funds after attending one of the speaker's seminars and following his instructions.

Winston and nearly 1,000 others in the room paid $50 apiece to sit in on the hour-long seminar. The speaker spoke primarily in generalities, but by the end of the session Winston was so enthused that he bought the $150 cassette tape instructional program. After listening to the tapes two or three times, Winston felt he had the technique mastered. He spent the next 10 days following the instructional tapes, finding a property, and attempting to buy it with no money down. To Winston's dismay, he struck out.

Q: Is it possible to buy property with no money down?

Yes, however, the buyer/investor has to find a seller who is desperate to sell and/or is ignorant or trusting.

Q: What type of financial approach does a "no money down" property take?

First, it takes a seller who has little equity in the property. Thus, the seller has little to lose and is willing to go for a fly-by-night proposition. For example, say a property is on the market and listed for $100,000. The property has an $80,000 mortgage, which illustrates one of the requirements needed—the owner has little equity. The seller also has to be anxious. Once these two factors are determined, the buyer approaches the seller with the following (or a similar) proposition. Follow the buyer through this typical, no money down transaction:

"You've had the property on the market for six months with no success. It is listed for $100,000, and if you do sell it $6,000 (or 6%, which is the approximate fee a broker collects from a sale) will come off the top leaving you with $94,000. Escrow and title costs will run another $2,000, leaving you $92,000. And, judging by the length of time the property has been on the market, it is probably overpriced. Thus, even if you do get a buyer for the property, the buyer will not give you more than $98,000, thus reducing the net to approximately $90,000."

Most sellers would agree that the above scenario is fairly accurate. They would acknowledge that the $100,000 gross would probably end up closer to $90,000, once expenses and fees were deducted. The seller who goes along with the above is ready for the no money down proposition.

The buyer/investor proceeds in the following manner. "I will do you a favor. Instead of buying the property from the real estate agent for the listed price (which will net you $90,000), I will give you the full $100,000, but you have to do me a favor. I'll give you a promissary note for $20,000, which will be secured by the property. You move out and I will take over the property and the $80,000 mortgage.

"The promissary note will be due and payable to you within one year. It will bear 12% interest, which means you make an additional $2,400. How can you miss?"

On the surface, the proposition sounds like a winner for the seller. The seller not only sells the property for the full $100,000, but gets $20,000, and if the buyer waits a year before paying it, also collects an additional 12%.

The buyer makes out, too. No funds have to be put up and the buyer has 12 months to produce the $20,000 (plus $2,400). In the meantime, the property can be earning money.

Q: Why is buying for no money down a proposition that can hurt both buyers and sellers, and raise a question of ethics at the same time?

What typically happens (if sellers go along with the proposition) is that buyers take over the property and try to sell it. They put it on the market for $105,000 or $110,000 in an effort to profit from the deal. Buyers are betting that they are better marketers than the sellers—and they may be. They have 12 months in which to find another buyer (for $105,000–$110,000). The new owner typically advertises the property for $5,000 to $10,000 down payment—which is low and extremely attractive to homebuyers. The investor tries to "sell" the unwary on their ability to refinance the property when the $20,000 (remaining down payment) plus interest becomes due in a year. While purchasers may scoff at this possible solution, their desire to get into the property may be overwhelming, thereby causing them to take a chance. In the meantime, while the new owners are trying to sell the property to naive prospects, they do not sit there and just make mortgage payments. They rent it.

Q: What should a buyer about to enter into a no money down arrangement ask for?

An agreement. Without one, there are major pitfalls.

Q: What do buyers have to play on when entering into a no money down transaction?

Seller desperation.

Q: Are time shares good investments?

No, and for several reasons. Just as desperation works to the buyer's advantage when it comes to no money down, it works to the investor's disadvantage when it comes to buying another well-known recent innovation in real estate—the time share. Time share is a concept whereby more than one person owns a property. Generally, the property is in a resort or vacation area, or some place where the owner/investor really cannot use it more than two or three weeks a year. Many time shares are located in mountain resorts or a vacation paradise such as Hawaii.

Q: Why have time shares proven to be popular if they are not good investments?

The investor gets a chance to own a second piece of property, that would normally be too expensive for them to buy, by simply sharing the ownership with other time-sharing partners. In many ways, time shares have some of the features of a limited partnership. Investors with limited capital can purchase something worth a great deal more than their funds will allow. But, unlike most limited partnerships, time shares can be used by the investors. In the case of most limited partnerships, the funds are invested in a commercial venture and the properties are rented. The limited partner usually benefits only when the property is sold or a dividend is declared.

Q: How did time shares come about?

Time shares started with sellers who owned vacation or resort property. Typically, this property is difficult to move. It does not have the mass market appeal of a residential tract in an urban area. Take, for instance, a $500,000 property in the ski resort community of Mammouth, California. Most buyers for this type of property are usually executives, entrepreneurs, or other highly successful business or professional people who can afford a second ($500,000 or more) home. Obviously, this is a limited market, and trying to find a buyer is difficult for the seller. But, suppose the seller finds 26 buyers, and he sells each buyer two weeks of usage at a reduced price. If the deal can be successfully put together, the seller not only unloads the property but makes a significant profit as well.

Q: What type of financial incentive do those marketing time shares try to use on investors?

The time share investment is usually sold by a polished, well-organized marketing company, not a real estate agent. The pitch usually starts out with a question to the investor similar to the following: "How much do you pay for one night's vacation? $100?" If the answer is affirmative, the time share salesperson goes on. "Let's assume that $100 a night is an average cost, which means if you take two weeks' vacation you are going to spend $1,400 (14 days × $100). Right?"

The answer is, of course, yes. From there, the time share salesperson goes on with another hypothetical question. "Let's look and see how you finance that vacation. If you took $20,000, put it in the bank, and earned 8% interest, you would have $1,600 a year. With tax on the earned interest, you might have enough ($1,400) left to take that vacation. The $20,000 stays the same; it never appreciates, right? Now, what happens five years from now if you are still trying to use the same $20,000 to finance your vacation? You know what will happen—it won't be enough because of inflation. Just assuming 5% inflation a year, means that $100 a night hotel room is going to cost around $125, and your two week vacation is going to be cut to 10 days. As time goes on, the vacation that $20,000 is going to finance becomes less and less; the days fewer and fewer. Even the $20,000 that you've been holding to finance the vacation has depreciated. You continue to lose."

Obviously, the investor—or anyone—would be agreeing. How can you argue with inflation? How can you argue with the desire to take two weeks' vacation a year? Once the seller has the investor agreeing, the seller takes him to the next plateau:

"How would you like to invest $30,000, use it to buy a two week vacation every year for the rest of your life, have an interest in real estate at the same time, and have a tax deduction as well?"

Q: What do time share investors actually own?

If there are 20 investors in a piece of property, the time share investor owns 1/20th. If there are 30, the investor owns 1/30th. Take, for instance, a time share that has 26 investors. For the money, the investor owns 1/26th of a piece of property, has 1/26th the appreciation, and has a two week vacation (the lodging portion) that is always paid.

Q: Can investors come out on top when it comes to a time share?

No. Time share investors may own an expensive piece of property at a minimal cost, but they have overpaid, as illustrated in the previous example. After paying a 50% premium on a piece of property it takes a great deal of appreciation to catch up. That's one of the tangible negatives. But, how about the intangibles? Do you (investor) want to go to the same vacation spot for the rest of your life? Chances are the answer is no. Most people like to vary vacations, and if they see a mountain resort one year they may want to see a tropical island the next. The time share concept does not allow for this consideration.

Time share investors can, of course, switch weeks with others and rotate the time of year they vacation, but they are still trapped into visiting the same place each year, and at the same time.

Q: What is the biggest problem investors face when they own time shares?

Selling it. They may be relatively inexpensive to get into, but they are hard to unload. Professional time share salespeople know how to move a portion of the property. They use direct mail, sweepstakes, and the promise of winning a new automobile, watch, or television set. They do anything and everything to get investors to a time share session. And once the investor is in the room, they find it difficult to leave without a commitment. Most time share salespeople are high pressure, and they do well.

Q: What happens to property appreciation with time shares?

The investor who purchases a time share and wants to sell it five years later will find it is difficult to factor in appreciation. The $500,000 piece of property that was sold for $30,000 a share to 20 investors, may only be worth $550,000, instead of the $600,000 (or more), because resort property generally appreciates slowly. It has a limited market, too.

Q: What are some of the other seldom thought of drawbacks to time shares?

Suppose the time share investors have to postpone a vacation because of pressing business problems? What happens? If luck holds, they may be able to get one of the other owners to switch. Or they may be able to rent the time share and recoup part of their loss. Either way, it is an inconvenient piece of property to own. It takes initial capital, usually is overpriced, takes an above average time to appreciate, and is difficult to sell. From an investor's standpoint, there are many properties around that would be much more worthwhile.

Q: What is "equity investing" or "equity financing?"

This is a recent financing innovation that is, in some ways, a scheme that benefits neither the buyer nor investor. It was designed to enable investors who were short of capital to become property owners. It first gained popularity in some of the high appreciation areas, such as the west and northeast sections of the country where appreciation ran double digits for several years.

In these areas, it did not take long before most people were priced out of the market. In fact, in places such as California, only about 10% of the 20 million plus people in the state can actually afford the down payment and monthly payment on an average piece of property. With conditions such as these, it was only logical that the "equity financing/investment" would come along.

Q: What is the premise behind equity financing?

The premise behind equity shared partnerships is that people will do almost anything to own property. It is geared primarily toward the first-time homeowner/investor, and works in the following manner: An investor puts up a percentage of the down payment (anywhere from 10 to 100% of it) and allows the buyer of the property to move into it. After five years, the property is either sold or the buyer refinances and pays off the equity investor. In other words, the money is put up by an investor, the buyer makes the payments, and in a specified amount of time the property is sold or refinanced and the investor receives principal plus interest back. The loan is secured by the property. On the surface, this appears to be a nice, clean way for investors to finance a property, earn a better than average return on their money, and have the monies secured by the deed on the property.

Q: What problems are there with equity sharing?

The most obvious is the investor/occupant relationship. Typically, the investor is going to be putting in most (or all) of the funds. As a result there is no incentive for the occupant/buyer/owner. If they fail to make a payment, what is lost? They have had a "rental" unit for a certain amount of months, and all they have to do is move on instead of paying the mortgage payments. If this happens, the seemingly clean arrangement can turn into a mess, with the investor owning a piece of property and making payments on it that may not be desired (or that the investor may not be able to afford). Based on this scenario, any investor who is going to get involved in an equity share partnership must make sure the occupant/owner puts up a significant portion of the down payment.

Q: If an investor were interested in equity ownership, what arrangement should be made with the person who is going to occupy and own the property?

The investor should make sure that the occupant/owner puts in at least 20% of the total down payment, plus the closing costs. They must have a financial investment in the property.

Q: If the occupant/owner has a minimal equity investment in the property, what problem may the investor face in a short amount of time?

Without having their own funds invested, what incentive is there for the occupant/owner to take care of the dwelling? One of the significant pitfalls in owning rental units is relying on the tenant to take care of the dwelling. In many cases, it does not happen because the tenant has nothing to lose. Hence, maintenance is deferred because the tenant refuses to do it, and the owner/landlord is called only when something breaks down.

Q: What problem arises with equity sharing arrangements when it comes to appreciation?

The homeowner/occupant believes that enough equity will be amassed in the property to sell or refinance after the five-year period. The homeowner or owner/occupant is planning to generate enough profit to produce sufficient monies for a down payment on another home, or to purchase this home. There is no guarantee this will happen. There is no better example of this than the real estate slowdown that started in 1988. Up until that point, most areas of the country had been appreciating at a rapid pace. Not all registered the double-digit increases of parts of California, but there were numerous sections that showed anywhere from 8 to 10% per year.

Based on those figures, equity sharing seemed to be a sensible, viable investment alternative. Unfortunately, in many parts of the country, anyone who bought a home during the late 1980s has seen a slowdown, stagnation, or even a slight decline in the value of the property. This is not unusual when looking at historic cycles, but it can be devastating to someone who is buying a property for a short-term (under five years) investment.

Q: What parts of the country are especially poor risks when it comes to equity share partnerships?

Although the equity share partnerships are based on the premise of holding for five years, in some areas of the country 60 months (historically) has not produced the required appreciation. Good examples are parts of the midwest and the southwest's oil belt. The midwest has always been an area that is slow to appreciate. Seldom do you see any dramatic, radical (up or down) movement. In fact, in many midwestern states appreciation just drifts along at 1%–2% a year, which is hardly enough to make an equity share partnership viable. The oil belt has taken a beating for nearly a decade, and is slowly recovering. Still, equity partnerships in the southwest do not bode well for investors.

Q: What does the profit split look like in a typical equity partnership?

To see the profit and how (and where) equity partnerships might fit, all an investor has to do is examine the average priced home in the United States. At the end of 1990, the figure was somewhere around $98,000. A 20% down payment ($19,600) would leave a mortgage of about $80,000 with monthly payments somewhere around $900 to $1,000 per month with taxes. If the property appreciated only 2% per year, at the end of five years (when it came time for the equity share partners to sell or refinance) an investor would be looking at the following:

Year	Appreciation (%)	Value	Increase
1	2	$ 98,000	$1,960
2	2	99,960	1,999
3	2	101,959	2,039
4	2	103,998	2,079
5	2	106,077	2,121

If the home sold for the full value ($106,077), the return would be approximately $8,000. If the investor put up the entire down payment ($19,600) and he had to split the profit with the buyer/occupant, he would be looking at a profit of about $4,000. From this there would be a real estate commission (about 6% of the selling price, or more than $6,300). Take this from the $8,000 and suddenly the profit is more like $1,700, or $850 apiece. Obviously, that is hardly enough for the buyer/occupant to put down on another dwelling, and it is a poor return for the investor who would be making $170 per year on a $19,600 investment. Even a federally insured certificate of deposit that paid a modest 7 to 8% interest per year ($1,100 to $1,370 per year in interest) would outpace this equity arrangement.

Q: *How can investors tilt the equity share partnership—that is try to ensure that it is viable?*

To ensure that the investment was even fairly viable, the investor should not be putting down anything more than 10% of the purchase price, and the equity split should be tilted with the investor collecting a higher percentage than the buyer/occupant. Even then, this investment would be questionable, and the only thing that would make it worth the risk was an appreciation that had a chance of surpassing the 2% per year.

Q: Before investing in an equity share arrangement, what precautions should investors take?

Investors should put down (on paper) various scenarios. They should determine when it will work and when it will not. The following examples do not take into consideration tax consequences.

Assume the buyer/occupant in both of the foregoing scenarios got involved with this type of investment simply because the buyer/occupant did not have the 20% ($44,000) required down payment to purchase the $220,000 residence.

	Example 1 10% per year appreciation	Example 2 5% per year appreciation
Location	Florida	Florida
Price of property	$220,000	$220,000
Mortgage	$176,000	$176,000
Down payment required	$ 44,000	$ 44,000
Funds from investor	$ 22,000	$ 22,000
Funds from owner/occupant	$ 22,000	$ 22,000
Cost per month (assume 1% of mortgage)	$ 1,760	$ 1,760
Holding period	Five years	Five years
New selling price	$354,000	$280,000
Cost of sale (8%)	$ 28,320	$ 22,400
Gross profit	$105,680	$ 37,600
Profit per partner	$ 52,840	$ 18,800

In the first scenario, after five years, the buyer/occupant now has a profit of $52,840 plus the original portion of the down payment of $22,000 or a total of $74,840. If the buyer/occupant desires to purchase the subject property or a similar property, the property will now cost $354,000. A 20% down payment will be $70,800.

The buyer/occupant obviously has the required down payment but still has to qualify for the new 80% mortgage of $280,000 and have the ability or desire to handle the increased mortgage payment. (Assuming that the monthly holding costs are still equal to 1% of the mortgage amount of $2,800 per month, this represents an increase in the buyer/occupant's monthly payment of $1,040.)

It is obvious that the first scenario can work provided the buyer/occupant's income is sufficient to justify the monthly payment.

In the second scenario, again after five years, the buyer/occupant now has a profit of $18,800 plus the original portion of the down payment of $22,000 or a total of $40,800. If the buyer/occupant desires to purchase the subject property or a similar property, the property will now cost $280,000. A 20% down payment will be $56,000.

Here the buyer/occupant obviously does not have the required down payment. In this situation, the buyer/occupant could make a 20% down payment on a $200,000 property. But, wait! To the buyer/occupant, this is going backward. This is not what was wanted. The buyer/occupant wanted a residence equal to or better than the one invested in. In this scenario, the buyer/occupant could attempt to purchase a home with an 85% loan to value ratio, having almost enough money to make the down payment on a $280,000 residence. An 85% loan would be $238,000, which would result in a monthly payment of $2,380, assuming that the monthly cost is equal to 1% of the mortgage. This represents an increase of $620 per month.

Q: What does the buyer/occupant often fail to calculate in an equity share partnership?

A considerable increase in the monthly payment must be expected if the buyer/occupant expects to remain in a residence of similar value.

Q: What occupations—and why—fit into an equity sharing investment?

The best prerequisite for an owner/occupant investor in an equity sharing investment would be to be employed in a profession that would experience a rapid rise in annual income over a period of a few short years to enable the owner/occupant to handle the expected increase in monthly payments. For example, dentists, doctors, lawyers, and accountants may fall into this category.

Q: What is the main affordability problem encountered by first-time investors?

Raising the initial capital for a down payment. Property has appreciated dramatically in some areas of the country, and in others, although it may not have soared, it is still difficult for first-time homebuyers to raise the capital. Despite the almost daily stories in the media about failed S&Ls and banks with problems, there is not a shortage of capital for real estate mortgages. There is, however, a difference between today and five or 10 years ago. That is, lenders are scrutinizing loans more carefully, and they are more wary of the credit worthiness of the borrower than ever before. Consequently, the first-time homebuyer or investor has to come up with more down payment and security than previously, and the higher costs have made homebuying today more difficult than at virtually any other time in our history.

The problem goes beyond lenders, however. Just examine the table below which compares key elements of the down payment, gross salary, price, and "months to save" from one period to another. Although the figures do not apply to every area, most communities have seen similar changes.

Year	Monthly payment	Gross (monthly) salary	Home price	20% down	Months required to save down payment
1960	$ 200	$1,200	$ 20,000	$ 4,000	4
1990	$1,800	$4,100	$200,000	$40,000	10
2000	$2,700	$7,000	$330,000+	$66,000	9–10

Thirty years ago, it took approximately the equivalent of four months' worth of an investor's salary to make the down payment on an average home. In 1990, it took 10 months and the prospects for the year 2000 are not much better. Affordability remains a problem that is going to stay with us for years. On the positive side, for those investing in real estate, it is obvious that appreciation makes property one of the best purchases that can be made over a long period of time.

Q: What is leverage and how does it favor real estate as an investment?

Leverage is something that weighs heavily on the side of property as an investment vehicle. Typically, an investor need not put more than 20% down to own a piece of property. In many cases, the investor can even purchase for 10%. Compare this to stocks, where 50% (that is, one-half the money) has to be paid at the time of purchase. With real estate it takes less money to control more.

Q: What ramifications does affordability have for investors?

Affordability has serious ramifications for investors as well as first-time homeowners. Obviously, the fewer number of people who are able to buy, the less demand. Slackened demand means slower appreciation. That means those who buy for investment rather than ownership are going to be holding properties longer and seeing smaller gains than real estate previously generated.

Q: How do demographics impact investing?

That segment of the population (25–44 years of age) that is the typical, first-time homebuyer is diminishing, and by the year 2000 will be significantly smaller than it is today. Real estate investors who plan to market to this group would do well to take heed of the diminishing numbers. The prime homebuyers in the year 2000 will be coming from the ranks of current (older) homeowners who already live in their own dwelling but may move because they want a smaller unit (i.e., their kids have been raised and have moved) or they want to move from a single family residence to a gated, more secure community. Given that scenario, it becomes obvious that typical tract building will be changing, and investors who do not pay attention to the market's movement could lose.

Q: How will the growing immigrant population impact homebuying, renting, and investment?

The growing immigrant population will impact homebuying and renting. Foreign groups have different cultures and in some cases 10 or 12 people in a single family residence is a way of life— not a crowd as is often perceived by Americans. Thus, investors should be cognizant of the areas in which they build or invest. Is there a growing foreign influence? If so, what kind of housing do they prefer? What kind of apartments or rental units do they seek?

Q: What are the most frequently asked questions posed by buyers?

The two most frequently asked questions are "how much down?" and "how much a month?" The full price has little significance. Many buyers get into a home by pooling savings for the down payment, and putting together monthly earnings for the mortgage payment.

Q: What ways are there to financially approach an investment in property?

First, there are those who pool funds and put everything they have into a dwelling, and then there are investors who have the capital to set aside reserves and not let the purchase strap them if trouble develops. The former are interested in the size of the monthly payment, while the latter look carefully at the return on investment.

Q: Despite the problems, does home ownership still make investment sense?

Home ownership is an investment that makes a great deal of sense. If an investor took, for instance, the $40,000 it takes to make a down payment today on a $200,000 dwelling, and put it in a certificate of deposit, it would earn somewhere around 8% or $3,200 a year. In five years, the earnings would be approximately $16,000.

If the same investor took $40,000 and made a down payment on a home, the return would far outstrip the certificate of deposit. For instance, if inflation averaged a "moderate" 5% during the next five years, and the value of the home kept pace (or even near-pace) to the rising cost, its value would climb from $200,000 to more than $250,000—a gain of $50,000. Although there is no guarantee the investor could sell the home, if it could be sold the return on investment would virtually triple the certificate of deposit.

Even the person who put aside $20,000 for a portion of a son's or daughter's college education would do well to look at real estate. Cycles are usually five years, and an investor who put $20,000 down on a dwelling at the beginning of it could purchase a $100,000 property, see it conservatively increase $15,000–$20,000, and sell it with a profit almost double the initial investment. The key, of course, is to buy at the beginning of the cycle. That takes care, patience, and study. For the investor who misses the cycle, the return will not be great and, in fact, the investor may be selling the property before it is desirable.

Q: What do economists who put down home investment fail to consider when they look at real estate?

In most cases, they have not reckoned on the "great American dream" which has not lost any of its fervor. People still want to own their own home, and that means there will continue to be demand, and demand means higher prices and the chances for a good, sensible investment.

Nevertheless, raising $20,000, $40,000, or any amount in today's escalating price economy is not easy. That is why there seems to be more financial alternatives than ever for the investor. Friends and families pool assets to buy single family residences, groups get together and form limited partnerships, and mutual funds are established that invest in real estate.

Q: What types of financing sources are available for investors who may not go to the typical bank?

135

For the buyer/investor there are financing alternatives. The Federal Housing Authority (FHA) and Veterans Administration (VA) are two. The key advantage to the buyer in both cases is the loan is usually for 30 years with a slightly lower rate of interest. The FHA loan is open to anyone, and will be of particular interest to first-time homebuyers. The VA loans are open only to veterans.

Q: Why do some sellers refuse to deal with buyers who want to utilize a VA loan?

VA loans restrict the amount of points a buyer can pay for a property. A point can simply be thought of as a percentage. One point equals 1%. When purchasing property, there are usually points connected with the transaction. The full price on a home may be $150,000 plus two points—or 2%, an additional $3,000 based on the total price of the loan.

The points are charged by the lender (bank, S&L), who does not care whether the buyer or seller pays. Traditionally, the buyer usually pays the points. But with lower cost government loans (FHA, VA) there is a limit or restriction on the amount of points a buyer can pay. Because of the restriction, many lenders do not want to deal with the government. They are not interested in putting someone in a dwelling without making as much money as they can. That is understandable, because the lender is in business to make money, and the one way to do this is by charging fees for the funds supplied. Points are part of the fees.

Q: If investors see a piece of property they truly want, and they plan to utilize a VA loan, how can they get around the point problem that often kills VA loan transactions?

There is a limitation on the points a buyer can be charged; however, the seller can agree to pay the points and make it up by raising the price of the property an equivalent amount. On the surface, this sounds fair. The lender gets the points, the seller the agreed on price, and the buyer the property. But it does not always work that way. For VA loans, an appraiser is sent out by the government and if the appraisal price does not match what the seller is asking, there may not be a transaction. The buyer cannot use the VA or FHA and pay more than the appraised amount. (Many buyers, if they want the property and there is a disparity in the appraisal and selling price, pay the seller cash to make up the difference.)

Q: How can investors find VA or FHA financing?

Not every lender supplies VA or FHA financing. Typically, FHA, VA, or any government funds are specialities, and buyers should query the real estate broker as to banks and/or lenders who specialize in it. Because of the point requirement and government red tape, there are many lenders who prefer to stay away from VA and FHA.

Q: When do VA loans make the most sense?

VA loans—which are a last resort for most sellers because of the point restrictions and other problems—become a logical tool for buyers during tough or slow times. Sellers who may need to unload a property will tone down objections to VA loans and point limitations if they have had a property on the market for a significant amount of time. In good times, of course, when properties move rapidly, a seller will seldom consider a VA loan. Whether FHA or VA loans fly as a financing vehicle depends primarily on timing and the economy.

Q: Why is there less emotion connected with investing in commercial real estate?

Buying a building, piece of land, or shopping center involves more objective arguments such as traffic flow, location, leases,

137

property condition, tenants, and recordkeeping. All these elements can be monitored and documented.

Unfortunately, when it comes to residential real estate, buying and selling becomes an emotional issue. The residence is a "part" of the seller, and offering an amount that is perceived as low insults the seller. There are ways to get the message across, without insulting the seller or the structure. For instance, the buyer can make subtle, innocent comments such as "Gee, I didn't realize how dark and gloomy this room was . . . did you ever think of painting it?" By registering dissatisfaction with one aspect of the property, the buyer is slowly bringing down the value of the entire property—without insulting the seller.

In many cases, the buyer does not even have to talk. A motion, body language, or an absence of a smile tells the seller that you are not pleased with the property—and the seller may have to deal to get you to purchase it.

Q: Why is it advisable to keep emotion out of the transaction?

Emotion impacts price. For example, usually the buyer and seller differ on one key element—price. The buyer who wants a property that is listed for $200,000 may see others in the neighborhood that are selling for $195,000, but they are not in as good condition. Knowing the conditions of the neighborhood, many buyers still come in and make a ridiculously low offer, hoping that the seller will drop the price. Instead, when the $150,000 offer is made for the $200,000 home, the seller gets angry. The seller is insulted, emotions enter the transaction, and the buyer does not get the property and the seller does not get the asked for price. This is not the way to negotiate price.

Q: How can buyers arrive at the right price for a piece of property?

See what properties sold for in the area five years previously. Making an offer along those lines is a tactic that some buyers often utilize. If the area has appreciated little, the buyer and seller will not be far apart. But if the community has shown an average (or above average) rate of appreciation, the buyer runs the risk of insulting the seller and starting off on the wrong foot once more. This, too, is not the way to negotiate price.

Q: What are some of the things buyers should keep in mind about sellers?

The first thing the buyer must realize is that sellers are astute; they differ from years ago, and most know the price of surrounding properties.

Buyers should be just as familiar (if not more so) with surrounding properties. They should be aware of what the properties sold for, what is available, and how long properties have been on the market. The buyer should check the inventory on the shelf, that is, the available supply of similar properties, and start with the lowest, comparable property. Offer 5%–10% less. That percentage is not an attempt to steal the property, but it does show the seller you know the market. It sets the stage for real negotiations.

Q: What types of sellers can investors expect to encounter?

Buyers usually run into one of three kinds of sellers: the seller who will not negotiate and wants full price, the seller who has a job transfer, and the seller who must sell because of death or divorce. Obviously, the latter two are transactions in which the buyer is going to find a seller who is in need and is willing to drop the price significantly. The former may not be and could just as well pull the property off the market. This seller does not have to sell.

In fact, the real estate slowdown that began in late 1988 was typified by these sellers. They did not have to sell, and when buyers began offering unrealistic prices, sellers simply started pulling properties off the market.

Obviously, the motivated seller is going to offer the better deal. The trick is to find a seller who is motivated. The property being sold may not be number one on your priority list, however, it may—because of the seller's circumstances—be a more worthwhile buy than the prime property.

Q: What should investors/buyers do in selecting a piece of property?

Buyers should (1) find an area in which they want to purchase a property, (2) find three acceptable properties and rank them in order of preference, (3) investigate each and determine the category into which each seller fits—is the seller a number one, two, or three scenario, and (4) go after the property for which you can negotiate the best deal. If all three properties are equivalent or close to it, buying number three and saving thousands of dollars may be much better than buying number one and overpaying thousands.

In the next chapter we will look at the agreements that follow once a buyer makes a choice. Unfortunately, agreements and contracts can be much more complex than any seller's personality.

6

Agreements, Contracts, and Tax

John Stephensen shifted uncomfortably in his chair as he listened to the judge hand down the stiff fine. He glanced across the courtroom and caught the eye of his insurance agent, and was immediately sorry that he had done so. The agent turned away, put his head down, and shook it slowly back and forth, as if what he had just heard the judge say was unbelievable.

To Stephensen and the crowded room full of real estate agents and brokers, the judge's comments were incomprehensible. But, so was the law. In a growing number of states, real estate law has become a hodgepodge that often defies common sense.

At the root of the melange is a controversial, difficult term to define—disclosure. To the buyer, disclosure is critical because it can mean the difference between purchasing a property or purchasing trouble.

Q: What is "full disclosure?"

As a rule, full disclosure means that the real estate agent must make a visual inspection to discover any "material facts that may affect the value or desirability of the property." They must disclose their findings to the prospective purchaser. Unfortunately, the definition of what is material and what is not may differ from state to state. "Material" can generally be defined as anything that may alter the decision of the purchaser to purchase or to alter the amount of the purchase price.

Q: Does the real estate agent have to disclose everything about the property?

Yes . . . and no. For example, at least one state has a law that says the buyer must be told if someone died in the house. But, at the same time, this state also prohibits the real estate agent from telling any buyer that someone died in the household from AIDS. This law is fairly new and is not expected to be adopted by many states.

Q: What obligation do sellers and agents have to buyers when it comes to disclosure?

For the most part, sellers (and agents) are obliged to disclose anything that may materially impact the value or desirability of the property. And they usually do. Many states adhere to these rules and have passed statutes relating to them. A problem arises, however, in defining what is "material." Whereas one state may feel the fact that someone died in a house is material, another may not. Thus, material is still a definition that is up to each state. Buyers, however, can certainly count on courts defining major structural defects as being material. Questions arise, however, when it comes to items such as "the school district" being considered material. Suffice it to say, the buyer should investigate.

Q: What kind of general guidelines are there for full disclosure?

The one guideline on which buyers can depend (unless they are dealing with an unscrupulous seller) is that material facts will be disclosed. If the home was recently rocked by a nearby explosion, and cracks appeared in the foundation, that should be disclosed. Most of the laws involving the agents' duty to investigate and disclose stem from problems involving the physical property and the improvements constructed on it, for example, broken or cracked foundations, unstable soil (soil that expands and contracts as moistened and then allowed to dry), improvements constructed, or repairs made without the required governmental permits.

Q: With disclosure laws, can buyers rely totally on the representation of the seller and real estate agent?

The buyer has a duty to observe anything that may not be readily apparent. For example, if it is obvious that the residence borders the fourth tee on a public golf course, one can assume that an errant golf ball may violate the air space of the property and do damage to the residence or harm to people on the property. The buyers would be held to "know" that these possibilities exist, and would have difficulty winning against an agent in court for failure to disclose. However, the result might be different if a grove of trees concealed the existence of the golf course.

For the most part, buyers can depend on the agent to let them know the important material issues. In fact, many agents have expanded their disclosure to include items that they are not required to disclose, such as the proximity of the property to shopping and schools. This is very different from years ago, when

143

residential buyers never knew what they were purchasing because there were few consumer protection laws. Today, of course, society has grown significantly more protective of the consumer, and buyers who are deceived find themselves well-protected (and compensated) by the law.

Q: Why are commercial buyers less protected by full disclosure laws?

Legislators have always felt that commercial buyers are more astute and aware. Brokers in commercial transactions are required to disclose all material facts "known"—they are not yet under a duty to investigate for the purpose of discovering defects that affect value or desirability. They are not in need of as much protective legislation from agents. For those buying commercial properties, the best rule is "caveat emptor," or buyer beware. It would not hurt the residential buyer to be wary as well. If, in the course of going through a property, something appears wrong or bothersome, ask about it. The question may bring an important disclosure fact to light.

Q: Do so-called "home warranties" protect the buyer?

During the past few years, some agents have tried to alleviate buyer concern by selling or giving them a "home warranty" or giving them the name of a "home inspecting company" that will check the property before the buyer takes possession. In some cases, the inspector has no more ability to inspect than the buyer. The inspector may simply be an entrepreneur who saw a niche in the market and a way to launch a business. On the surface, home inspections make sense. Wouldn't you want someone checking out a $100,000 (or more) investment? Most buyers would; however, the inspector is not always the ideal person to do so.

Q: What problems arise with home inspectors?

Inspectors frequently go through houses and list many minor deficiencies instead of finding the major problems. For example, a drippy faucet or chipped piece of tile is not going to impact the value or desirability of a property. A foundation that is cracked certainly may. Unfortunately, most home inspection companies simply list the obvious, and they do not always get into areas where there may be serious flaws. The philosophy of many of these companies is that if they come up with a long list, the buyer will be satisfied that the inspection was complete. Yet, the concern is not the length of the list but the seriousness or materiality of an item.

Q: What should buyers check before purchasing a home warranty?

Before purchasing one a buyer should check the exclusions. Look for the "ifs" and "buts" in the policy. Most are loaded with them, and the reason they are inexpensive to purchase is because many major repair items are not covered. But, in this era of consumer suspicion, home warranty companies have found a profitable business niche and as long as buyers are willing to pay for the policies, they will continue to sell them. As a rule, the buyer should count on spotting flaws themselves, and not rely on inspection companies or warranties. Buyers should also be asking the right questions of the agent, and in doing so any significant problems will be disclosed.

Q: What is a "due on sale clause" and how can it impact the investor?

One potentially damaging agreement is the so-called "due on sale clause," which is contained in most promissory notes. When the buyer decides to purchase a property, he should ascertain whether or not there is a due on sale clause in existence.

The due on sale clause is simply a term and condition added to or made a part of a loan agreement between the borrower (homeowner) and the lender. With it the lender has the option to declare all sums of unpaid principal and/or interest due and payable on the transfer of title (of the property) or any interest therein.

In simple language, this means that should the borrower/homeowner transfer any interest in their property—which is the security for the repayment of the loan made by the lender— the lender has the option to declare all sums to be repaid immediately. Typical situations that "trigger" the due on sale clause are (1) the borrower/homeowner leases the property (which has been put up as security for a loan) for more than a year, (2) grants an option to purchase the property to someone, (3) conveys all interest in the property to someone else, or (4) grants an easement to a neighbor.

Should any of these acts take place without the consent of the lender, the lender can declare the loan in default. In other words, the borrower/homeowner has violated the terms and conditions of the loan agreement. A failure to pay a monthly installment of principal and interest is also a default, and whenever the loan is in default the lender has the power to start foreclosure proceedings.

Q: Is there any recourse for the borrower when a loan is in default?

Most states have laws that allow the borrower a few months to reinstate a loan that is in default as a result of the borrower's failure to make the monthly payments of principal and interest when they were due. These laws usually require the borrower to make up all the back payments, including late charges, and to reimburse the lender for all costs and fees incurred during the foreclosure process. The exception to all this is when the default is declared by the lender because the borrower/homeowner transferred the property or any interest therein. In this case, the borrower/homeowner or the successor (the buyer) must resolve the situation immediately.

One solution is to have the new owner refinance the property by securing a new loan from a different lender. Another would be to have the buyer go to the lender and ask for a new loan. In this case, the lender decides whether to qualify the buyer. Should the new owner qualify, the lender may also change the terms of the loan, by increasing the interest rate and charging the new owner additional fees and costs before allowing the buyer to assume the seller's loan.

Q: What is the difference between "assuming" an existing loan and accepting one without prior consent of the lender?

Buyers should be aware that whenever they accept title to a property with an existing loan without getting the prior consent of the lender, the buyer is said to be taking title to the property "subject to" the existing loan and the lender may foreclose. When the buyer approaches the lender before the transaction is completed, receives the lender's consent, and agrees in writing to abide by the terms and conditions of the existing loan, the buyer is said to be taking title to the property and "assuming" the existing loan.

Q: How can a buyer determine the existence of a due on sale clause?

In most states, there is a consumer law that requires the lender to set forth the terms and conditions of the due on sale clause in a separate sheet of paper that has to be signed by the borrower and attached to the promissory note as an addendum. In large print, on the addendum, there is a note that says there is a due on sale clause in the loan agreement.

Q: What is the prepayment privilege clause, and how does it impact an investor who buys a property?

This clause permits the lender to charge the borrower several months of unearned interest in the event the borrower elects to pay off the balance of the loan before maturity. Many states have laws that permit this penalty only during the first five years of the loan, and they limit the penalty to six months of unearned interest. Those six months, however, can represent substantial monies.

The theory behind the clause is that the lender has a great deal of upfront expenses from the loan. Since the lender's upfront expenses are not fully offset by the loan fees paid by the borrower (if the loan is paid off too early), the lender may not make the anticipated profit.

Q: How does the prepayment privilege clause work?

Suppose you purchase a property and obtain a 30-year amortized loan in the amount of $100,000 with interest at 10%. At the end of six months, you inherit a sum of money sufficient to pay off the loan. If the promissory note contained a prepayment penalty of six months of unearned interest (if the loan were prepaid during the first year), the prepayment penalty would be calculated as follows: The balance of the loan would be $99,728.98. Since the annual interest is 10%, 12 months of interest would be $9,972.90. Six months of interest would be one-half the annual interest, or $4,986.45, a considerable sum.

Had the loan been paid off in the third or fourth year, the penalty would be significantly less since many state laws require the amount of the principal to be reduced by 20% per year for purposes of calculating the prepayment penalty. Therefore, had the loan been paid off in the fourth year, for instance, the penalty would be calculated by reducing the actual loan balance by 80% of the original loan amount ($100,000 × 80%) or $80,000. This would leave a balance of less than $20,000 for purposes of calculating the prepayment penalty. The annual interest of this amount would be approximately $2,000, and six month's interest would be less than $1,000.

Obviously, the cost of borrowing increases significantly if the loan is prepaid soon after it is made. If it is anticipated that the loan is going to be prepaid during the first few years, it would be wise to obtain a loan without a prepayment penalty, even if the annual interest rate is slightly higher.

Q: What is "antideficiency legislation" and how does it impact buyers?

"Antideficiency" statutes basically provide a limitation on the personal liability of a borrower in certain transactions where the loan is secured by real property. In other words, in the event of a foreclosure lawsuit, the borrower (buyer) would have limited liability if antideficiency laws exist.

Q: What are the basic types of loans that are secured by real property?

There are two. The first is a "purchase money mortgage," which is a loan in which the proceeds are used to buy the real property. Some states provide that the first or senior obligation (loan) on single family residences from one to four units fall under this first definition. In addition, obligations created at or about the time of the purchase favor of the seller. An example would be a promise by the buyer to pay the remainder of the purchase price to the seller which promise would be contained in a promissory note and secured by the real estate sold.

The second category of loans is the so-called "hard money loans." Any loan that is not a purchase money loan is a hard money loan. For example, assume that you recently purchased a property for $200,000 and obtained a first mortgage from Bank XYZ for $150,000 and the seller (Mr. Jones) carries back a second mortgage for $25,000. Two months after you purchased the property, you decided to build a recreation room and went to ABC Bank and obtained a third mortgage of $30,000. By applying the definitions given above, the first and second mortgages are purchase money mortgages and the third mortgage to ABC Bank is a hard money mortgage.

Q: How does antideficiency legislation protect the buyer?

Assume that you missed the monthly installments and you are in default. The lender of each of the obligations can commence foreclosure proceedings. If you are in a state that has antideficiency legislation, the Bank of XYZ and Jones can look only to the property for repayment of their obligations. You are not personally liable. But there is a catch. Since antideficiency statutes normally apply only to purchase money mortgages, the holder of the third mortgage, ABC Bank, can obtain a judgment against you and you will remain personally liable for the repayment of this loan.

Q: How does antideficiency legislation protect the buyer/investor?

Obviously, antideficiency legislation was meant to protect the borrower/investor from any lending abuses and it behooves any investor to check the state laws and regulations to see if this legislation exists before entering into any agreement. Generally, states with antideficiency legislation are quite cognizant of investors and sympathetic toward them. This creates an environment that is certainly more inviting to the investor than states that do not have this legislation. It means that the first-time investor in a bind can count on some support (support that will protect assets not connected to the disputed property). This type of legislation usually exists in the more progressive and less traditional states. A real estate attorney can inform the investor of which states have antideficiency legislation.

Q: What problems will investors encounter who want to have a late penalty clause in a rental contract?

Most states are quite sensitive and responsive when it comes to rental agreements that investors ask tenants to sign. This is especially true if the agreement penalizes the tenant for late payment. If, for instance, the $800 rent payment is due on the first and carries a penalty of $50 if it is not paid on that date, the court will most likely disallow the penalty portion at trial.

For investors who become landlords and want to collect the rent on time with a penalty (if it is late), there is another approach. For an investor/owner who wants to rent a property for $800 a month, but also wants a penalty if the rent is late, the way to structure the agreement is to have it show the actual rent as $850 per month ($800 rent plus $50 for the late fee). The contract does not say the $50 is a late fee. It only lists the rent as $850. Of course, the renter will object, saying you agreed to $800 a month. The owner gets around this issue by putting a provision in the contract that says the rent is $850 a month, however, for tenants who make their payments on or before the first of the month, the rent will be reduced $50 a month to $800. The renter gets a rent of $800 a month and the owner obtains a penalty if the payment is not on time. Some courts recognize such discounts as penalties "in disguise" and may disallow them.

Q: What is the most important agreement the investor will encounter?

Unquestionably, the most important agreement the investor will encounter is "offer to purchase." This is the form that is filled out once the investor decides on a property. The offer varies from state to state. The offer to purchase is prepared by the buyer with the assistance of the real estate agent. (This offer is designed for residential transactions, however, it is typically utilized in the commercial purchase of up to four units.) It is designed to spell out (in detail) the terms and conditions of the purchase and sale of the property, to protect both the buyer and seller. You can find a typical example of this document at the end of the chapter (Figure 6.1). Individual items in the document will be referred to in separate sections of the chapter. (Although this purchase agreement is not identical in each state, many of the sections described in the remainder of this chapter are standard in purchase agreements throughout the country.)

Q: Which is more binding—a contract or agreement? What are the differences?

Notice an important statement at the top of Figure 6.1. It says, "This is more than a receipt for money. It is intended to be a legally binding contract. Read it carefully." The point is that not all agreements are contracts, but all contracts are agreements. In other words, a contract is more binding than an agreement. It is the contract that comes into dispute and winds up in court, whereas the agreement is not always legally enforceable. The offer to purchase is a contract. A contract is a legally enforceable agreement. An agreement that is not legally enforceable has no real value.

The first part of the agreement calls for a deposit, which is typically made payable to the escrow holder. The deposit is normally held uncashed until the offer is accepted.

Q: Why should the interest rate always be spelled out in the agreement?

In Figure 6.1, Section 1, Financing, there are several things the buyer should note. One of the most important is item "D," which outlines the type of loan the buyer will obtain. The interest rate should always be spelled out. Never leave it open-ended or insert the phrase "interest rate at the best prevailing rate." Between the time this offer is approved by the seller and returned to the buyer, many things can happen. The prime rate may be raised, which will impact and increase the cost of money (the interest rate).

Money is like any other commodity. If it becomes scarce (via a higher rate) the cost (interest rate) is going to go up.

Q: What actual dollar impact does a one point increase in a loan have on the average monthly payment?

If there is a national emergency or crisis, the interest rates can go up more than a point, which will, of course, significantly impact the monthly payment. For example, look at Tables 6.1 and 6.2 and compare an $80,000 mortgage at 9% ($643 per month) to one at 10% ($702), an increase of $59 per month, $700 per year, and more than $21,000 during the 30-year life of the mortgage.

Q: What is the cost of the average-priced single family residence in the United States?

In 1990, the average-priced single family residence in the United States was just over $90,000.

Q: What would the typical mortgage payment be for an average-priced home in the United States, and how would an increase in the interest rate impact that payment?

With a 30-year fixed-rate mortgage at 9%, buyers would be paying just over $804 per month. If inflation (and interest rates) rise, however, a 1% gain would turn that into a $877 a month payment, or $73 more per month, $876 per year, and more than $26,000 during the life of the mortgage.

Table 6.1.

9% MONTHLY PAYMENT
NECESSARY TO AMORTIZE A LOAN

AMOUNT	10 YEARS	15 YEARS	20 YEARS	25 YEARS	26 YEARS	27 YEARS	28 YEARS	29 YEARS	30 YEARS
$ 50	.64	.51	.45	.42	.42	.42	.41	.41	.41
100	1.27	1.02	.90	.84	.84	.83	.82	.82	.81
250	3.17	2.54	2.25	2.10	2.08	2.06	2.05	2.03	2.02
500	6.34	5.08	4.50	4.20	4.16	4.12	4.09	4.06	4.03
750	9.51	7.61	6.75	6.30	6.24	6.18	6.13	6.08	6.04
1000	12.67	10.15	9.00	8.40	8.31	8.24	8.17	8.11	8.05
2000	25.34	20.29	18.00	16.79	16.62	16.47	16.33	16.21	16.10
3000	38.01	30.43	27.00	25.18	24.93	24.70	24.49	24.31	24.14
4000	50.68	40.58	35.99	33.57	33.23	32.93	32.66	32.41	32.19
5000	63.34	50.72	44.99	41.96	41.54	41.16	40.82	40.51	40.24
10000	126.68	101.43	89.98	83.92	83.08	82.32	81.63	81.02	80.47
15000	190.02	152.14	134.96	125.88	124.61	123.47	122.45	121.53	120.70
20000	253.36	202.86	179.95	167.84	166.15	164.63	163.26	162.04	160.93
25000	316.69	253.57	224.94	209.80	207.69	205.79	204.08	202.54	201.16
30000	380.03	304.28	269.92	251.76	249.22	246.94	244.89	243.05	241.39
35000	443.37	355.00	314.91	293.72	290.76	288.10	285.71	283.56	281.62
40000	506.71	405.71	359.90	335.68	332.29	329.26	326.52	324.07	321.85
45000	570.05	456.42	404.88	377.64	373.83	370.41	367.34	364.58	362.09
50000	633.38	507.14	449.87	419.60	415.37	411.57	408.15	405.08	402.32
51000	646.05	517.28	458.87	428.00	423.67	419.80	416.32	413.19	410.36
52000	658.72	527.42	467.86	436.39	431.98	428.03	424.48	421.29	418.41
53000	671.39	537.57	476.86	444.78	440.29	436.26	432.64	429.39	426.45
54000	684.05	547.71	485.86	453.17	448.60	444.49	440.81	437.49	434.50
55000	696.72	557.85	494.85	461.56	456.90	452.72	448.97	445.59	442.55
56000	709.39	567.99	503.85	469.95	465.21	460.96	457.13	453.69	450.59
57000	722.06	578.14	512.85	478.35	473.52	469.19	465.30	461.79	458.64
58000	734.72	588.28	521.85	486.74	481.82	477.42	473.46	469.90	466.69
59000	747.39	598.42	530.84	495.13	490.13	485.65	481.62	478.00	474.73
60000	760.06	608.56	539.84	503.52	498.44	493.88	489.78	486.10	482.78
61000	772.73	618.71	548.84	511.91	506.75	502.11	497.95	494.20	490.82
62000	785.39	628.85	557.84	520.31	515.05	510.34	506.11	502.30	498.87
63000	798.06	638.99	566.83	528.70	523.36	518.57	514.27	510.40	506.92
64000	810.73	649.14	575.83	537.09	531.67	526.81	522.44	518.51	514.96
65000	823.40	659.28	584.83	545.48	539.98	535.04	530.60	526.61	523.01
66000	836.07	669.42	593.82	553.87	548.28	543.27	538.76	534.71	531.06
67000	848.73	679.56	602.82	562.27	556.59	551.50	546.93	542.81	539.10
68000	861.40	689.71	611.82	570.66	564.90	559.73	555.09	550.91	547.15
69000	874.07	699.85	620.82	579.05	573.20	567.96	563.25	559.01	555.19
70000	886.74	709.99	629.81	587.44	581.51	576.19	571.41	567.12	563.24
71000	899.40	720.13	638.81	595.83	589.82	584.42	579.58	575.22	571.29
72000	912.07	730.28	647.81	604.23	598.13	592.66	587.74	583.32	579.33
73000	924.74	740.42	656.80	612.62	606.43	600.89	595.90	591.42	587.38
74000	937.41	750.56	665.80	621.01	614.74	609.12	604.07	599.52	595.43
75000	950.07	760.70	674.80	629.40	623.05	617.35	612.23	607.62	603.47
76000	962.74	770.85	683.80	637.79	631.35	625.58	620.39	615.72	611.52
77000	975.41	780.99	692.79	646.19	639.66	633.81	628.56	623.83	619.56
78000	988.08	791.13	701.79	654.58	647.97	642.04	636.72	631.93	627.61
79000	1000.74	801.28	710.79	662.97	656.28	650.27	644.88	640.03	635.66
80000	1013.41	811.42	719.79	671.36	664.58	658.51	653.04	648.13	643.70
81000	1026.08	821.56	728.78	679.75	672.89	666.74	661.21	656.23	651.75
82000	1038.75	831.70	737.78	688.15	681.20	674.97	669.37	664.33	659.80
83000	1051.41	841.85	746.78	696.54	689.51	683.20	677.53	672.44	667.84
84000	1064.08	851.99	755.77	704.93	697.81	691.43	685.70	680.54	675.89
85000	1076.75	862.13	764.77	713.32	706.12	699.66	693.86	688.64	683.93
90000	1140.09	912.84	809.76	755.28	747.66	740.82	734.67	729.15	724.17
95000	1203.42	963.56	854.74	797.24	789.19	781.97	775.49	769.65	764.40
100000	1266.76	1014.27	899.73	839.20	830.73	823.13	816.30	810.16	804.63
105000	1330.10	1064.98	944.72	881.16	872.26	864.29	857.12	850.67	844.86
110000	1393.44	1115.70	989.70	923.12	913.80	905.44	897.93	891.18	885.09
115000	1456.78	1166.41	1034.69	965.08	955.34	946.60	938.75	931.69	925.32
120000	1520.11	1217.12	1079.68	1007.04	996.87	987.76	979.56	972.19	965.55
125000	1583.45	1267.84	1124.66	1049.00	1038.41	1028.91	1020.38	1012.70	1005.78
130000	1646.79	1318.55	1169.65	1090.96	1079.95	1070.07	1061.19	1053.21	1046.01
140000	1773.47	1419.98	1259.62	1174.88	1163.02	1152.38	1142.82	1134.23	1126.48
150000	1900.14	1521.40	1349.59	1258.80	1246.09	1234.69	1224.45	1215.24	1206.94

Reproduced from Pub. No. 493, Comprehensive ARM Payment Tables, copyright 1985, pages 34 and 42, Financial Publishing Company, Boston, MA 02215

Table 6.2.

10% MONTHLY PAYMENT
NECESSARY TO AMORTIZE A LOAN

AMOUNT	10 YEARS	15 YEARS	20 YEARS	25 YEARS	26 YEARS	27 YEARS	28 YEARS	29 YEARS	30 YEARS
50	.67	.54	.49	.46	.46	.45	.45	.45	.44
100	1.33	1.08	.97	.91	.91	.90	.89	.89	.88
250	3.31	2.69	2.42	2.28	2.26	2.24	2.22	2.21	2.20
500	6.61	5.38	4.83	4.55	4.51	4.48	4.44	4.42	4.39
750	9.92	8.06	7.24	6.82	6.76	6.71	6.66	6.62	6.59
1000	13.22	10.75	9.66	9.09	9.01	8.95	8.88	8.83	8.78
2000	26.44	21.50	19.31	18.18	18.02	17.89	17.76	17.65	17.56
3000	39.65	32.24	28.96	27.27	27.03	26.83	26.64	26.48	26.33
4000	52.87	42.99	38.61	36.35	36.04	35.77	35.52	35.30	35.11
5000	66.08	53.74	48.26	45.44	45.05	44.71	44.40	44.13	43.88
10000	132.16	107.47	96.51	90.88	90.10	89.41	88.80	88.25	87.76
15000	198.23	161.20	144.76	136.31	135.15	134.12	133.20	132.38	131.64
20000	264.31	214.93	193.01	181.75	180.20	178.82	177.60	176.50	175.52
25000	330.38	268.66	241.26	227.18	225.25	223.53	222.00	220.62	219.40
30000	396.46	322.39	289.51	272.62	270.30	268.23	266.39	264.75	263.28
35000	462.53	376.12	337.76	318.05	315.35	312.94	310.79	308.87	307.16
40000	528.61	429.85	386.01	363.49	360.40	357.64	355.19	353.00	351.03
45000	594.68	483.58	434.26	408.92	405.44	402.35	399.59	397.12	394.91
50000	660.76	537.31	482.52	454.36	450.49	447.05	443.99	441.24	438.79
51000	673.97	548.05	492.17	463.44	459.50	455.99	452.86	450.07	447.57
52000	687.19	558.80	501.82	472.53	468.51	464.94	461.74	458.89	456.34
53000	700.40	569.55	511.47	481.62	477.52	473.88	470.62	467.72	465.12
54000	713.62	580.29	521.12	490.70	486.53	482.82	479.50	476.54	473.89
55000	726.83	591.04	530.77	499.79	495.54	491.76	488.38	485.37	482.67
56000	740.05	601.78	540.42	508.88	504.55	500.70	497.26	494.19	491.45
57000	753.26	612.53	550.07	517.96	513.56	509.64	506.14	503.02	500.22
58000	766.48	623.28	559.72	527.05	522.57	518.58	515.02	511.84	509.00
59000	779.69	634.02	569.37	536.14	531.58	527.52	523.90	520.67	517.77
60000	792.91	644.77	579.02	545.23	540.59	536.46	532.78	529.49	526.55
61000	806.12	655.51	588.67	554.31	549.60	545.40	541.66	538.32	535.32
62000	819.34	666.26	598.32	563.40	558.61	554.35	550.54	547.14	544.10
63000	832.55	677.01	607.97	572.49	567.62	563.29	559.42	555.97	552.88
64000	845.77	687.75	617.62	581.57	576.63	572.23	568.30	564.79	561.65
65000	858.98	698.50	627.27	590.66	585.64	581.17	577.18	573.62	570.43
66000	872.20	709.24	636.92	599.75	594.65	590.11	586.06	582.44	579.20
67000	885.41	719.99	646.57	608.83	603.66	599.05	594.94	591.26	587.98
68000	898.63	730.74	656.22	617.92	612.67	607.99	603.82	600.09	596.75
69000	911.85	741.48	665.87	627.01	621.68	616.93	612.70	608.91	605.53
70000	925.06	752.23	675.52	636.10	630.69	625.87	621.58	617.74	614.31
71000	938.28	762.97	685.17	645.18	639.70	634.81	630.46	626.56	623.08
72000	951.49	773.72	694.82	654.27	648.71	643.76	639.34	635.39	631.86
73000	964.71	784.47	704.47	663.36	657.72	652.70	648.22	644.21	640.63
74000	977.92	795.21	714.12	672.44	666.73	661.64	657.10	653.04	649.41
75000	991.14	805.96	723.77	681.53	675.74	670.58	665.98	661.86	658.18
76000	1004.35	816.70	733.42	690.62	684.75	679.52	674.85	670.69	666.96
77000	1017.57	827.45	743.07	699.70	693.76	688.46	683.73	679.51	675.74
78000	1030.78	838.20	752.72	708.79	702.77	697.40	692.61	688.34	684.51
79000	1044.00	848.94	762.37	717.88	711.78	706.34	701.49	697.16	693.29
80000	1057.21	859.69	772.02	726.97	720.79	715.28	710.37	705.99	702.06
81000	1070.43	870.44	781.67	736.05	729.80	724.22	719.25	714.81	710.84
82000	1083.64	881.18	791.32	745.14	738.81	733.17	728.13	723.64	719.61
83000	1096.86	891.93	800.97	754.23	747.82	742.11	737.01	732.46	728.39
84000	1110.07	902.67	810.62	763.31	756.83	751.05	745.89	741.29	737.17
85000	1123.29	913.42	820.27	772.40	765.84	759.99	754.77	750.11	745.94
90000	1189.36	967.15	868.52	817.84	810.88	804.69	799.17	794.23	789.82
95000	1255.44	1020.88	916.78	863.27	855.93	849.40	843.57	838.36	833.70
100000	1321.51	1074.61	965.03	908.71	900.98	894.10	887.97	882.48	877.58
105000	1387.59	1128.34	1013.28	954.14	946.03	938.81	932.36	926.61	921.46
110000	1453.66	1182.07	1061.53	999.58	991.08	983.51	976.76	970.73	965.33
115000	1519.74	1235.80	1109.78	1045.01	1036.13	1028.22	1021.16	1014.85	1009.21
120000	1585.81	1289.53	1158.03	1090.45	1081.18	1072.92	1065.56	1058.98	1053.09
125000	1651.89	1343.26	1206.28	1135.88	1126.23	1117.63	1109.96	1103.10	1096.97
130000	1717.96	1396.99	1254.53	1181.32	1171.28	1162.33	1154.35	1147.23	1140.85
140000	1850.12	1504.45	1351.04	1272.19	1261.37	1251.74	1243.15	1235.47	1228.61
150000	1982.27	1611.91	1447.54	1363.06	1351.47	1341.15	1331.95	1323.72	1316.36

Reproduced from Pub. No. 493, Comprehensive ARM Payment Tables, copyright 1985, pages 34 and 42, Financial Publishing Company, Boston, MA 02215

Q: Under what conditions can buyers be in breach of a contract and lose their deposit?

One way is by making a mistake on the purchase agreement and inserting "best prevailing rate" instead of a specific rate. If the rates rise, buyers who want to back out could lose their deposit, because, at the time, they were provided with the best rate. Consequently, if they want to back out, they may be considered to be in breach of contract and could be financially responsible for damages to the seller.

Q: Why is it important to be as exact as possible with a real estate agreement?

There is no room for confusion. Buyers do not need anyone to interpret the contract if it is exact and specific. For example, by inserting an exact interest rate, buyers show they are conditioning their obligation to purchase on the availability of a particular type of loan at a particular interest rate. If they cannot obtain it, they can be legally relieved from performance without penalty. Remember to always insert the approximate monthly payment, based on the interest rate that is stipulated in the contract.

Q: Why do lenders scrutinize the "occupancy" item in the purchase agreement?

Section 2 (Occupancy) of Figure 6.1 is critically important to buyers. Lenders examine this line to see if buyers intend to occupy the property. If they are not the prime occupant, that indicates to the lender that the buyer is investing rather than planning on living in the property. To the lender, investors pose a greater risk than buyers who plan to be occupants. Absentee owners do not have as much to lose as the buyer/occupant. Absentee owners can give up the property and lose nothing more than their down payment and monthly payment. They may have another residence in which they can live. On the other hand, buyer/

occupants usually have no other place to move. They depend on the property to provide their family with shelter as well as serve as an investment.

Q: Why do buyer/occupants generally get lower interest rates than investors?

The one who has the most to lose is the buyer/occupant. It also follows that the person with more to lose is going to try harder to retain and maintain the residence, not giving up at the first sign of difficulty. Lenders realize this fact and they reward the buyer/occupants with lower interest rates. Although the difference may not be significant, an owner/occupant can plan on paying 0.25% less in interest than the investor. On a $100,000 property with an $80,000 mortgage, this can mean a difference of $14.91 in monthly payments and more than $5,000 during the lifetime of a 30-year loan.

Q: What is meant by supplements in a real estate agreement?

Section 3 of Figure 6.1 refers to attachments or supplements. Supplements are add-ons to the agreement that either the buyer or seller requests. They become part of the contract, and before it can be effective, the supplements must be agreed to by both parties. For example, a typical supplement might state that the present home of the buyer must be sold before the buyer is obligated to purchase this new property. Selling the old home becomes a condition of the contract. If the buyer cannot sell, the contract is voided and the deposit returned.

In supplements buyers usually spell out any difficulties they may have before purchasing the property. It may, as previously stated, involve the selling of another piece of property. Or, perhaps, they are making repairs on their present home and intend to sell it when the improvements are completed. Then, something happens, for example, they lose their job. That prevents the agreement from being concluded in a timely manner, and it could cost buyers their deposit—unless the supplements spelled out conditions under which the transaction could be terminated.

Q: In what way can supplements in an agreement protect sellers as well as buyers?

A supplement might say that the seller can occupy the property for a certain number of days or months after it is purchased by the buyer. This would fall under the "interim occupancy agreement," which is another form that should be filled out and attached to the contract. Or, perhaps, the buyer is going to lease the property to the seller following the purchase. This, too, should be included. VA and FHA amendments refer to special types of financing. As mentioned in Chapter 5, the VA loan restricts the amount of points a buyer can pay. Sellers have to agree to accept these types of loans if they are requested and they want to sell the property to the purchaser.

Q: What is an escrow holder? What do they do?

The escrow holder (Section 4, Escrow, of Figure 6.1) is an intermediary, and an agent of both the buyer and seller. The escrow holder is given the buyer's deposit, and holds onto all funds until the agreement is finalized. The escrow holder notifies the seller when the deposit has been received and if the check has cleared the bank, and also draws up a set of instructions, itemizing things that have to be done before the property is sold and transferred. For instance, perhaps the seller must supply a termite inspection. The escrow holder would track this requirement and make sure it is fulfilled before any funds are transferred to the seller. Some states do not have escrow companies. In these states closing agents may be an attorney or title companies.

Q: What is the role of the title company in a transaction?

The term title (Section 5 of Figure 6.1) is familiar to most investors, but it is important to understand the key role the title company plays in a transaction.

Title companies either maintain or have access to ownership records of properties. Most title companies cover an entire county, some just a portion of the county, depending on the size and number of transactions that are conducted through the year. The title company reviews documents on the property that have been filed with city or county, and determines if the property can be transferred and can the transfer be insured. For example, suppose a carpet company did some work for a carpenter who was remodeling a room on the property. If the company was never paid, it might have recorded a mechanic's lien against the property. The document would be recorded with the county recorder, and the title company would not insure the transfer of the title of the property until the lien was paid or released. The title company would detect this lien in its search, and notify the seller through the escrow holder of its existence.

Once the escrow holder knows the title to the property can be transferred to the purchaser according to the escrow instructions, the escrow holder forwards the deed to the title company with an instruction and authorization to cause the deed to be recorded. The proceeds that are due the seller will be paid by the escrow holder.

Q: How is the escrow holder compensated?

Generally, for services, the escrow holder works for a fee, which is usually relative to the sales price. It might be $100–$200 plus $1.50 per every thousand dollars of the purchase price.

Q: What is an "independent escrow?"

So-called "independent escrows" could fall under the jurisdiction of the department of corporations and do not generally have common ownership with the real estate agent. Some real estate firms handle their own escrows, and usually do so in cases in which the buyers and sellers have to travel too far. If real estate brokers also act as the escrow holder, they are normally regulated by the department of real estate.

One thing buyers should understand is that although the enclosed agreement says "escrow," it is not actually an escrow document. With this contract, the buyer and seller are "agreeing to agree" to execute an escrow agreement that is consistent with the terms and conditions contained in the real estate purchase contract. In other words, they are similar to a pair of negotiators, and their terms have been spelled out via this contract. Those terms are then put into a formal escrow agreement. Normally the escrow agreement will contain all of the provisions of the sales agreement.

Q: How do legal problems develop when calendar days are mentioned in an agreement instead of specific dates?

In the "calendar days" item under "Title" in the agreement, there is room for confusion on both the buyer and seller's part. For example, a buyer who is given a preliminary report by the title company that contains unacceptable items may want to cancel the agreement to purchase. To do this the buyer must submit objections and disapprovals in writing within "X calendar days" of receipt of a copy of the preliminary report that was issued. The problem is (1) when did the buyer receive the report, (2) when was it sent, and (3) who is going to prove it. This section can become argumentative, especially if the buyer wants to withdraw. The escrow holder will normally ask the purchaser to sign a document acknowledging what day the purchaser received the preliminary report. This sets the clock in motion. Assume the purchaser only had five days to approve or disapprove. If, on the fourth day, the purchaser still has questions, the other party should be notified that additional time is needed. If it is not granted, or if the purchaser is still unsure, the purchaser should cancel the agreement.

If possible, it is best to enter a specific date and time instead of the "calendar days." Everyone understands a date and deadline, and there is no room for ambiguity. But, when it comes to calendar days, there is a great deal of latitude for misunderstanding, especially when the beginning date is also a date that can be ambiguous, for example, "within five calendar days from the acceptance of the offer." In this case, the exact day of acceptance of the offer becomes the critical day. That day can be ascertained by applying "contract law." This is not always easily agreed on and if the date becomes critical, lawyers will be needed (and, perhaps even a judge) to determine it.

Q: What type of items do preliminary reports contain?

A portion of the preliminary report will indicate any bonds or encumbrances on the property. Buyers frequently overlook this portion of the report, yet it can save them thousands of dollars. For example, a builder or subdivider may have gone out and sold bonds on a development. The purpose of the bonds was to put in streets, street lights, and sewers. Assume the improvements cost $1.5 million and there were 100 homes in the tract. Each property would be encumbered with its share of the debt, $15,000. The bonds are usually paid off through tax bills on the property. Each year, when owners receive their bills, if they carefully examine the items they will find the bond item and the amount the owner is paying each year to satisfy the debt with interest.

When one of the 100 homes is sold, notice of the bond's existence is provided in the preliminary report. Unfortunately, many buyers do not pay attention to this (sometimes) involved, technical document. If they did, they would find in most cases the bond can be assumed by the new owner. It is normally assumable, that is, they do not usually contain "due on sale" clauses.

Thus, when the new owner takes over, the first tax bill will reflect the payment for the bond.

The buyer can demand as part of the agreement that the bond be paid off before the transaction is completed. The payment would be deducted from the seller's proceeds. If it happens, it is similar to a reduction in the liens or obligations against the property. Of course, the buyer would still be paying the full purchase price, however, taxes would be reduced over time since the bond (which is added to his property taxes) was paid by the seller. The key is to examine and understand the preliminary report.

Q: What is vesting and how does it relate to the buyer's taxes?

From a tax standpoint, vesting (Section 6 of Figure 6.1) is one of the most important items that a buyer will fill in on the document. Vesting refers to who (or how many) parties will hold title to the property. In whose name will it be? This is especially important for married couples who are the buyers. Most of the time, the couple puts the property in "joint tenancy." Most couples prefer this arrangement because transfer of title to the surviving joint tenant is a relatively simple procedure in most states, and does not require probate. The impact of that decision is illustrated by the following.

Assume a couple bought their first property for $200,000 and the title was vested as "John Smith and Joan Smith, husband and wife as joint tenants." In this case, the husband actually owns an individual one-half ($100,000) and the wife the other individual one-half ($100,000). This is their tax basis as well. If they were to obtain a divorce and sell the property for a profit (i.e., $300,000) each would automatically then have $150,000 in proceeds, and they would be taxed accordingly.

In other words, the IRS would figure that each invested $100,000 and made a $50,000 profit when they sold it for $150,000. What each would pay in taxes depends greatly on their individual situations and, of course, the rapidly changing tax laws. In this scenario, the joint tenancy works fine.

But, suppose they do not get a divorce and, instead, they remain happily married and hold onto the property as it appreciates. In 10 years, it is worth $400,000. Shortly thereafter, the husband dies and his $200,000 share is transferred immediately to his widow. Thus far, it sounds easy. No probate. No lawyers.

At the date of the husband's death, the IRS provides that his interest is transferred to the surviving spouse at fair market value. The husband's one-half interest is, therefore, $200,000. The surviving widow now has an adjusted basis for IRS purposes. Her new basis is $300,000 (her deceased husband's interest at $200,000 plus her original basis of $100,000).

Now, after a year, the widow decides that the house is too big and she wants to sell it. She does, for a net of $400,000, and is shocked when the IRS tells her she has to pay capital gains tax. This means that she has to pay tax on a $100,000 gain (the net sale price of $400,000, less her adjusted basis of $300,000). This can be a significant problem, aside from being a shock. The one good thing about joint tenancy is that ownership is transferred without a problem. The downside is if the surviving owner decides to sell, the tax consequences may be devastating.

Q: What does vesting in "community property" do for the buyer's taxes?

It is an alternative. Assume that the property is vested as "John Smith and Joan Smith, husband and wife as community property," not joint tenancy. Assume, too, that the same scenario unfolds. The property is purchased for $100,000 and it appreciates to $400,000. The husband dies and the widow wants to sell the property. She sells it for the $400,000. Something unusual happens. She finds that her capital gains—instead of being based upon a $100,000 profit as it is in joint tenancy—is zero!

163

Q: What is the advantage of vesting in community property?

When title to the property is held by married persons as community property, and one of the spouses dies, both the descendent's interest and the surviving spouse's interest are "stepped up" to fair market value as of the date of death. Thus, the potential tax liability is significantly less than for joint tenancy.

Q: Does joint tenancy have a place when it comes to holding title?

Community property can be a much better way of holding title for a property owner than joint tenancy. Today, there is no reason for a married couple to hold a property in joint tenancy unless, of course, the tax laws change. Community property, as a method of holding title, is generally ignored by buyers because they are unaware of the tax ramifications. The real estate agent or licensee is not a tax authority, and cannot be expected to know the answers. Even if the real estate agent knows the tax law, the agent is not authorized by the laws in most states to provide such information.

Q: Considering the tax advantages, why don't more buyers opt for community property?

This decision is made when property is purchased. The sales person who is filling out the paperwork has little or no knowledge of tax laws, joint tenancy, or community property. Typically, when it comes to the vesting portion, most buyers ask "how does everyone else do it?" The answer from the agent is "joint tenancy." The agent's sole function is to sell property. It takes a real estate attorney or an accountant to interpret agreements and answer questions about joint tenancy and community property.

Q: How can a buyer find a real estate attorney or CPA?

Buyers can utilize either when purchasing property. Whichever one is selected, the buyer should ask "how much of their practice is devoted to real estate and real estate taxation?" If the answer is more than half, they have usually found the professional who can usually give them the best tax advice. A good lawyer or CPA will also gather much more information about the parties and their financial status. Generally, as their total assets become larger, tax planning and estate planning become more of a necessity.

Q: What does the term "prorations" mean in an agreement?

Prorations (Section 7 of Figure 6.1) means that taxes and other payments and assessments will be paid according to the date of transfer of title or the deed is recorded. This is normal and it provides that both parties will pay that portion of these expenses that are applicable to the time they own(ed) the property.

Although this matter may seem matter-of-fact, it can lead to disagreements between buyer and seller if it is not read and understood by both parties. The seller may have prepaid some real property taxes, that is, paid them before they were due. If this happens, then the seller is entitled to reimbursement from the buyer for that portion of the prepaid tax that applies to the period of time the buyer owns the property.

Assume, for example, that the seller did not occupy the property but had it rented to a tenant. Generally, rental agreements provide the rent be paid in advance. If the tenant paid the seller the rent of $500 on the first of the month and the deed to the buyer was recorded on the 15th day of the month, the seller would be required to pay $250 of the rent collected to the buyer, because that portion of the rent is owed for the period the buyer owned the property.

Q: What is the significance of "possession" in a purchase agreement? Why is it important to buyers?

Possession (Section 8 of Figure 6.1) takes some thought. When does the buyer gain possession? The answer is usually when the transaction is finalized and the deed is recorded. Normally, this is at the close of escrow. But astute buyers ask for possession a day prior to the close of escrow. When that happens, they can inspect the property to ensure that all parts of the agreement have been fulfilled. Suppose, for instance, there is trash or lumber that should have been removed. On inspection, the buyer finds the trash and lumber are still there. The buyer calls the seller who states that it will not be removed until escrow is closed. The buyer can call escrow and get it to close a day early, so the trash and lumber can be removed and the buyer can move in the following day—as planned.

Often, buyers are moving from one house to another and they have not left themselves much leeway. The seller does not want to leave until the funds are obtained, and sometimes there are unplanned delays. If the deed is not recorded until late afternoon, the seller will not get the proceeds until the end of the day. The buyer is ready to move, but not the seller.

Q: What are the differences between "fixtures and fittings" and "personal property?" How do they impact the purchase of a property and the purchase agreement?

Sometimes fixtures (Section 11 of Figure 6.1) can create problems. "All permanently installed fixtures and fittings" are usually included in the contract. However, there can be ambiguity in the definition. At times, attorneys can argue a fine line. For instance, a homeowner may purchase standard readymade drapes from a department store and install a universal curtain hanger, as well, and put the readymade drapes up. Some attorneys will argue that the readymade drapes are not "fixtures and fittings" but personal property. But, if the homeowner goes out and has drapes custom-made and fitted for the residence, there is usually no argument—the drapes are "fixtures and fittings" because they would not readily fit in another house.

In this category, it is not always how the item is affixed to the property. When disagreements arise, it becomes a matter of judgment and, too frequently, the judgment is decided in a court. The disposition of fixtures and fittings frequently leads to arguments. To avoid the confrontation, spell out what goes and what stays beforehand. Make sure it is in the contract.

Frequently, sellers will improperly remove items from the property at closing. When the buyer takes possession and discovers the missing items they become irate. They usually attack the real estate agents and normally blame them—perhaps because they are the easiest parties in the transaction to reach. It is the sellers who should be contacted by the buyer. Selling disputes of this nature should not involve the real estate agents. They did not take the items; the sellers are the wrongdoers and the agent has no way of requiring the seller to return the items.

Q: How should smoke detector requirements in a purchase agreement be handled?

Recently, many states have started to require that smoke detectors (Section 12 of Figure 6.1) be installed before a property can be transferred. In many older properties, smoke detectors do not exist, and even in some new ones the owners have not installed any. It is the responsibility of the seller to see that they are installed. Yet, it is the buyer who is going to be living with them. The buyer should price the smoke detectors, and ask the seller for credit for the funds needed to purchase the detectors the buyer desires. Do not leave it up to the seller to produce the detectors. Remember, the seller is leaving and in many cases will not care how good or bad the detectors happen to be. This is something that should remain in the buyer's domain.

Q: What is the importance of a "Transfer Disclosure" statement in a purchase agreement? Why should buyers insist on one?

The Transfer Disclosure statement (Section 13 of Figure 6.1) is something that every state should require (unfortunately, they do not) for agreements between buyers and sellers concerning the purchase and sale of single family residences. The statement mandates that the seller disclose to the buyer everything known about the property that could materially impact the property's value. The concept behind this statement is that the seller has been living on the property and is better acquainted with it than either the buyer or the real estate agents. Therefore, if there is anything that may impact the value of the property that is not evident, the seller should disclose that information in a statement of this type.

Q: How does "as is" in a purchase agreement benefit the seller?

Some states have an "as is" provision in an agreement instead of a Transfer Disclosure statement. The "as is" benefits the seller. Basically, it puts the buyer on notice to thoroughly examine the property. "As is" may as well say "buyer beware." (Interestingly, even when this clause is inserted into a contract, some states do not recognize it. Some states maintain that a seller who has not disclosed known latent defects may be liable for those defects. When buyers run into these statements, they should take extreme care to have the property inspected, and they should be looking at everything from the foundation to the condition of the wiring.)

The "as is" statement is a definite red flag, and only a buyer who is foolish would ignore it and proceed with the transaction without a thorough investigation. Once these forms are completed, and submitted to the buyer, the buyer has three days to rescind the agreement and back out, if the buyer disapproves of the disclosure. Not all states have statutes permitting rescission based on a disclosure of property condition report.

Q: What is the tax and financial impact of buying property from a foreign corporation or entity in this country?

The tax withholding (Section 14 of Figure 6.1) in the purchase agreement is another red flag issue. Its primary purpose is to make buyers aware that if they are purchasing property from a foreign corporation or entity, there may be tax liabilities on the part of the seller. The escrow company should be informed. Although it does not happen frequently, the buyer runs the risk of being liable for the tax liability if the funds are not withheld from the seller's proceeds. While the escrow holder will normally perform this function for the buyer, it is the buyer's responsibility to cause the funds to be withheld. If the seller is a foreign corporation and, for some reason, fails to pay the taxes due, the buyer may be liable.

Q: What is a Multiple Listing Service (MLS)?

The so-called Multiple Listing Service (MLS) (Section 15 of Figure 6.1) is an organization that is part of every real estate community. The MLS collects information on properties for sale and makes the information available to all members. It also keeps records on sales, selling price, and related information. It will provide statistics and summaries to MLS members. A broker may be an MLS member without becoming a member of the local board of realtors.

Q: How does the MLS benefit buyers and sellers?

An agent, having obtained a listing from a seller, will file the listing with the MLS, which means that any agent who is a member of the local MLS has access to the information. The days of exclusive listings, in which agents from other companies have no opportunity to sell a property, are disappearing. Obviously, there is an advantage to having a property listed and placed in the MLS. More agents have access to the information and, hopefully, more buyers are brought around. When the agent submits the terms and conditions of the sale to the MLS, it provides other agents in the area with valuable market data. With it, they can more intelligently price properties and sell them. A buyer, who for some reason does not want the information released, can request this section be stricken from the agreement.

[Note: On the typical purchase agreement we have included (Figure 6.1) Section 16 is unusual in that in order for any of the items (A through K) to be effective, all buyers and sellers must initial. If only the purchasers initial a particular paragraph, and the buyers do not, the paragraph and condition do not apply.]

Q: *What makes an inspection a worthwhile expense for buyers?*

The first item (A) (Section 16 of Figure 6.1) permits the buyer to bring in an independent inspector to search for any flaws in the soils or structure. The inspection is at the buyer's expense, but it is a worthwhile expense, especially if the property is in an area in which the earth is subject to movement, that is, earthquakes. Structural damage is often not immediately obvious following a quake, and it takes time—and another jolt—before the damage affects the stability of the property. A geological inspection should uncover any problems in this area.

In fact, the first three items (A–C) of Section 16 stem from a situation in which the seller, the listing agent, and contractor who built the property were all sued by the purchaser. The lawsuit (Easton versus Strassburger) established the broker's duty to conduct an investigation of the property. Until this case went to trial, buyers seldom sued agents because the agents had (and were held to) a duty to disclose what they "knew" about a particular property. Usually, it was the buyer versus the seller, and the agent was off the hook. The Easton versus Strassburger case changed everything.

Q: What was the Easton versus Strassburger case, and how has it impacted full disclosure by sellers and agents?

The case involved a buyer who discovered there was a serious problem with the property she purchased for $170,000. Half the structure was built on fill dirt and the other half on cut. (Fill dirt is soil that is used to level a lot.) Many structures are built on fill, however, the soil must be properly compacted so there will be no movement when rains come. Unfortunately, this particular property was apparently not compacted properly and shortly after the purchase it rained, and the property moved, causing extensive damage.

In the trial by jury, the court found that the seller, listing agent/broker, and contractor were all negligent to a different degree. For example, the listing agent/broker was found to be 5% negligent, which meant he had to pay 5% of the damages. All other defendants were held to be 90% negligent and a nonparty to the litigation (another broker) was found to be 5% negligent. Since liability in this type of case is joint and several, it is possible that a party who is only 1% liable may be required to pay the entire judgment if codefendants are unable to contribute.

In the case, the jury awarded the plaintiff $197,000. Estimates to repair the $170,000 property were as high as $213,000. The fair market value of the property, in its damaged condition, was around $20,000.

Most important, the court decided that the agent/broker had a "duty of discovery." In other words, the agent/broker dealt with property all the time and had the obligation to discover if there was anything wrong with the property and inform the buyer. This imposed a duty on the agent/broker to conduct, in all future sales, a reasonably diligent visual inspection for the purpose of discovering material facts that could affect the value and desirability of the property and to disclose these findings to prospective buyers. Previously agent/brokers had the responsibility to disclose only what was within their personal knowledge. Proving that a broker "knew" some material fact that was not disclosed to the buyer was difficult, if not impossible. With this ruling, that is no longer the case. This case is rapidly becoming the standard throughout the country.

Q: Are there any hidden legal burdens that might impact the broker and the buyer's investment?

Today, in many states, agent/brokers are responsible for discovering material facts concerning the property they sell. In some states, there is significant burden put on the broker. (Sales associates work under the broker's license in a real estate office.) The broker cannot fully delegate this obligation to the sales associate, and the broker cannot escape the liability by hiring someone else to do the inspection. In other words, this legal obligation has involved the broker more than ever in the sale and, thus, is greater protection for the buyer. Not every state, of course, recognizes this legal burden; however, it is spreading. With the emphasis on consumerism, it will not be long before most states recognize this burden.

(Note: Although item B of Section 16 does not pertain to any serious material defects, it is important for both seller and buyer to initial it since it guarantees the buyer that things such as lawns and pools will be in as good a condition when escrow closes as they were when the contract was negotiated.)

Q: What is the significance of a "pest control stipulation" in the purchase agreement?

Item D of Section 16, the pest control stipulation, is something that all agents know about. In many states, pest control inspection is required as part of the purchase, and if there is an infestation the seller has to pay for the exterminator to come in and clear it up. Frequently, sellers will put a limitation on the amount of funds they will spend for pest control inspection and repairs. If, for instance, it is agreed that the seller is responsible for up to $2,500 for pest control treatment, and a firm cannot be found that will do it for less than $2,700, that does not mean the pest control item is thrown out or the transaction terminated. Under most state laws, the seller has to inform the buyer, and the buyer has the option of paying the extra $200 and requiring the seller to absorb the remaining $2,500.

Of course, if a property is located in a hazardous flood area (item E of Section 16), the buyer should know about it. Just as floods are a prime concern to many midwestern and southern areas of the country, earthquakes are problems for those in California. Item F of Section 16 addresses this issue and, once again, requires that both the buyer and seller initial to become a part of the agreement.

In some instances, states have passed energy conservation laws that require sellers to insulate certain portions of the property. If the insulation has not been completed, it is the seller's responsibility. The buyer can handle it by authorizing escrow to withhold sufficient funds to pay for the conservation materials.

Q: Who pays for home protection plans? Are they worth it?

Home protection plans (item H of Section 16) are usually paid for by the buyer, but, once again, they are generally not worth the expenditure. It would be more fruitful for the buyer to hire a structural engineer or contractor, who knows what to look for, to examine the stability of a home.

Q: What are CC&Rs, and to what type of investments do they usually apply?

Item I of Section 16 indicates that the seller will disclose any meaningful or significant covenants, conditions, and restrictions (CC&Rs) that apply to a condominium and its use. There are usually a set of CC&Rs that, together with homeowner association documents, is written and governs the use of all condominium and townhouse projects. Buyers must read these documents because there may be restrictions and regulations within them that they cannot abide. For example, suppose the buyers have a 10-year-old dog who has been a close companion to their young son or daughter. CC&Rs may prohibit dogs in the development. If the buyers never ask about their animal and the seller never mentions the restriction, the transaction may be completed before the problem surfaces. Other possible violations of CC&Rs range from prohibiting automobiles from being parked outside the condominium or on the street to restrictions on when the recreation area or swimming pool can be used. If the purchase involves a condominium or townhouse, the buyer should definitely inspect the CC&Rs.

Q: How does a liquidated damage clause impact a buyer's deposit?

Item J of Section 16 is of special importance because of the "liquidated damage" clause and the fact that buyers can lose their deposit. The section stems from the commercial (not commercial investment) transactions field. For example, a company might design an unusual widget that requires special tooling and dies to manufacture. The company representative visits a manufacturer and states what is wanted.

The manufacturer checks costs and discovers it is going to cost $100,000 for the special machine, and another $15,000 for the dies, because the widgets are unlike anything previously built. The manufacturer has another problem aside from the initial cost—suppose the company cancels after the first 1,000 widgets are built. How will the costs be recouped? Why take the risk?

In commercial law, an attorney is usually given the facts and hashes out the agreement. In most of these contracts, there is a "liquidated damages" clause, which partially protects the manufacturer in the event the company cancels the agreement before the machinery and dies are amortized. The amount of liquidated damages normally diminishes as the contract comes closer to completion. Thus, when the company purchases the last of its 100,000 widgets, and the machinery has been amortized, there are no liquidated damages involved. But if the company finds it cannot sell the widgets, and cancels the contract after half the widgets have been made, the liquidated damage clause may provide for a $50,000 penalty from the company. The penalty helps pay for the tooling and dies, which are of little use to some other firm.

Q: How do liquidated damages in real estate transactions work?

Liquidated damages in a real estate transaction apply when the buyer and seller have come to an agreement, and the buyer has asked for a number of conditions to be fulfilled. The seller has completed all of them. Suddenly, the buyer breaches the contract and the deal is dead. A breach of the buyer is defined as failing to proceed when the buyer is under an obligation to proceed. In simple terms, the buyer fails to perform and has no legal excuse for not doing so.

For instance, suppose the seller has enhanced the property per the buyer's instructions in a way that no other buyer may want. The seller is stuck—but not quite. With the liquidated damage clause, the seller is entitled to keep 3% of the purchase price as damages, or the actual deposit, whichever is less. The buyer's liability for breaching the contract is thereby limited. In this situation, the seller does not need to establish damages, only that the buyer breached the contract in order to prevail. It should be noted that in California, should the buyer default the buyer may still get the deposit returned if the buyer can establish that the seller did not sustain a monetary loss. Laws relating to liquidated damages vary greatly from state to state.

Q: Can buyers (and sellers) be content with the knowledge that liquidated damage clauses are easy for courts to determine?

175

No, in fact in many instances courts have a difficult time coming to a verdict. Take, for instance, a buyer who agrees to purchase a property for $200,000, and later backs out or breaches the contract for some reason. Now, suppose this occurs during a period of high inflation, and a week after the buyer backs out, the seller finds another purchaser who pays $220,000 for the property. Has the seller been damaged? After all, the seller's profit has increased by $20,000. The fact that the seller has not been damaged may be irrelevant if the liquidated damage clause has been properly signed. But, suppose the buyer signs a contract and backs out during a soft or declining real estate market. If the price is depreciating, this would be a good clause for the buyer, who simply gives up 3% of the price, or the actual deposit, whichever is less.

Or, for example, there was a recent case in which a buyer came into a broker's office and saw a property that was listed for $200,000. He immediately knew it was the home his wife wanted. He went home and within an hour had brought back his wife who was equally as excited. The buyer made an offer and wrote a check for $10,000 as a deposit. The agent agreed and the contract was written with a 90-day escrow, and contained the liquidated damage provision.

Five days after the contract was accepted by the seller, the buyer discovered that his wife really did not want the house. She was excited only because she thought he wanted it. Both looked at each other in amazement and raced down to the real estate office to cancel the agreement. They were able to cancel it but it cost them 3% of their deposit.

In another instance, a buyer purchased a $200,000 property with the contract containing a liquidated damage clause. Judging by the buyer's reaction, the seller knew the buyer was anxious to get in as soon as possible so the seller began to move the furniture and even bought a new home 300 miles away, where a new position had been accepted. The day before escrow was slated to close the buyer called the seller and indicated a change in mind. The buyer would not buy the property and suggested the seller take the 3%, or $6,000, as compensation for any trouble.

Q: What general statement can be made about liquidated damage clauses when it comes to escrow, and buyers and sellers?

At the beginning of escrow, the liquidated damage clause favors the seller. In other words, it is the seller who makes the least amount of commitments. But as escrow comes nearer to closing, the seller has to make more commitments. The seller has to buy a new home somewhere else, has to hire a moving company to store or handle the furniture, and ensure that the property is as it should be for the buyer. And it is the seller who is damaged most if the contract is broken near the end of escrow. In many cases, sellers are damaged far beyond the maximum of 3% of the purchase price, or the actual deposit. However, if this clause is signed by both buyer and seller, that is all the seller gets.

Q: What is the most important thing for buyers to understand about liquidated damage clauses?

Buyers should understand that liquidated damage clauses are in most contracts and they are one of the most important provisions in the contract. If buyers have doubts as to whether they want to go through with a transaction, they are better off not signing the agreement and saving themselves thousands of dollars.

Q: What is the advantage of having an "arbitration of disputes" clause in a contract?

An arbitration of disputes clause (item K in Section 16) can be inserted in any real estate contract, and in many cases it may save the buyer and seller considerable expense. Arbitration is an alternative solution to trial by judge or jury. Generally, justice is swifter in arbitration proceedings. Our courts spend 75% of their time litigating criminal matters, and, as a result, civil matters, such as breach of contract cases, may take years before a judge and/or a courtroom is available.

Q: What is the difference between a "listing" and "selling" agent?

Listed under Section 21 of Figure 6.1 is the "listing agent" and the "selling agent." In real estate sales the listing agent is the broker with whom the seller contracted to market the seller's property. The listing agreement spells out what the listing agent will do for the seller. The authority contained in the listing will usually allow the agent to provide a copy of the listing to the MLS, place a sign on the property, advertise it, and do other marketing-oriented activities that will help sell it.

The "selling agent" is actually the agent who succeeds in obtaining a buyer for the property. This could, of course, be the listing agent, or it could be an agent from another company.

Q: Who gets the real estate commission and how much is it?

Typically, the selling and listing agents (companies) split the commission that is earned on the property. Thus, if a property sells for $200,000, and there was an agreement between owner and agent for a 6% commission, the commission would be $12,000. The selling agent's company would retain $6,000 and the listing agent's company would receive the other $6,000. Of course, if the selling and listing agent are the same, the entire $12,000 would go to one company. The amount of the commission is normally negotiated between the listing agent and the seller of the property at the time the listing agreement is signed.

Once an agreement is signed and financing arranged, the investor/buyer's next question and consideration is taxation. What happens when the investor decides to sell? With the changing tax laws, is there any specific formula or techniques that investors should keep in mind?

Q: What is a tax deferred exchange?

A tax deferred exchange is probably one of the most popular vehicles for deferring taxes. Assume that someone purchased a property 20 years ago for $100,000. Today, that property is worth $600,000. With a commercial structure, the buyer can depreciate only the building, not the ground. If the buyer started with $100,000, and depreciated the property (building) over a 20-year period, a total of perhaps $80,000 would have been depreciated. Depreciation is useful in that it is a deduction from income, thereby reducing the owner's overall tax liability.

Now, suppose the investor wants to sell the property. If it sells for $600,000, the investor has made a gain of $500,000 (the property was bought for $100,000). But according to the government the gain is actually $580,000 because the tax basis has been reduced by the $80,000 depreciation. Under the old laws, the investor would pay a capital gains tax (the gain on the investment) based on the $580,000 profit. The tax, once again, under the old law, would be a maximum 20% of the $580,000, or $116,000. The profit would be an astounding $484,000.

Compare this to an investor taking $100,000 and putting it into a tax free bond and leaving it for 20 years. The return at the end of that period would be around $300,000—or $184,000 less than the real estate venture.

Q: What is the advantage of a tax deferred exchange today?

The capital gains tax (at present) is a maximum of 34% (and Congress argues each year about the amount). With a gain of $580,000 × 0.34, the investor would be paying tax of $197,000, yielding a return of $382,000 versus the $484,000, which is a significant difference. This increased tax burden has provided an incentive for investors to take the entire $580,000 profit and roll it into another property. Under this scenario, the investor can sell one property, invest in another (and defer capital gains taxes), and borrow on the equity of the second property if cash is needed. And the borrowing becomes another tax deduction, because the interest paid on the loan is deductible.

In raising the capital gains tax, Congress intended to increase the amount of tax it would collect from investors. Instead, they have actually decreased the taxes collected because, whenever possible, the astute investor simply rolls one sale into another and delays the tax. Today, instead of investing in a property, holding it, selling it, and paying the tax, the investor purchases the property, holds it, and then exchanges it via a tax deferred exchange.

Q: What is the 1031 exchange?

The tax deferred exchange falls under IRS section 1031, and is commonly known as a 1031 exchange, even though other code sections may apply as well. It takes more than just switching one property for another, and investors who want to avoid tax and exchange properties should definitely consult a tax attorney and a CPA early in the process. The attorney should be someone familiar with real estate law, as well.

Interestingly, exchange is really a form of barter that goes back almost to the beginning of time. One of the landmark cases that allowed for the real estate exchange as it is known today took place about 10 years ago and is known as the U.S. versus Starker. The Starker case established the initial groundrules for delayed exchanges; these rules should be followed to the letter.

The IRS says that once an investor disposes of a property via a title company, facilitator, or accommodator, the investor is divested of that property. The investor no longer owns it.

Q: What is an accommodator or facilitator in a real estate transaction?

The accommodator or facilitator is a person or entity who holds title to the seller's property, conveys the property to the buyer, holds the purchase price, and awaits the seller's instructions to purchase the replacement property. Care should be taken in selecting the accommodator or facilitator, because when the investor sells the property, it is first deeded to the facilitator who, in turn, deeds it to the new owner. The facilitator holds the buyer's monies for the sold property in an interest-bearing trust account. Because of this enormous responsibility, investors should make sure that the accommodator or facilitator is well financed. Before trusting your property and money to an accommodator, carefully verify their ability to perform and employ an attorney to make sure that sufficient safeguards are in place. The larger the accommodating company, the better. Smaller companies can obtain letters of credit from their bank ensuring the funds will be available when needed.

The fees for this service are competitive, however, investors should be more concerned about the security of their monies than saving a few dollars on fees. An ideal method would be to set up the accommodator, with your attorney or accountant as a co-signator. The account should require two signatures, one from the investor or the investor's CPA or attorney and the other from the accommodator. No one can get the monies without the investor's signature, or that of the investor's attorney or accountant.

Q: What happens if money passes through the investor's hands during a 1031 or other similar exchange?

The funds should never pass through the investor's hands. If the money from the sale of the property is accessible to the seller, the exchange will not qualify for the tax deferred treatment, and all capital gains taxes will become due.

Q: How long does an investor have to complete an exchange before the IRS nullifies it?

From the date the title is transferred to the purchaser, the investor has 45 days to identify a new property, and escrow on that new property must be closed within six months. In other words, six months from the date title is transferred on the property being sold, the investor must acquire, through the accommodator, the replacement property.

Although it sounds like a great deal of time, six months goes by relatively quickly, especially when the investor is trying to negotiate the acquisition of the replacement property. The lesson is to move quickly. In fact, it is a good idea for the investor to have a new property in mind before escrow has closed on the old one.

Q: What key rules should investors keep in mind when it comes to exchanges?

Two key rules to follow are (1) always buy up and (2) keep the debt at or above the obligation on the property sold. In other words, if an investor is selling a $300,000 building, to defer taxes and follow guideline (1) the investor should make sure the price of the next property purchased (within the six month time frame) is more than $300,000. Rule (2) refers to the amount of debt the investor had on the old building. Suppose it was $100,000. To be safe and follow rule (2), when buying the new building the investor should owe $100,000 or more.

Investors should always exceed the value of the old building and exceed the debt on the old building as well. Both items should be reviewed by a CPA and/or someone familiar with real estate transactions. Although there are many real estate agents familiar with 1031 exchanges, the sensible thing to do is go to the expert, a CPA or real estate attorney who specializes in the field.

Some typical exchanges are illustrated in Figures 6.2, 6.3, and 6.4.

REAL ESTATE PURCHASE CONTRACT AND RECEIPT FOR DEPOSIT
THIS IS MORE THAN A RECEIPT FOR MONEY. IT IS INTENDED TO BE A LEGALLY BINDING CONTRACT. READ IT CAREFULLY.
CALIFORNIA ASSOCIATION OF REALTORS® (CAR) STANDARD FORM

☐

_____, California, _____, 19_____

Received from _____

herein called Buyer, the sum of _____ Dollars $_____

evidenced by ☐ cash, ☐ cashier's check, ☐ personal check or ☐ _____, payable to _____

_____, to be held uncashed until acceptance of this offer as deposit on account of purchase price of

_____ Dollars $_____

for the purchase of property, situated in _____, County of _____, California,

described as follows: _____

1. FINANCING: The obtaining of Buyer's financing is a contingency of this agreement.

   A. DEPOSIT upon acceptance, to be deposited into _____ $ _____

   B. INCREASED DEPOSIT within _____ days of acceptance to be deposited into _____ $ _____

   C. BALANCE OF DOWN PAYMENT to be deposited into _____ on or before _____ $ _____

   D. Buyer to apply, qualify for and obtain a NEW FIRST LOAN in the amount of . . . . $ _____

     payable monthly at approximately $_____ including interest at origination not to exceed _____%.

     ☐ fixed rate, ☐ other _____ all due _____ years from date of origination. Loan fee not to

     exceed _____ Seller agrees to pay a maximum of _____ FHA/VA discount points.

     Additional terms _____

     _____

   E. Buyer ☐ to assume, ☐ to take title subject to an EXISTING FIRST LOAN with an approximate balance of . . . . . $ _____

     in favor of _____ payable monthly at $_____ including interest at _____% ☐ fixed rate,

     ☐ other _____. Fees not to exceed _____.

     Disposition of impound account _____

     Additional terms _____

   F. Buyer to execute a NOTE SECURED BY a ☐ first, ☐ second, ☐ third DEED OF TRUST in the amount of . . . . $ _____

     IN FAVOR OF SELLER payable monthly at $_____ ☐ or more, including interest at _____% all due

     _____ years from date of origination, ☐ or upon sale or transfer of subject property. A late charge of _____

     _____ shall be due on any installment not paid within _____ days of the due date.

     ☐ Deed of Trust to contain a request for notice of default or sale for the benefit of Seller. Buyer ☐ will, ☐ will not execute a request

     for notice of delinquency. Additional terms _____

     _____

   G. Buyer ☐ to assume, ☐ to take title subject to an EXISTING SECOND LOAN with an approximate balance of . . . . $ _____

     in favor of _____ payable monthly at $_____ including interest at _____%

     ☐ fixed rate, ☐ other _____. Buyer fees not to exceed _____.

     Additional terms _____

     _____

   H. Buyer to apply, qualify for and obtain a NEW SECOND LOAN in the amount of . . . . $ _____

     payable monthly at approximately $_____ including interest at origination not to exceed _____% ☐ fixed rate,

     ☐ other _____, all due _____ years from date of origination.

     Buyer's loan fee not to exceed _____ Additional terms _____

     _____

   I. In the event Buyer assumes or takes title subject to an existing loan, Seller shall provide Buyer with copies of applicable notes and Deeds

     of Trust. A loan may contain a number of features which affect the loan, such as interest rate changes, monthly payment changes, balloon

     payments, etc. Buyer shall be allowed _____ calendar days after receipt of such copies to notify Seller in writing of disapproval.

     FAILURE TO NOTIFY SELLER IN WRITING SHALL CONCLUSIVELY BE CONSIDERED APPROVAL. Buyer's approval shall not be

     unreasonably withheld. Difference in existing loan balances shall be adjusted in ☐ Cash, ☐ Other _____

     _____

   J. Buyer agrees to act diligently and in good faith to obtain all applicable financing. _____

     _____

     _____

   K. ADDITIONAL FINANCING TERMS: _____

     _____

     _____

     _____

   L. TOTAL PURCHASE PRICE . . . . $ _____

2. OCCUPANCY: Buyer ☐ does, ☐ does not intend to occupy subject property as Buyer's primary residence.

3. SUPPLEMENTS: The ATTACHED supplements are incorporated herein:

   ☐ Interim Occupancy Agreement (CAR FORM IOA-11)   ☐ _____

   ☐ Residential Lease Agreement after Sale (CAR FORM RLAS-11)   ☐ _____

   ☐ VA and FHA Amendments (CAR FORM VA/FHA-11)   ☐ _____

4. ESCROW: Buyer and Seller shall deliver signed instructions to _____ the escrow holder, within _____ calendar days

   of acceptance of the offer which shall provide for closing within _____ calendar days of acceptance. Escrow fees to be paid as follows: _____

   _____

        Buyer and Seller acknowledge receipt of copy of this page, which constitutes Page 1 of _____ Pages.

        Buyer's Initials (_____) (_____)   Seller's Initials (_____) (_____)

             OFFICE USE ONLY ────

             Reviewed by Broker or Designee _____

             Date _____

M-MB-Feb.-91

BROKERS COPY
REAL ESTATE PURCHASE CONTRACT AND RECEIPT FOR DEPOSIT (DLF-14 PAGE 1 OF 4)

Figure 6.1. (Represented with permission, California
Association of Realtors.® Endorsement not implied.)

☐

Subject Property Address: _____

5. TITLE: Title is to be free of liens, encumbrances, easements, restrictions, rights and conditions of record or known to Seller, other than the following: (a) Current property taxes, (b) covenants, conditions, restrictions, and public utility easements of record, if any, provided the same do not adversely affect the continued use of the property for the purposes for which it is presently being used, unless reasonably disapproved by Buyer in writing within _____ calendar days of receipt of a current preliminary report furnished at _____ expense, and (c) _____

Seller shall furnish Buyer at _____ expense a California Land Title Association policy issued by _____ _____ Company, showing title vested in Buyer subject only to the above. If Seller is unwilling or unable to eliminate any title matter disapproved by Buyer as above, Buyer may terminate this agreement. If Seller fails to deliver title as above, Buyer may terminate this agreement; in either case, the deposit shall be returned to Buyer.

6. VESTING: Unless otherwise designated in the escrow instructions of Buyer, title shall vest as follows: _____

(The manner of taking title may have significant legal and tax consequences. Therefore, give this matter serious consideration.)

7. PRORATIONS: Property taxes, payments on bonds and assessments assumed by Buyer, interest, rents, association dues, premiums on insurance acceptable to Buyer, and _____ shall be paid current and prorated as of ☐ the day of recordation of the deed; or ☐ _____. Bonds or assessments now a lien shall be ☐ paid current by Seller, payments not yet due to be assumed by Buyer; or ☐ paid in full by Seller, including payments not yet due; or ☐ _____. County Transfer tax shall be paid by _____. The _____ transfer tax or transfer fee shall be paid by _____. **PROPERTY WILL BE REASSESSED UPON CHANGE OF OWNERSHIP. THIS WILL AFFECT THE TAXES TO BE PAID.** A Supplemental tax bill will be issued, which shall be paid as follows: (a) for periods after close of escrow, by Buyer (or by final acquiring party if part of an exchange), and (b) for periods prior to close of escrow, by Seller. TAX BILLS ISSUED AFTER CLOSE OF ESCROW SHALL BE HANDLED DIRECTLY BETWEEN BUYER AND SELLER.

8. POSSESSION: Possession and occupancy shall be delivered to Buyer, ☐ on close of escrow, or ☐ not later than _____ days after close of escrow, or ☐ _____

9. KEYS: Seller shall, when possession is available to Buyer, provide keys and/or means to operate all property locks, and alarms, if any.

10. PERSONAL PROPERTY: The following items of personal property, free of liens and without warranty of condition, are included: _____

11. FIXTURES: All permanently installed fixtures and fittings that are attached to the property or for which special openings have been made are included in the purchase price, including electrical, light, plumbing and heating fixtures, built-in appliances, screens, awnings, shutters, all window coverings, attached floor coverings, TV antennas, air cooler or conditioner, garage door openers and controls, attached fireplace equipment, mailbox, trees and shrubs, and _____ except _____

12. SMOKE DETECTOR(S): State law requires that residences be equipped with an operable smoke detector(s). Local law may have additional requirements. Seller shall deliver to Buyer a written statement of compliance in accordance with applicable state and local law prior to close of escrow.

13. TRANSFER DISCLOSURE: Unless exempt, Transferor (Seller), shall comply with Civil Code §§1102 et seq., by providing Transferee (Buyer) with a Real Estate Transfer Disclosure Statement: (a) ☐ Buyer has received and read a Real Estate Transfer Disclosure Statement; or (b) ☐ Seller shall provide Buyer with a Real Estate Transfer Disclosure Statement within _____ calendar days of acceptance of the offer after which Buyer shall have three (3) days after delivery to Buyer, in person, or five (5) days after delivery by deposit in the mail, to terminate this agreement by delivery of a written notice of termination to Seller or Seller's Agent.

14. TAX WITHHOLDING: (a) Under the Foreign Investment in Real Property Tax Act (FIRPTA), IRC §1445, every Buyer of U.S. real property must, unless an exemption applies, deduct and withhold from Seller's proceeds 10% of the gross sales price. The primary FIRPTA exemptions are: No withholding is required if (i) Seller provides Buyer with an affidavit under penalty of perjury, that Seller is not a "foreign person," or (ii) Seller provides Buyer with a "qualifying statement" issued by the Internal Revenue Service, or (iii) Buyer purchases real property for use as a residence and the purchase price is $300,000 or less and Buyer or a member of Buyer's family has definite plans to reside at the property for at least 50% of the number of days it is in use during each of the first two 12-month periods after transfer. (b) In addition, under California Revenue and Taxation Code §§18805 and 26131, every Buyer must, unless an exemption applies, deduct and withhold from the Seller's proceeds 3⅓% of the gross sales price if the Seller has a last known street address outside of California, or if the Seller's proceeds will be paid to a financial intermediary of the Seller. The primary exemptions are: No withholding is required if (i) the Seller has a homeowner's exemption for the subject property, for local property taxes, for the year in which the title transfers, or (ii) the property is selling for $100,000 or less, or (iii) the Franchise Tax Board issues a certificate authorizing a lower amount or no withholding, or (iv) the Seller signs an affidavit stating that the Seller is a California resident or a corporation qualified to do business in California. (c) Seller and Buyer agree to execute and deliver as directed any instrument, affidavit, or statement reasonably necessary to carry out those statutes and regulations promulgated thereunder.

15. MULTIPLE LISTING SERVICE: If Broker is a Participant of an Association/Board multiple listing service ("MLS"), the Broker is authorized to report the sale, its price, terms, and financing for the publication, dissemination, information, and use of the authorized Board members, MLS Participants and Subscribers.

16. ADDITIONAL TERMS AND CONDITIONS:
ONLY THE FOLLOWING PARAGRAPHS 'A' THROUGH 'K' *WHEN INITIALLED BY BOTH BUYER AND SELLER* ARE INCORPORATED IN THIS AGREEMENT.
Buyer's Initials   Seller's Initials

_____/_____   _____/_____   **A. PHYSICAL AND GEOLOGICAL INSPECTION:** Buyer shall have the right, at Buyer's expense, to select a licensed contractor and/or other qualified professional(s), to make "Inspections" (including tests, surveys, other studies, inspections, and investigations) of the subject property, including but not limited to structural, plumbing, sewer/septic system, well, heating, electrical, built-in appliances, roof, soils, foundation, mechanical systems, pool, pool heater, pool filter, air conditioner, if any, possible environmental hazards such as asbestos, formaldehyde, radon gas and other substances/products, and geologic conditions. Buyer shall keep the subject property free and clear of any liens, indemnify and hold Seller harmless from all liability, claims, demands, damages, or costs, and repair all damages to the property arising from the "Inspections." All claimed defects concerning the condition of the property that adversely affect the continued use of the property for the purposes for which it is presently being used (☐ or as _____) shall be in writing, supported by written reports, if any, and delivered to Seller within _____ calendar days FOR "INSPECTIONS" OTHER THAN GEOLOGICAL, and/or within _____ calendar days FOR GEOLOGICAL "INSPECTIONS," **of acceptance of the offer.** Buyer shall furnish Seller copies, at no cost, of all reports concerning the property obtained by Buyer. When such reports disclose conditions or information unsatisfactory to the Buyer, which the Seller is unwilling or unable to correct, Buyer may cancel this agreement. Seller shall make the premises available for all Inspections. BUYER'S FAILURE TO NOTIFY SELLER IN WRITING SHALL CONCLUSIVELY BE CONSIDERED APPROVAL.
Buyer's Initials   Seller's Initials

_____/_____   _____/_____   **B. CONDITION OF PROPERTY:** Seller warrants, through the date possession is made available to Buyer: (1) property and improvements, including landscaping, grounds and pool/spa, if any, shall be maintained in the same condition as upon the date of acceptance of the offer, and (2) the roof is free of all known leaks, and (3) built-in appliances, and water, sewer/septic, plumbing, heating, electrical, air conditioning, pool/spa systems, if any, are operative, and (4) Seller shall replace all broken and/or cracked glass; (5) _____.
Buyer's Initials   Seller's Initials

_____/_____   _____/_____   **C. SELLER REPRESENTATION:** Seller warrants that Seller has no knowledge of any notice of violations of City, County, State, Federal, Building, Zoning, Fire, Health Codes or ordinances, or other governmental regulation filed or issued against the property. This warranty shall be effective until the date of close of escrow.

Buyer and Seller acknowledge receipt of copy of this page, which constitutes Page 2 of _____ Pages.
Buyer's Initials (_____) (_____)   Seller's Initials (_____) (_____)

┌─ OFFICE USE ONLY ─┐
Reviewed by Broker or Designee _____
Date _____

EQUAL HOUSING OPPORTUNITY
M-MB-Feb.-91

BROKERS COPY
REAL ESTATE PURCHASE CONTRACT AND RECEIPT FOR DEPOSIT (DLF-14 PAGE 2 OF 4)

Figure 6.1. (*cont.*)

☐

Subject Property Address _____

_____/ _____/   **D. PEST CONTROL:** (1) Within _____ calendar days of acceptance of the offer, Seller shall furnish Buyer at the expense of ☐ Buyer, ☐ Seller, a current written report of an inspection by _____
a licensed Structural Pest Control Operator, of the main building, ☐ detached garage(s) or carport(s), if any, and ☐ the following other structures on the property:

_____

(2) If requested by either Buyer or Seller, the report shall separately identify each recommendation for corrective measures as follows:
    "Section 1": Infestation or infection which is evident.
    "Section 2": Conditions that are present which are deemed likely to lead to infestation or infection.
(3) If no infestation or infection by wood destroying pests or organisms is found, the report shall include a written Certification as provided in Business and Professions Code § 8519(a) that on the date of inspection "no evidence of active infestation or infection was found."
(4) All work recommended to correct conditions described in "Section 1" shall be at the expense of ☐ Buyer, ☐ Seller.
(5) All work recommended to correct conditions described in "Section 2," if requested by Buyer, shall be at the expense of ☐ Buyer, ☐ Seller.
(6) The repairs shall be performed with good workmanship and materials of comparable quality and shall include repairs of leaking showers, replacement of tiles and other materials removed for repairs. It is understood that exact restoration of appearance or cosmetic items following all such repairs is not included.
(7) Funds for work agreed to be performed after close of escrow, shall be held in escrow and disbursed upon receipt of a written Certification as provided in Business and Professions Code § 8519(b) that the inspected property "is now free of evidence of active infestation or infection."
(8) Work to be performed at Seller's expense may be performed by Seller or through others, provided that (a) all required permits and final inspections are obtained, and (b) upon completion of repairs a written Certification is issued by a licensed Structural Pest Control Operator showing that the inspected property "is now free of evidence of active infestation or infection."
(9) If inspection of inaccessible areas is recommended by the report, Buyer has the option to accept and approve the report, or within _____ calendar days from receipt of the report to request in writing further inspection be made. BUYER'S FAILURE TO NOTIFY SELLER IN WRITING OF SUCH REQUEST SHALL CONCLUSIVELY BE CONSIDERED APPROVAL OF THE REPORT. If further inspection recommends "Section 1" and/or "Section 2" corrective measures, such work shall be at the expense of the party designated in subparagraph (4) and/or (5), respectively. If no infestation or infection is found, the cost of inspection, entry and closing of the inaccessible areas shall be at the expense of the Buyer.
(10) Other _____

_____

_____/ _____/   **E. FLOOD HAZARD AREA DISCLOSURE:** Buyer is informed that subject property is situated in a "Special Flood Hazard Area" as set forth on a Federal Emergency Management Agency (FEMA) "Flood Insurance Rate Map" (FIRM), or "Flood Hazard Boundary Map" (FHBM). The law provides that, as a condition of obtaining financing on most structures located in a "Special Flood Hazard Area," lenders require flood insurance where the property or its attachments are security for a loan.
The extent of coverage and the cost may vary. For further information consult the lender or insurance carrier. No representation or recommendation is made by the Seller and the Broker(s) in this transaction as to the legal effect or economic consequences of the National Flood Insurance Program and related legislation.

_____/ _____/   **F. SPECIAL STUDIES ZONE DISCLOSURE:** Buyer is informed that subject property is situated in a Special Studies Zone as designated under §§ 2621-2625, inclusive, of the California Public Resources Code; and, as such, the construction or development on this property of any structure for human occupancy may be subject to the findings of a geologic report prepared by a geologist registered in the State of California, unless such a report is waived by the City or County under the terms of that act.
Buyer is allowed _____ calendar days from acceptance of the offer to make further inquiries at appropriate governmental agencies concerning the use of the subject property under the terms of the Special Studies Zone Act and local building, zoning, fire, health, and safety codes. When such inquiries disclose conditions or information unsatisfactory to the Buyer, which the Seller is unwilling or unable to correct, Buyer may cancel this agreement. BUYER'S FAILURE TO NOTIFY SELLER IN WRITING SHALL CONCLUSIVELY BE CONSIDERED APPROVAL.

_____/ _____/   **G. ENERGY CONSERVATION RETROFIT:** If local ordinance requires that the property be brought in compliance with minimum energy Conservation Standards as a condition of sale or transfer, ☐ Buyer, ☐ Seller shall comply with and pay for these requirements. Where permitted by law, Seller may, if obligated hereunder, satisfy the obligation by authorizing escrow to credit Buyer with sufficient funds to cover the cost of such retrofit.

_____/ _____/   **H. HOME PROTECTION PLAN:** Buyer and Seller have been informed that Home Protection Plans are available. Such plans may provide additional protection and benefit to a Seller or Buyer. The CALIFORNIA ASSOCIATION OF REALTORS® and the Broker(s) in this transaction do not endorse or approve any particular company or program:
a) ☐ A Buyer's coverage Home Protection Plan to be issued by _____
    Company, at a cost not to exceed $_____, to be paid by ☐ Buyer, ☐ Seller; or
b) ☐ Buyer and Seller elect not to purchase a Home Protection Plan.

_____/ _____/   **I. CONDOMINIUM/P.U.D.:** The subject of this transaction is a condominium/planned unit development (P.U.D.) designated as unit _____ and _____ parking space(s) and an undivided interest in community areas, and _____
_____. The current monthly assessment charge by the homeowner's association or other governing body(s) is
$_____. As soon as practicable, Seller shall provide Buyer with copies of covenants, conditions and restrictions, articles of incorporation, by-laws, current rules and regulations, most current financial statements, and any other documents as required by law. Seller shall disclose in writing any known pending special assessment, claims, or litigation to Buyer. Buyer shall be allowed _____ calendar days from receipt to review these documents. If such documents disclose conditions or information unsatisfactory to Buyer, Buyer may cancel this agreement. BUYER'S FAILURE TO NOTIFY SELLER IN WRITING SHALL CONCLUSIVELY BE CONSIDERED APPROVAL.

_____/ _____/   **J. LIQUIDATED DAMAGES: If Buyer fails to complete said purchase as herein provided by reason of any default of Buyer, Seller shall be released from obligation to sell the property to Buyer and may proceed against Buyer upon any claim or remedy which he/she may have in law or equity; provided, however, that by initialling this paragraph Buyer and Seller agree that Seller shall retain the deposit as liquidated damages. If the described property is a dwelling with no more than four units, one of which the Buyer intends to occupy as his/her residence, Seller shall retain as liquidated damages the deposit actually paid, or an amount therefrom, not more than 3% of the purchase price and promptly return any excess to Buyer. Buyer and Seller agree to execute a similar liquidated damages provision, such as CALIFORNIA ASSOCIATION OF REALTORS® Receipt for Increased Deposit (RID-11), for any increased deposits. (Funds deposited in trust accounts or in escrow are not released automatically in the event of a dispute. Release of funds requires written agreement of the parties, judicial decision or arbitration.)**

Buyer and Seller acknowledge receipt of copy of this page, which constitutes Page 3 of _____ Pages.
Buyer's Initials (_____) (_____)   Seller's Initials (_____) (_____)

┌─────── OFFICE USE ONLY ───────┐
Reviewed by Broker or Designee _____
Date _____
└───────────────────────────────┘

🏠 EQUAL HOUSING OPPORTUNITY

M-MB-Feb-91

Figure 6.1. (*cont.*)

K. ARBITRATION OF DISPUTES: Any dispute or claim in law or equity arising out of this contract or any resulting transaction shall be decided by neutral binding arbitration in accordance with the rules of the American Arbitration Association, and not by court action except as provided by California law for judicial review of arbitration proceedings. Judgment upon the award rendered by the arbitrator(s) may be entered in any court having jurisdiction thereof. The parties shall have the right to discovery in accordance with Code of Civil Procedure § 1283.05. The following matters are excluded from arbitration hereunder: (a) a judicial or non-judicial foreclosure or other action or proceeding to enforce a deed of trust, mortgage, or real property sales contract as defined in Civil Code § 2985, (b) an unlawful detainer action, (c) the filing or enforcement of a mechanic's lien, (d) any matter which is within the jurisdiction of a probate court, or (e) an action for bodily injury or wrongful death, or for latent or patent defects to which Code of Civil Procedure § 337.1 or § 337.15 applies. The filing of a judicial action to enable the recording of a notice of pending action, for order of attachment, receivership, injunction, or other provisional remedies, shall not constitute a waiver of the right to arbitrate under this provision.

Any dispute or claim by or against broker(s) and/or associate licensee(s) participating in this transaction shall be submitted to arbitration consistent with the provision above only if the broker(s) and/or associate licensee(s) making the claim or against whom the claim is made shall have agreed to submit it to arbitration consistent with this provision.

"NOTICE: BY INITIALLING IN THE SPACE BELOW YOU ARE AGREEING TO HAVE ANY DISPUTE ARISING OUT OF THE MATTERS INCLUDED IN THE 'ARBITRATION OF DISPUTES' PROVISION DECIDED BY NEUTRAL ARBITRATION AS PROVIDED BY CALIFORNIA LAW AND YOU ARE GIVING UP ANY RIGHTS YOU MIGHT POSSESS TO HAVE THE DISPUTE LITIGATED IN A COURT OR JURY TRIAL. BY INITIALLING IN THE SPACE BELOW YOU ARE GIVING UP YOUR JUDICIAL RIGHTS TO DISCOVERY AND APPEAL, UNLESS THOSE RIGHTS ARE SPECIFICALLY INCLUDED IN THE 'ARBITRATION OF DISPUTES' PROVISION. IF YOU REFUSE TO SUBMIT TO ARBITRATION AFTER AGREEING TO THIS PROVISION, YOU MAY BE COMPELLED TO ARBITRATE UNDER THE AUTHORITY OF THE CALIFORNIA CODE OF CIVIL PROCEDURE. YOUR AGREEMENT TO THIS ARBITRATION PROVISION IS VOLUNTARY."

"WE HAVE READ AND UNDERSTAND THE FOREGOING AND AGREE TO SUBMIT DISPUTES ARISING OUT OF THE MATTERS INCLUDED IN THE 'ARBITRATION OF DISPUTES' PROVISION TO NEUTRAL ARBITRATION."

Buyer's Initials   Seller's Initials

_____ / _____   _____ / _____

17. **OTHER TERMS AND CONDITIONS:** _____

_____

_____

_____

18. **ATTORNEY'S FEES:** In any action, proceeding or arbitration arising out of this agreement, the prevailing party shall be entitled to reasonable attorney's fees and costs.

19. **ENTIRE CONTRACT:** Time is of the essence. All prior agreements between the parties are incorporated in this agreement which constitutes the entire contract. Its terms are intended by the parties as a final expression of their agreement with respect to such terms as are included herein and may not be contradicted by evidence of any prior agreement or contemporaneous oral agreement. The parties further intend that this agreement constitutes the complete and exclusive statement of its terms and that no extrinsic evidence whatsoever may be introduced in any judicial or arbitration proceeding, if any, involving this agreement.

20. **CAPTIONS:** The captions in this agreement are for convenience of reference only and are not intended as part of this agreement.

21. **AGENCY CONFIRMATION:** The following agency relationship(s) are hereby confirmed for this transaction:

LISTING AGENT: _____ is the agent of (check one):
(Print Firm Name)

☐ the Seller exclusively; or   ☐ both the Buyer and Seller

SELLING AGENT: _____ (if not the same as Listing Agent) is the agent of (check one):
(Print Firm Name)

☐ the Buyer exclusively; or   ☐ the Seller exclusively; or   ☐ both the Buyer and Seller.

22. **AMENDMENTS: This agreement may not be amended, modified, altered or changed in any respect whatsoever except by a further agreement in writing executed by Buyer and Seller.**

23. **OFFER:** This constitutes an offer to purchase the described property. Unless acceptance is signed by Seller and a signed copy delivered in person, by mail, or facsimile, and received by Buyer at the address below, or by _____ calendar days of the date hereof, this offer shall be deemed revoked and the deposit shall be returned. Buyer has read and acknowledges receipt of a copy of this offer. This agreement and any supplement, addendum or modification relating hereto, including any photocopy or facsimile thereof, may be executed in two or more counterparts, all of which shall constitute one and the same writing.

REAL ESTATE BROKER _____   BUYER _____

By _____   BUYER _____

Address _____   Address _____

                                                   _____

Telephone _____   Telephone _____

ACCEPTANCE

The undersigned Seller accepts and agrees to sell the property on the above terms and conditions and agrees to the above confirmation of agency relationships (☐ subject to attached counter offer).

Seller agrees to pay to Broker(s) _____

compensation for services as follows: _____

Payable: (a) On recordation of the deed or other evidence of title, or (b) if completion of sale is prevented by default of Seller, upon Seller's default, or (c) if completion of sale is prevented by default of Buyer, only if and when Seller collects damages from Buyer, by suit or otherwise, and then in an amount not less than one-half of the damages recovered, but not to exceed the above fee, after first deducting title and escrow expenses and the expenses of collection, if any. Seller shall execute and deliver an escrow instruction irrevocably assigning the compensation for service in an amount equal to the compensation agreed to above. In any action, proceeding, or arbitration between Broker(s) and Seller arising out of this agreement, the prevailing party shall be entitled to reasonable attorney's fees and costs. The undersigned has read and acknowledges receipt of a copy of this agreement and authorizes Broker(s) to deliver a signed copy to Buyer.

Date _____ Telephone _____   SELLER _____

Address _____   SELLER _____

Real Estate Broker(s) agree to the foregoing.

Broker _____   By _____   Date _____

Broker _____   By _____   Date _____

┌─ OFFICE USE ONLY ─
Reviewed by Broker or Designee _____
Date _____

Page 4 of ____ Pages.

M-MB-Feb.-91

Figure 6.1. (cont.)

Jones has owned Blackacre for several years and wishes to exchange his property for Whiteacre in order to defer any capital gains tax. Brown, who owns Whiteacre, desires to receive cash for his property and expresses no interest in owning Blackacre. Smith has money and would like to purchase Blackacre and has stated that he is not interested in purchasing Whiteacre.

While depicted for purposes of illustration as Steps 1 and 2, the delivery and exchange of all deeds of conveyance and monies actually occur normally within the same business day and are considered to be accomplished "simultaneously", therefore the term Simultaneous Exchange.

STEP 1

STEP 2

Figure 6.2. Simultaneous exchange.

187

A secured promissory note in the original amount of $30,000 bearing interest at 12% per annum, payable $300, or more per month, all sums of principal and unpaid interest are due and payable in 5 years.

Assume that the owner of the foregoing Note has held it and collected the payments for a period of 6 months and is in need of cash. The Note owner has offered the Note for sale at a 15% discount from the remaining balance.

Should you elect to purchase the Note what is your average annual return?

ANALYSIS OF THE SECURED NOTE:

T = Remaining Term, expressed in years (54 months or 4.6 years)
I = Total interest to be earned over the remaining life of the Note
  $30,000 × 12% = $3,600 per year = $300 per month
  $300 × 54 months = $16,200
D = Discount Allowed ($30,000 × 15% = $4,500)
C = Cost of Note ($30,000 − $4,500 = $24,500)
Y = Average Annual Return on Investment, expressed in dollars
A = Average Annual Rate of Interest Earned on Investment

FORMULA: $\dfrac{I + D}{T} = Y \qquad \dfrac{Y}{C} = A$

EXAMPLE: $\dfrac{\$16,200 + \$4,500}{4.6} = \$4,500 \qquad \dfrac{\$4,500}{\$24,500} = 18.3673\%$

CAUTION: WHEN PURCHASING OR ACCEPTING AN ASSIGNMENT OF A SECURED NOTE (1) BE SURE TO GET THE ORIGINAL DOCUMENTS, (2) ALWAYS PURCHASE AN ENDORSEMENT TO AN EXISTING POLICY OF TITLE INSURANCE OR PURCHASE A POLICY OF TITLE INSURANCE.

Figure 6.3. Investing in secured promissory notes.

Jones has owned Blackacre for several years and wishes to exchange his property for another parcel of real property in order to defer any capital gains tax. Jones has not yet selected the parcel of property he wishes to acquire.

While depicted for purposes of illustration as Steps 1, 2 and 3, Step 1 occurs first. Then, at any time within 6 months of the completion of Step 1, Steps 2 and 3 will be completed "simultaneously". In the event Steps 2 and 3 are not completed within said 6 month period the transaction will not qualify as a deferred exchange for tax purposes and the capital gain will be realized and taxable.

STEP 1

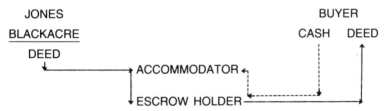

STEP 2 (Within 45 days of the completion of Step 1, Jones identifies the property he wishes to acquire [Brownacre] and notifies the Accommodator of his decision, in writing)

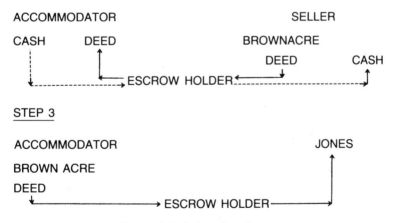

Figure 6.4. Delayed exchange.

189

7
Those Elusive Terms

Real estate, like any industry, has a language of its own. But real estate is also a profession that deals extensively with investors who may not be attuned to all the acronyms and terms that a broker or sales associate might spout. In an effort to clear up the confusion, we have devoted this chapter to many of those terms that are often heard but seldom understood. Some may be familiar, whereas others may be words or phrases you have never seen before. In either case, all are important to the industry, and especially to the investor who will find that an understanding of the "lingo" is a definite aid when dealing with the industry.

Q: What is Abstract of Judgment?

This refers to a court judgment in a civil action. It contains a summary of the essential provisions of the judgment, which, when recorded in the county recorder's office, creates a lien on the property of the defendant only in that county.

Q: What is Abstract of Title?

This refers to a summary of the recorded documents relating to the title of property from which an attorney may give an opinion as to the condition of title (see Title). Although it is still in use, it is rapidly giving way to title insurance (see Title Insurance).

Q: What is Accelerated Depreciation?

A general accounting term, including any method of depreciation greater than straight line depreciation (see Straight Line Depreciation) of a property.

Q: What is Access Right?

A right to enter (ingress) or leave (egress) anyone's property. May be express or implied. An express easement is one that was reserved or was granted in writing. An implied easement is one that is created by application of the law.

For example, there are two houses on a lot, each with separate owners. The owner of the front property has allowed the owner of the back property to use the front property's walkway for access to the back property. The right to enter is implied and by law it cannot be taken from the owner of the rear home even though this owner does not own the walkway.

Q: What is Accrued Depreciation?

The amount reserved each year in the accounting system for the eventual replacement of a building or other asset.

Q: What is an Acre?

A measure of land equal to 160 square rods (43,560 square feet) in any shape. Usually land is subdivided into smaller lots for housing and/or commercial development.

Q: What is an Adjustable Mortgage Loan (AML)?

Mortgage loans under which the interest rate is periodically adjusted to more closely coincide with current interest rates. The amounts and times of adjustment are agreed to at the inception of the loan. Some loans are adjusted according to the Consumer Price Index (CPI) while others are adjusted according to any other index agreed to by the borrower and lender. These loans are also called "Adjustable Rate Loans," "Adjustable Rate Mortgages" (ARMs), "Flexible Rate Loans," and "Variable Rate Loans." They emerged during the early 1980s, when due on sale clauses were held to be unenforceable and when interest rates soared to as much as 18 to 20%. (Due on sale clauses are now enforceable.) In an effort to keep housing relatively affordable and to afford some protection to lenders, adjustable rate mortgages were introduced.

Q: What is Ad Valorem?

"According to value." A method of taxation using the value of the thing taxed to determine the amount of tax. Taxes can be either "Ad Valorem" or "Specific." For example, a tax of $10 per $1,000 of value per house is Ad Valorem. A tax of $10 per house, regardless of value, is Specific.

Q: What is Adverse Possession?

A method of acquiring title to property belonging to another. The person claiming ownership must actually possess the property under some claim or right. This person's use of the property must be exclusive, continuous, and against the interest of the true owner. Many states require possession for five years and the payment of real property taxes.

Q: What is Agency?

Any relationship in which one party (agent) acts for or represents another (principal) under the authority of the latter. An Agency involving real estate is generally required to be in writing, such as one involving listings, sales, or trusts.

Q: What is an Agency Listing Agreement?

In some states, the term describes a listing under which the broker's commission is protected against a sale of the property made by other agents. In other words, an agent approaches the owner of a property, and the owner agrees to list the property (for sale) with the agent. Agents from other companies may sell the property. However, only the first agent is entitled to the commission. In this type of listing, should the owner sell the property to a buyer who had no relationship with the agent, no commission or fee is paid to the agent.

Q: What is an Agreement?

A general term usually describing a common view of two or more people regarding the rights and obligations of each with regard to a given subject. This is not necessarily a contract, although all contracts are agreements. A contract is a document that embraces an enforceable agreement. Contracts are enforceable; agreements may be enforceable.

Q: What is an Agreement of Sale?

This has two separate meanings, depending on the area of the country. In some states it means the same as a "purchase agreement" (see Purchase Agreement). In other states it is synonymous with the term "land contract" (see Land Contract).

Q: What are Air Rights?

The right to the use of the air space above a property, without the right to use the surface of the property.

Q: What is Alienation of Title?

A harsh-sounding term that simply means the transfer of property from one owner to another.

Q: What is an Alienation Clause?

This is similar to a "due-on-sale clause" (see Due-on-Sale Clause). It is a type of acceleration clause, calling for a debt under a mortgage or deed of trust, to be due in its entirety on transfer of ownership of the property.

Q: What is an All-Inclusive Deed of Trust?

See Wrap-Around Mortgage.

Q: What is Amortization?

Payment of debt in equal installments of both principal and interest, rather than interest only payments. In other words, fully amortized loans are loans in which the principal is paid off at the same time as the interest. There is no balloon payment at the end of the mortgage period. In most states, the last payment may not be more than 50% greater than any other payment.

Q: What is Annual Percentage Rate (APR)?

The yearly interest percentage of a loan as expressed by the actual rate of interest paid. For example, 6% add-on interest would be much more than 6% simple interest although each is 6%. The APR is disclosed as part of the federal truth in lending laws, and is a good way for investors to determine how much interest they are actually going to pay over the life of the loan, as well as to compare various loans.

Q: What is an APPEL (Accelerating Payoff Progressive Equity Loan)?

This is a residential property loan that calls for a payment increase over the first six years. Level payments are made for the remaining years and the loan is paid off during the 15th year. There is no prepayment penalty.

Q: What is an Appraisal?

An opinion of value based on a factual analysis. Legally, an estimation of value by two disinterested persons with suitable qualifications.

Q: What is Appreciation?

An increased value of a property due to either a positive improvement of the area or the elimination of negative factors. Sometimes, this term is incorrectly used to describe an increase of value through inflation.

Q: What is Appurtenance?

Something that belongs to something else (for example, a barn to a house or an easement to land). It can be either directly attached or not. The appurtenance is part of the property and passes with it on sale or transfer, regardless of whether it is described in the deed of conveyance.

Q: What is an Arbitrary Map?

A map drawn by a title company to be used in locating property in areas in which legal descriptions are difficult and complex.

Q: What is an Arbitration Clause?

A clause in a lease or other contract calling for the decision of a third party (arbiter) regarding disputes. A growing alternative to the judicial system.

Q: What is an Arch Rib Roof?

A roof design used primarily in industrial buildings, and having the shape of an arch or crescent.

Q: What is Arrears?

Payment made after it is due is in arrears. Interest is paid in arrears since it is paid to the date of payment rather than in advance, as is rent. For example, a rent payment made July 1 pays the rent to August 1. An interest payment made July 1 pays the interest from June 1 to July 1.

Q: What is "As Is" Condition?

The premises are accepted by the buyer or tenant in the condition existing at the time of the sale or lease. This includes all physical defects. State laws vary greatly concerning as is clauses in contracts for residential dwellings.

Q: What is Assess?

To fix a value or appraise. Most commonly used in connection with real property taxes and the value fixed on the property for determining those taxes.

Q: What is Assignment?

To transfer property, or an interest in property to another.

Q: What is an Assignee?

One who receives an assignment.

Q: What is an Assumption Fee?

A lender's charge for paperwork involved in processing records for a new buyer assuming an existing loan.

Q: What is Back Title Letter?

In states in which attorneys examine title for title insurance purposes, this letter is given by a title insurance company to an attorney. It gives the attorney the condition of the title of a piece of property as of a certain date. The attorney can then begin his examination of the title as of that date.

Q: What is a Backup Offer?

A secondary offer to purchase property from another party. It is used in the event the first offer fails. A backup offer is especially useful when the initial offer contains difficult contingencies. For example, a buyer may make an offer on a piece of property, but it may be contingent on the sale of the buyer's present home.

Q: What is a Balloon Note?

A note calling for periodic payments that are not sufficient to fully amortize the face amount of the note prior to maturity. Thus, at maturity, a principal sum known as a "balloon" is due. In some states the holder of the note must give the borrower several months' notice of the pending balloon payment.

Q: What is Base Line?

A survey line used in the government survey to establish township lines. The base line runs east and west through a principal meridian (a line running north and south). The base line can also mean a horizontal elevation line used as the centerline in a survey for a highway route.

Q: What is Base Molding?

Molding installed along the top of the baseboard.

Q: What is Base Rent?

A specific amount used as a minimum rent in a lease, which uses a percentage or overage to compile additional rent. Investors should carefully examine any lease documents to see if this term is used. If it is, they should then check the agreement to see if there is a clause that outlines how additional monthly rent is calculated. The base rent can be quite low, but the total rent may be relatively high.

Q: What is Basis for Depreciation?

The value of property for purposes of depreciation. For example, with a purchased asset, the basis is cost, whether paid for or not. With real property, only the improvements can be depreciated—not the land.

Q: *What is Basis Point?*

A finance term measuring a yield of 1/100th of 1% annually. Frequently, lenders use the term with investors to indicate the fee involved for a loan. They may say "50 basis points," which is actually ½ of 1%. If they said 100 basis points and the loan were for $100,000, the fee involved would be $1,000.

Q: *What is a Bearing Wall?*

A wall that supports the weight of a part of a structure in addition to its own weight.

Q: *What is Bedrock?*

Solid rock beneath the soil, as distinguished from rocks or boulders mixed with soil.

Q: *What is Bench Mark?*

Surveying mark made in some object that is permanently fixed in the ground, showing the height of that point in relation to sea level. Used in topographic surveys.

Q: *What is Beneficial Interest?*

The equitable, rather than legal ownership of property, such as under a land contract. Under a land contract, the seller retains legal title subject to the buyer's equitable interest in the property. A land contract is an agreement that is similar in nature to an "installment sale." The buyer normally gives the seller a lower down payment than usual, prompting the seller to retain legal title until the buyer has a substantial interest (equity) in the property. The terms of the land contract will specify when the seller is required to convey the legal title to the buyer.

Q: What is a Beneficiary?

One for whose benefit a trust is created. In states in which deeds of trust are commonly used instead of mortgages, the lender (mortgagee) is called the beneficiary.

Q: What is a Beneficiary's Demand?

Written instructions by a beneficiary under a deed of trust stating and demanding the amount necessary for issuance of re-conveyance. There are three parties to a deed of trust. The trustor (borrower), the lender (beneficiary), and the trustee. When a deed of trust is used to secure an obligation, the borrower executes the deed of trust, which conveys title to the trustee named in the deed of trust. The trustee has two functions. In the event of the trustor's default (failure to make payment, for example), the beneficiary may instruct the trustee to commence foreclosure pro-ceedings. The other function performed by the trustee is the reconveyance. When the beneficiary has been paid in full, a re-quest to issue reconveyance is sent to the trustee and the trustee "reconveys" the title to the property to the trustor/owner of the property.

Q: What is Bequest?

Personal property left by will.

Q: What is a Berm?

A mound used to control drainage by diverting all or part of the flow.

Q: What is a Bill of Sale?

An instrument by which one transfers personal property.

Q: What is a Binder?

(1) A report issued by the title insurance company setting forth the condition of title to a certain property, as of a certain date. It also sets forth conditions that, if satisfied, will cause a policy of insurance to be issued at a later date to the purchaser. Also called a commitment. (2) A policy of title insurance used primarily by investors calling for a reduced rate for a future policy if the property is sold within a specified time period. Normally a "binder" is a commitment and is purchased at the time the investor purchases the property. The binder affords a considerable savings to the investor.

Q: What is a Blanket Mortgage?

(1) A mortgage covering more than one property of the mortgagor, such as a mortgage covering all the lots of a builder in a subdivision. (2) A mortgage covering all real property of the mortgagor, both presently owned by the buyer and all property to be acquired at some future date, if any.

Q: What is a Block?

(1) In a city, a square or rectangular area surrounded by streets. (2) In some states, a part of a subdivision's legal description, such as, Lot 1, Block 1, Tract 1.

Q: What is a Blueprint?

A plan of a building in such detail as to enable workmen to construct the building from the print. The name comes from the photographic process that produces the plan in blue.

Q: What is a Boardfoot?

Unit of measurement for lumber. One boardfoot equals 144 cubic inches or 12″ × 12″ × 1″.

Q: What is a Bona Fide Purchaser?

One who purchases in good faith for a fair value without knowledge of any adverse claims of others.

Q: What is Book Depreciation?

Depreciation reserved (on the books) by an owner for future replacement or retirement of an asset. (See Accrued Depreciation.)

Q: What is a Boundary?

In real estate, a separation, natural (river) or artificial (fence), that marks the division of two contiguous properties.

Q: What is Braced Framing?

Framing reinforced with posts and braces, forming a rigid frame.

Q: What is a Breach of Contract?

Failure to perform a contract, in whole or part, without legal excuse.

Q: What is a Breach of Covenant?

The failure to do or refrain from doing that which was promised.

Q: What is a Breach of Warranty?

In real estate, the failure of the seller to pass title as either expressed or implied (by law) in the conveyance document. For example, a seller who delivers and records a deed to party A and then delivers the same deed on the same property to party B is said to have breached the warranty of title to party B.

Q: What is Bridge Financing?

A form of interim loan, generally made between a short-term loan and a permanent (long-term) loan, when the borrower needs to have more time before taking the long-term financing.

Q: What is Brokerage?

The act of bringing together principals (buyer–seller; land-lord–tenant, etc.) for a fee or commission. In real estate transactions, a state issued license is required before someone can act as an agent of a buyer, seller, etc.

Q: What is Brokerage Commission?

See Commission.

Q: What is a Broker (Real Estate)?

One who is licensed by the state to carry on the business of representing others in dealings in real estate. A broker may receive a fee or commission for bringing together parties in real estate transactions.

Q: What is a Building Code?

A comprehensive set of laws that regulates the construction of buildings, including design, materials used, construction use, repair, remodeling, and other similar factors.

Q: What is a Building Permit?

A permit given by a local government to construct a building or make improvements to real property.

Q: What is Build to Suit?

A method of improving property whereby the owner/lessor builds improvements to suit the buyer/tenant, according to the buyer/tenant's specifications. The cost of construction is figured into the rental amount of the lease, which is usually for a term sufficient to amortize the expense of the improvements, or is added to the purchase price of the land.

Q: What is Buydown?

A payment of a fee to the lender from an interested party, causing the lender to reduce the interest rate of a loan, resulting in a reduced monthly payment. The buydown is usually for the first one to five years of the loan. A developer of a tract of homes will use this technique as a marketing device to stimulate sluggish sales.

Q: What is a Cancellation Clause?

A clause in a contract setting forth the conditions under which one party or the other may cancel or terminate the agreement. These clauses should always be reviewed by a lawyer.

Q: What are Capital Assets?

Assets of a permanent nature used to produce income. In real estate this could be a building, land, etc.

Q: What are Capital Gains?

Gains realized from the sale of capital assets. Generally the difference between the initial cost and selling price, less certain deductible expenses, such as depreciation. Used mainly for income tax purposes.

Q: What is Capitalization?

The determining of the present value of income property by taking the annual net income (either known or estimated) and discounting by using a rate of return commonly acceptable to buyers of similar properties. For example, if the income of a property is $10,000 per year, capitalizing it at a rate of 10% would mean the property would be worth $100,000 (10 × $10,000).

Q: What is the Capitalization Rate?

The percentage (acceptable to buyer) used to determine the value of income property through capitalization. Also referred to as the cap rate. Examine the example above.

Q: What are Carrying Charges or Costs?

These are costs involved in keeping a property that is intended to produce income (either by sale or rent) but has not yet done so.

Q: What is Cash Flow?

In investment properties, the actual cash the investor will receive after deduction of operating expenses and debt service (loan payment) from gross income.

Q: What is Caveat Emptor?

"Let the buyer beware." A legal term stating that the buyer takes the risk regarding the quality or condition of the item purchased, unless it is protected by warranty or there is a misrepresentation. Consumer laws have almost eliminated the effect of this legal maxim because of the responsibility put on sellers and brokers for disclosure of material facts regarding residential dwellings. This term is still applicable in commercial transactions.

Q: What are CC&Rs (Covenants, Conditions, and Restrictions)?

A term used in some areas to describe the restrictive limitations that may be placed on property by the recordation of a document. In other areas, these are simply called restrictions. CC&Rs are prominent when it comes to condominiums and townhouse developments, because they detail the requirements and limitations to which owners and occupants must adhere.

Q: What is a Certificate Backed Mortgage?

A variation of the buydown. The seller purchases a savings certificate (usually with the proceeds of the sale) from the lender. The lender sets the buyer's interest rate below market (generally 2% above the certificate rate). Should the seller withdraw the certificate funds, the buyer's rate rises to market rate.

Q: What is the Chain of Title?

The chronological order of documents affecting a parcel of land, from the original owner (usually the government) to the present owner.

Q: What is a Chattel Mortgage?

A lien on personal property. Also called a security interest or financing statement.

Q: What is Closing?

In real estate sales, the final procedure in which documents are recorded, and the sale (or loan) is completed.

Q: What is a Cloud on Title?

An invalid encumbrance on property. For example, A sells parcel 1 to B. The deed is mistakenly drawn to read parcel 2. A cloud is created on parcel 2 by the recording of the erroneous deed. The cloud must be removed or corrected prior to the issuance of title insurance.

Q: What is a Commission?

An amount, usually as a percentage, paid to an agent (real estate broker) as compensation for professional brokerage services. The amount is generally expressed as a percent of the sale price or rental income.

Q: What is Compaction?

The pressing together and joining of soil to make it more solid. A report showing the density of the soil and its makeup is required in some areas before permits for construction will be issued. This is especially true in areas where the soil has a high clay content.

Q: What is Compound Interest?

Interest paid on accumulated interest as well as the principal. In some states, the compounding of interest is a violation of usury laws.

Q: What is Condition?

In real estate law, some limiting restriction to a grant or conveyance of property, stating that on the occurrence or nonoccurrence of a certain event, the estate shall be changed in some manner.

Q: What is Condition Precedent?

A condition to be performed before an agreement becomes effective.

Q: What is Conditions Subsequent?

A condition following an agreement, the happening of which changes the estate.

Q: What is a Condominium?

A structure of two or more units, the interior space of which is individually owned, with the balance of the property (both land and building) owned "in common" by the owners of the individual units of the tract.

Q: What is Constructive Notice?

Notice given by a published announcement in a newspaper, a recording, or some other method which satisfies the legal requirements for notifying the parties involved, but may not actually notify them. In most states, constructive notice is the equivalent of actual notice.

Q: What is a Contract?

An agreement between two or more persons or entities that creates or modifies a legal relationship. Generally based on offer and acceptance.

Q: What is a Contract of Sale?

In some areas of the country, synonymous with land contract. In other areas, synonymous with purchase agreement.

Q: What is a Cost of Living Index?

A government-generated indicator of the increase or decrease of living costs for the average person on a monthly basis. There are several indexes maintained by the government. (See also Escalation Clause.)

Q: What is a Counter Offer?

An offer (instead of acceptance) in response to an offer. For example, A offers to buy B's house for X dollars. B, in response, offers to sell to A at a higher price. B's offer to A is a counter offer. A counter offer rejects an offer. Once an offer is rejected, it cannot be accepted later.

Q: What is a Covenant?

Generally, almost any written agreement.

Q: What is a CPM (Certified Property Manager)?

A designation conferred by the Institute of Real Property Management on one who has completed certain required courses and has been active in property management. For the investor searching for a property manager, the CPM indicates the manager has had experience and education in the field.

Q: What are Cuts?

In construction, the excavation of land into a terrace or terraces, to control flooding, locate a highway, building, or affect the grade for some other purposes.

Q: What is a Declaration of Homestead?

See Homestead.

Q: What is a Declaration of Restrictions?

Restrictions recorded by a subdivider to cover an entire tract or subdivision. See CC&Rs.

Q: What is a Deed?

Actually, any one of many conveyances or financing instruments. An instrument that conveys or transfers title to real property.

Q: What is a Deed of Reconveyance?

See Reconveyance.

Q: What is a Deed of Trust?

An instrument used in many states in place of a mortgage. Property is transferred to a trustee by the borrower (trustor) in favor of the lender (beneficiary), and reconveyed on payment in full of the loan. The Deed of Trust is the security for the promissory note.

Q: What are Deed Restrictions?

Limitations on the use of property, usually contained in a deed of conveyance, which bind all future owners. Similar to CC&Rs.

211

Q: What is Deferred Maintenance?

When improvements made to real property have not been maintained at regular intervals.

Q: What is Delivery?

In conveyancing, this refers to the necessity of placing the deed to the property in the actual or constructive possession of the grantee (purchaser). Usually accomplished by delivery of a deed to the buyer or agent of the buyer, or by recording said deed at the grantee's request. A deed that has been signed by the seller conveying title to the buyer is placed in the seller's desk. It has not been delivered and therefore the title has not been transferred to the purchaser.

Q: What is the Department of Real Estate?

The department of the state government that is responsible for the licensing and regulation of people engaged in the real estate business. The Real Estate Commissioner usually heads it.

Q: What is Depreciable Life?

A tax term meaning the number of years used to determine depreciation of an asset.

Q: What is a Disclaimer?

Statement in a publication attempting to limit liability in the event information contained therein is inaccurate.

Q: What is Documentary Transfer Tax?

A state tax on the conveyance of real property, based on the sale price or equity transferred. In most states, it is 55 cents for each $500 of the taxable amount of the transaction. In addition to the transfer tax, some cities impose an additional tax based on a percentage of the sale price.

Q: What is a Dominant Tenant?

A parcel of land that benefits from an easement. For example, an easement exists over parcel A for access to parcel B. Parcel B is the dominant tenant, parcel A is the servient tenant.

Q: What is Double Escrow?

Two concurrent escrows on the same property, having the same party as buyer and seller of the property. For example, Escrow 1: A buys from B. Escrow 2: A sells the same property to C. A is using C's money to buy B's property. The process is illegal in many states unless full disclosure is made.

Q: What is Dry-Wall Construction?

Type of construction using the manufactured interior wall consisting of plaster between heavy sheets of paper, in contrast to lath and plaster.

Q: What is Dual Agency?

The representation of opposing principals (buyer and seller) by the same broker. Full disclosure of a dual agency relationship must be made to both buyer and seller in most states.

Q: What is a Due-on-Sale Clause?

A clause within a contract, loan, or agreement that says the seller must pay a loan in full when the property owned is sold. Many lenders' loan agreements provide that the due-on-sale clause can be enforced when the owner leases the property for more than 6 months or upon granting an option to purchase the property.

Q: What is an Easement?

A right created by grant, reservation, agreement, prescription, or necessary implication, affecting the land of another. For example, it may give one party the right to cross another's land.

Q: What is Encumbrance (Incumbrance)?

A claim, lien, charge, or liability attached to real property.

Q: What is Equity?

The market value of a property, less the amount of existing liens.

Q: What is an Escalation Clause?

A clause in a lease providing for an increased rental at a future time. It is usually tied to some indicator, such as "cost of living index" maintained and published by the government.

Q: What is an Exclusive Listing?

A written contract between a property owner and a real estate broker, whereby the owner promises to pay a fee or commission to the broker if certain real property of the owner is sold during a stated period. The broker receives the fee or commission regardless of whether the broker or the owner arranges the sale. At the same time, the broker promises to put forth his best efforts to sell the property, and may make specific advertising and promotion promises.

Q: What is Fannie Mae?

See FNMA.

Q: What is Federal Fair Housing Law?

Title VIII of the Civil Rights Act, which forbids discrimination in the sale or rental of residential property because of race, color, sex, religion, or national origin.

Q: What is Federal Home Loan Mortgage Corporation?

A semigovernmental purchaser of mortgages.

Q: What is a Federal Tax Lien?

A lien attaching to property for nonpayment of a federal tax (estate, income, etc.).

Q: What is Fee Simple?

An estate under which the owner is entitled to unrestricted powers to dispose of the property. Synonymous with the term "ownership." Sometimes abbreviated as the "fee."

Q: What is Federal Housing Administration (FHA)?

The agency that insures the holders of first mortgages, enabling lenders to loan a higher percentage of the sale price than in normal transactions.

Q: What is the FHLMC (Freddie Mac)?

Federal Home Loan Mortgage Corporation. A federal agency purchasing first mortgages, both conventional and federally insured, from members of the Federal Reserve System and the Federal Home Loan Bank System.

Q: What is Fiduciary?

One acting in a relationship of trust regarding financial transactions.

Q: What is a Finder's Fee?

A fee paid to someone who finds a buyer or seller for a broker, buyer, etc. The term is sometimes used to describe a fee paid to an unlicensed person. If the finder performs any service for which a real estate license is required, the fee will not be payable, unless the finder has a valid real estate license.

Q: What is a First Mortgage?

A mortgage having priority over all other voluntary liens against certain property.

Q: What is FNMA (Fannie Mae)?

The Federal National Mortgage Association. A private corporation dealing with the purchase of first mortgages at discounts.

Q: What is FNMA Buydown?

FNMA accepts loans containing a buydown provision on single family residential, owner-occupied units. A prepayment (points) will bring a lower rate of interest during the first one to five years of the mortgage.

Q: What is Foreclosure?

A proceeding, in or out of court, to eliminate all rights, title, and interest of the owner(s) of property so as to sell the property to satisfy a lien against it.

Q: What is the Front Foot Cost?

A determination of the value of property based on a value per foot as measured along the frontage of a parcel. Usually used with commercial property.

Q: What is the General Contractor?

One who contracts for the construction of an entire building or project, rather than for a portion of the work. The general contractor hires subcontractors, such as plumbers and carpenters, coordinates their work, and is responsible for payment to them.

Q: What is a General Index (GI)?

A term referring to a section of the public records containing liens against individuals that may affect the transfer of real property.

Q: What is a General Partnership?

A partnership made up of two or more general partners without special (limited) partners.

217

Q: What is a G.I. Loan?

See Veteran's Administration (VA) Loan.

Q: What is GNMA (Ginnie Mae)?

Government National Mortgage Association. A federal association that works with FHA and offers special assistance in obtaining and purchasing mortgages.

Q: What are GNMA (Government National Mortgage Association) Options?

A method of purchasing GNMA securities.

Q: What is a Grace Period?

A period of time past the due date for a payment (mortgage, insurance, etc.) during which a payment can be made and still not be considered delinquent.

Q: What is a Grant?

To transfer an interest in real property.

Q: What is a Grantee?

One to whom a grant is made.

Q: What is a Grantor?

One who grants property, or property rights.

Q: What is Gross Income?

A term used in commercial investment. It refers to the total income (either actual or estimated) from a business or property.

Q: What is Gross Income Multiplier?

A figure that, when multiplied by the annual gross income, will theoretically determine the market value of the property. For example, a property generates $100,000 in gross income per year, and the Gross Income Multiplier (10) gives it a market value of $1 million, which may serve as a price guide for the investor.

Q: What is Growing Equity Mortgage (G.E.M.)?

A fixed rate, graduated payment loan, allowing low beginning payments and a shorter term because of higher payments as the loan progresses.

Q: What is Hard Money Mortgage?

A mortgage or deed of trust given in return for a loan of cash.

Q: What is Historical Cost?

The cost of an improvement when first constructed.

Q: What is a Homeowners' Association?

An association of people who own homes in the area formed for the purpose of maintaining or enhancing values of the properties in the area.

Q: What is a Homestead?

An exemption allowed homeowners on their primary residence against the action of creditors. No protection is afforded the homeowner against voluntary liens.

219

Q: What is Home Warranty Insurance?

Private insurance insuring buyers against specified defects in the home they have purchased. Policies and coverage vary.

Q: What is Hypothecate?

To mortgage or pledge without delivery of the security to the lender.

Q: What is Idem Sonans?

Sounding the same. Legally, names misspelled will not void a document provided the written name sounds the same as the correctly spelled legal name. Example: Anderson/Andersen.

Q: What is Implied Contract?

A binding contract created by the actions of the principals, rather than by written or oral contract.

Q: What is Impound Account?

Account held by the lender for payment of taxes, insurance, or other periodic debts against the property.

Q: What is Income Approach?

An appraisal method to determine the value of rental property by use of the estimated net income over the life of the structure.

Q: What is Incumbrance (Encumbrance)?

A claim, lien, charge, or liability against (and binding) the property.

Q: What is Indexing?

To alter mortgage term, payment, or rate according to inflation and/or suitable mortgage rate index. (See Rate Index.)

Q: What is In Perpetuity?

Of endless duration; forever.

Q: What is an Installment Contract?

A method of purchasing by installment, usually monthly payments. When used in conjunction with the sale of real property, it is referred to as a land sale contract.

Q: What is an Installment Sale?

A term used to describe a sale that may qualify for the application of special tax treatment. A sale in which the purchase price is paid in two or more installments.

Q: What is an Insured Mortgage?

A mortgage insured against loss to the mortgagee in the event of default.

Q: What is an Interest Extra Note?

A note stating an equal (usually monthly) payment on principal, plus interest. As the interest decreases the total payment decreases. The amount applied to principal remains the same.

Q: What is an Interest Included Note?

A note having equal payments (usually monthly). Interest is figured on the declining principal balance. As the principal decreases, interest also decreases.

Q: What is an Interest Only Mortgage?

Periodic payments are of interest only. The principal amount borrowed is generally repaid in one payment.

Q: What is an Interest Rate Cap?

The maximum interest rate increase of an adjustable rate mortgage. For example, a 12% loan with a 5% rate cap would have a maximum interest for the life of the loan that could not exceed 17%.

Q: What is an Interpleader?

A court action that may be filed to settle a dispute arising out of who gets certain funds (buyer or seller, for example) that are being held in escrow. When buyer and seller cannot agree, the escrow holder may file an interpleader action. A court action brought by the holder of funds (escrow holder) that names all possible claimants of the funds (buyer, seller, broker). The holder of the funds deposits them with the court and the court decides who gets what. In some states, a party to an escrow who wrongfully refuses to sign written authorization releasing escrowed funds may be liable for attorney's fees and trebled damages.

Q: What is an Involuntary Lien?

A lien, such as a tax lien or judgment, that attaches to the property without the consent of the owner.

Q: What is a Joint Protection Policy?

A policy of title insurance that insures both the owner and lender under the same policy.

Q: *What is Joint Tenancy?*

A form of ownership of property providing for right of survivorship between two or more joint tenants.

Q: *What are Joint Tenants?*

Those holding under joint tenancy.

Q: *What is Judicial Foreclosure?*

Foreclosure through court action, rather than a power of sale as contained in the deed of trust.

Q: *What is a Jumbo VA Loan?*

A loan for an amount greater than the allowable 100% financed amount. For example, the maximum allowable VA loan is $110,000. The purchase price is $130,000. The difference is $20,000. Seventy-five percent of the difference is $15,000. The total jumbo loan is $110,000 plus $15,000 = $125,000. The jumbo loan allows for 75% of the difference between the maximum VA loan and the purchase price.

Q: *What is a Junior Mortgage?*

Any mortgage of lesser priority than the first mortgage.

223

Q: What is a Land Contract?

An installment contract for the sale of land, in which the seller retains legal title and the buyer receives equitable title.

Q: What is a Landlocked Parcel?

A parcel of land surrounded entirely by privately owned land with no access to a public right of way.

Q: What is a Land Patent?

See Patent.

Q: What is a Late Charge?

A penalty for failure to pay a payment on time. It is usually not allowed as interest for income tax purposes.

Q: What is a Latent Defect?

A hidden or concealed defect. One that could not be discovered by inspection, and using reasonable care. Example: a defect within a wall; an unstable soils condition resulting in the intrusion of water or resulting in the uneven settlement of the improvements.

Q: What is Leasehold Improvements?

Improvements made by the lessee.

Q: What is a Leasehold Interest?

The interest that the lessee has in the value of the lease itself in condemnation proceedings.

Q: What is a Lease with Option to Purchase?

A lease under which the lessee has the right to purchase the property. The price and terms of the purchase must be set forth in the agreement for the option to be valid. Note: if the loan contains a due-on-sale clause the lender may elect to demand the loan be paid in full.

Q: What is a Legal Description?

A method of geographically identifying a parcel of land.

Q: What is Liber?

The latin word for book. Used in some states when referring to the book and page of a recorded document.

Q: What is a Lien?

An encumbrance against a property.

Q: What is Lis Pendens?

A recorded legal notice to show that legal action has commenced which relates to the property. Generally, a cloud on title that must be eliminated prior to obtaining title insurance.

Q: What is a Listing Agent?

The real estate agent having an agreement with the owner of real property to represent the seller in the marketing of the property.

Q: What is a Loan Origination Fee?

A one-time fee charged by the lender for setting up the loan package.

Q: What is a Loan Package?

The file containing all items necessary for the lender to decide to make or not to make a loan on a particular property to a particular borrower.

Q: What is a Maintenance Fee?

As applied to condominiums and planned developments, the amount charged each unit owner to maintain the common area and to provide a fund for future repairs. Example: reroofing, repaving, etc. Usually a monthly fee.

Q: What is Market Price?

The sale price of a property.

Q: What is Market Value?

The estimated price a willing buyer would pay and a willing seller would accept.

Q: What is Market Value Approach?

A method of appraising the value of a property by comparing similar properties in the area that were recently sold.

Q: What is a Master Plan?

A zoning plan for an entire governmental area such as a city. The plan theoretically allows for the development of the area in an orderly and sound manner.

Q: What is a Mechanic's Lien?

A lien created for the purpose of securing priority of payment for the value of work performed and materials furnished in construction/repair/improvement of land. A mechanic's lien is considered to be a voluntary lien.

Q: What is Metes and Bounds?

Description of land by boundary lines, with their terminal points and angles.

Q: What is Misrepresentation?

A statement or conduct by a person that represents to another a fact that is not true. A seller, broker, or builder may have duty to disclose certain facts about a property to a buyer, and failure to do so is a misrepresentation. Depending on the extent of the misrepresentation there could be a suit or other action for damages.

Q: What is Month-to-Month Tenancy?

A right to occupy a property for a period of one month. While the actual period of occupancy may extend from several months to years, the owner or tenant may terminate the tenancy or adjust the rent payable with a one month notice.

Q: What is a Mortgage?

(1) To hypothecate as security real property for the payment of a debt. The borrower (mortgagor) retains possession and use of the property. (2) The instrument by which real estate is hypothecated as security for the repayment of a loan.

Q: What is a Mortgage Banker?

A company providing mortgage financing with its own funds rather than simply bringing together lender and borrower, as does a mortgage broker. Although the mortgage banker uses its own funds, these funds are generally borrowed and the financing is either short term, or, if long term, the mortgages are sold to investors within a short time after creation.

Q: What is a Mortgage Broker?

One who, for a fee, brings together borrower and lender.

Q: What is a Mortgagee?

The party lending the money and receiving the mortgage.

Q: What is Mortgage Insurance?

Insurance written by an independent mortgage insurance company protecting the mortgage lender against loss incurred by a mortgage default.

Q: What is Mortgage Life Insurance?

A term life insurance policy for the amount of the declining balance of a loan secured by a mortgage or deed of trust.

Q: What is Mortgage Servicing?

Controlling the necessary duties of a mortgagee, such as collecting payments, releasing the lien on payment in full, foreclosing if in default, and other related services.

Q: What is a Mortgagor?

The party who borrows the money and gives the mortgage.

Q: What is a Multifamily Dwelling?

A building legally divided to be occupied by more than one family.

Q: What is the National Association of Realtors (NAR)?

An association of people engaged in the real estate business. Organized in 1908.

Q: What is a Multiple Listing?

An exclusive listing submitted to all members of an association, so that each may have an opportunity to sell the property.

Q: What is the National Association of Real Estate Boards (NAREB)?

A national trade association whose members include not only real estate brokers, but appraisers, property managers, and other affiliated groups.

Q: What is Negative Amortization?

A condition created when a loan payment is less than interest alone. Even though payments are made on time, the amount owed increases.

Q: What is Negative Cash Flow?

When the income from an investment property is less than the usual expenses.

Q: What is Net After Taxes?

The income produced from property after income tax and all other expenses are paid.

Q: What is Net Before Taxes?

The net income before payment of income tax, but after payment of property taxes and other expenses of ownership.

Q: What is a Net Income Multiplier?

The number that, when multiplied by the net income, gives the selling price of the property. It is found by dividing the sales price by the net income.

Q: What is a Net Lease?

A lease requiring the tenant to pay, in addition to a fixed rental, the expenses of the property leased, such as taxes, insurance, and maintenance. In some states, the terms "net, net, net," "triple net," and other such repetitions are used.

Q: What is a Net Listing?

A listing under which a real estate agent receives any amount over a given amount to the seller. This may be illegal in some states.

Q: What is a Nonexclusive Listing?

A listing under which the real estate broker has an exclusive listing as opposed to the other agents, but the owner may sell the property without paying commission to the broker.

Q: What is a Nonjudicial Foreclosure Sale?

Sale by a trustee under a deed of trust, or mortgagee under a power of sale of a mortgage. This is an alternative to a court proceeding sometimes referred to as a statutory foreclosure.

Q: What is a Notice of Default?

A notice filed to show that the borrower under a mortgage or deed of trust has defaulted in the performance of the borrower's obligations.

Q: What is a Notice of Nonresponsibility?

A notice filed by the owner of a property to show that the owner did not contract for the work being done on the property. If properly filed, mechanic's liens will not attach to the property.

Q: What is an Offer and Acceptance?

Necessary elements of a contract to sell real estate.

Q: What is Off-Site?

Not on the property to be sold. For example, the developer of a housing tract sells only the house and lot, but must build (off-site) the streets and sewers.

Q: What are Off-Site Improvements?

Development of land to make adjacent land suitable for development. It includes sidewalks, curbs, streets, sewers, etc.

Q: What is the "Once in a Lifetime" Tax Exclusion?

A forgiveness of a portion of the tax due on a residence by a senior citizen (over 55 years of age). As the term denotes, the exclusion can be taken only once.

Q: What is an Open End Mortgage?

A mortgage permitting the mortgagor to borrow additional money under the same mortgage.

Q: What is an Open Listing?

A written authorization to a real estate agent by a property owner, stating that a commission will be paid to the agent on acceptance by the seller of an offer that meets specified price and terms.

Q: What is an Option?

A right that acts as a continuing offer to the presenter of the offer to purchase or lease property at an agreed on price and terms within a specified time.

Q: What is an Origination Fee?

A fee made by a lender for making a real estate loan. Usually, a percentage of the loan.

Q: What is an "Or More" Clause?

A clause in a note, mortgage, or deed of trust allowing additional payments to be made without penalty. The words "or more" appear after the specified minimum payment.

Q: What is Partition Action?

A court proceeding resulting in a division of the interest of two or more owners of real or personal property, or the forced sale of such property in which the proceeds are divided between the owners in proportion to their interest.

Q: What is a Partnership?

As defined by the Uniform Partnership Act: "An association of two or more persons to carry on as co-owners, a business for profit."

Q: What is a Patent?

Instrument of conveyance of title to public (government) land.

Q: What is Personal Property?

Any property that is not designated by law as real property.

Q: What is a Personal Property Loan?

A loan that is secured by both real and personal property. The minimum ratio of personal to real property is set by law.

Q: What is a Piggyback Loan?

A loan made jointly by two or more lenders on the same property, under one mortgage or trust deed. A 90% loan, for example, may have one lender loaning 80% and another (subordinate) lender loaning the top 10% (high risk portion).

Q: What is a Planned Unit Development?

A subdivision of five or more individually owned lots with one or more other parcels owned in common, or with reciprocal rights in one or more other parcels.

Q: What is a Planning Commission?

A board of city, county, or local government that applies building guidelines and approves proposed building projects.

Q: What is a Point?

In financing, equal to 1%. When referring to mortgages or deeds of trust, the term is used to describe the percentage of discount rather than interest (for which the word "percent" is used). The points are paid by the seller in FHA and VA insured loans, and by either buyer or seller (or both) in conventional loans.

Q: What is a Power of Attorney?

An authority by which one person (principal) enables another (attorney) to act for that person. The result is an agency relationship.

Q: What is Power of Sale?

Clause in a mortgage or deed of trust giving the mortgagee or trustee the power to sell the property in the event of the default of the mortgagor, trustor (borrower).

Q: What is Prepayment Penalty?

A penalty contained in a promissory note, secured by a mortgage or deed of trust that is imposed when the loan is paid before it is due. Some states provide that prepayment of a portion of the loan may be made without penalty, provided the property securing the loan is a dwelling.

Q: What is Private Mortgage Insurance?

Insurance against a loss by a lender in the event of default by the borrower (mortgagor).

Q: What is a Promisee?

One to whom a promise has been made.

Q: What is a Promisor?

One who makes a promise.

Q: What is a Promissory Note?

A promise in writing and executed by the maker to pay a specified amount during a limited time, or on demand, or at sight, to a named person or to a bearer.

Q: What is Property Management?

The branch of the real estate business dealing with the management of property. The property can be a rented house, office complex, or large industrial development.

Q: What is a Property Management Agreement?

The contract between the owner and the property management company.

Q: What is Pro Rate?

To divide in proportionate shares, such as taxes, insurance, or rent, that the buyer and seller share at the time of closing or other agreed on time. For example, if the seller owns the property for nine months of the year, the seller's share of taxes for that year would be nine months while the buyer's share would be three months.

Q: What is a Purchase Agreement?

An agreement between buyer and seller of real property setting forth the price and terms of the sale.

Q: What is Purchase Money Mortgage?

(1) A mortgage given from buyer to seller to secure all or a portion of the purchase price. (2) Any mortgage from which the funds are used to purchase the property.

Q: What is a Quitclaim Deed?

A deed operating as a release, intended to pass any title, interest, or claim that the grantor (originator of the Quitclaim) may have in the property.

Q: What is a Rate Index?

An index used to adjust the interest rate of an adjustable mortgage. For example, the change in U.S. Treasury Securities (T-Bills) with a one year maturity may be used as a rate adjustor.

Q: What is Rate of Return?

The annual percentage return on investment in property.

Q: What is Raw Land?

Land in its natural state. Land that has not been subdivided.

Q: What is a Real Estate Board?

A board composed of regular members, real estate brokers and salespeople, and affiliate members (i.e., lenders), who come together for the purpose of furthering real estate in a particular area.

Q: What is a Real Estate License?

State license granted to broker and/or salesperson.

Q: What is Reconveyance?

An instrument used to transfer the title from a trustee to the equitable owner of real estate, when the title is held as collateral security for a debt. Most commonly used on payment in full of a trust deed.

Q: What is Reformation?

An action to correct a deed or other document that, through mistake or fraud, does not express the real agreement or intent of the parties.

Q: What is a Regional Shopping Center?

The largest type of shopping center, having one or more major department stores as so-called anchor tenants.

Q: What is Regulation Z?

Government regulation requiring that a credit purchaser be advised in writing of all costs connected with the credit portion of the purchase.

Q: What is Reinstatement?

Payment of a note, mortgage, deed of trust, etc. to cure a default and return to good standing.

Q: What is Real Estate Investment Trust (R.E.I.T.)?

A method of investing in real estate in a group with certain tax advantages.

Q: What is a Renegotiable Rate Mortgage?

A real property loan calling for an adjustment in the interest rate at a given time. For example, a loan with a 15-year amortization is adjusted to current rates after two years. The lender agrees to make the adjusted loan at the new rate as long as the old loan is not in default. The Federal Reserve Board allows the origination to be treated either as a balloon payment loan or a variable rate loan. However, points must be figured into the Annual Percentage Rate (A.P.R.) based on the time of renegotiation.

Q: What is Rescind?

To void or cancel in such a way as to treat the contract or other object of the rescission as if it never existed. To return the parties to their respective positions that existed prior to the signing of a contract.

Q: What is the Real Estate Settlement and Procedures Act (RESPA)?

A federal statute that requires disclosure of certain costs in the sale of residential (one to four units) properties.

Q: What is Resubdivision?

Subdividing an existing subdivision.

Q: What is a Safety Clause?

A clause in a listing agreement protecting the broker from having the buyer and seller wait until the listing agreement expires in order to consummate a transfer of the property in an attempt to avoid a commission that may be due the broker.

Q: What is a Sale-Leaseback?

A sale to a buyer and subsequent lease from that buyer back to the seller.

Q: What is a Sales Contract?

Another name for a sales agreement, purchase agreement, etc.

Q: What is Scope of Authority?

The authority of an agent to act for or contractually bind a principal. An agent may bind a principal when the agent not only has actual authority, but also implied or apparent authority.

Q: What is the Secondary Mortgage Market?

The buying and selling of first mortgages or trust deeds by banks, insurance companies, government agencies, and other mortgagees. This enables lenders to keep an adequate supply of money for new loans.

Q: What is a Second Mortgage?

A mortgage that ranks after a first mortgage in priority. Properties may have two, three, or more mortgages, deeds of trust, or land contracts, as liens at the same time. Legal priority determines whether they are called first, second, etc.

Q: What is a Selling Agent?

The real estate agent obtaining the buyer rather than the agent who lists the property. The listing and selling agent may, however, be one in the same. (See Dual Agency.)

Q: What is Separate Property?

Property owned by husband or wife in which the other has no legal ownership interest.

Q: What is a Set Back Ordinance?

Part of a zoning ordinance. Regulates the distance from the lot line to the point where improvements may be constructed.

Q: What is a Settlement Statement?

A statement prepared by a broker, escrow, or lender giving a complete breakdown of costs involved in a real estate sale.

Q: What is Shared Appreciation?

The gaining or retaining of equity in a property by someone other than the buyer. For example, the seller may retain a 25%

interest in the property. This makes the buyer responsible for 75% of the purchase price and, therefore, lowers the necessary financing by 25%. This obviously makes the property more affordable for the buyer. By agreement, expenses are shared as well as any increase in value when the property is sold.

Q: What is a Shopping Center?

A general term covering a number of types of clustered retail stores with common parking and ownership or management.

Q: What is a Short-Term Lease?

A general term, indicating a lease under five years in some states, under ten years in others.

Q: What is Simple Interest?

Interest computed on principal alone, as opposed to compound interest.

Q: What is a Slab?

(1) A concrete slab used as a floor and foundation in homes without a basement. (2) Any concrete floor, even if in an upper story.

Q: What is a Sole Proprietorship?

Individual ownership of a business as opposed to a partnership or corporation.

Q: What is a Standby Commitment?

A commitment to issue a loan, usually for a term of one to five years, after completion of construction, in the event a permanent loan cannot be found. The standby loan is usually at a higher interest rate than a permanent loan, and a standby fee is charged.

Q: What is the Statute of Frauds?

State laws requiring certain contracts to be in writing to be enforceable. All contracts for the sale of real property must be in writing to be enforceable. (A few exceptions do exist.)

Q: What is a Straight Note?

A promise to repay a loan, signed by the debtor and containing the date executed, amount, to whom, date due, rate of interest, and how it is payable. A straight note is not amortized.

Q: What are Street Improvement Bonds?

Interest bearing bonds issued by local government to secure assessments for street improvements. The owners of property assessed may pay in lump sum or pay installments on the bonds including interest.

Q: What is a Subcontractor?

One who works under a general contractor, such as a plumber, carpenter, or electrician.

Q: What is a Subdivision?

Commonly a division of a larger parcel(s) of land into smaller parcels (lots).

Q: What is a Subdivision Map?

The map submitted by a subdivider to the proper governmental authority for approval and subsequent recordation to establish a subdivision.

Q: What is a "Subject To" Clause?

A clause stating that the grantee takes the title "subject to" an existing mortgage as opposed to assuming the obligation. See Due-on-sale.

Q: What is a Substitution of Trustee?

A document that is recorded to change the trustee under a deed of trust.

Q: What are Surface Rights?

The rights to use the surface of land, including the right to drill or mine through the surface when subsurface rights are involved.

Q: What is a Take Out Loan?

The permanent, long-term financing of real estate after completion of construction.

Q: What is Tax Base?

The assessed valuation of real property, which is multiplied by the tax rate to determine the amount of tax due.

Q: What is a Tax Lien?

A lien for nonpayment of property taxes. Attaches only to the property on which the taxes are unpaid.

Q: What is Tenancy by the Entirety?

A form of ownership by husband and wife whereby each owns the entire property. In the event of the death of one, the survivor owns the property without probate.

Q: What is Tenancy in Common?

An undivided ownership in real estate by two or more persons or entities. The interests of each need to be specific but need not be equal. In the event of the death of one of the owners there is no right of survivorship. The portion of the property owned by the decedent passes to the decedent's heirs.

Q: What is a Tentative Map?

A map submitted by a subdivider to a planning commission for approval.

Q: What is a Thermal Window?

An insulating window of two panes of glass with air space between.

Q: What is a Third Party?

A general term that includes anyone not a party to a contract or agreement.

Q: What is "Time is of the Essence?"

Clause used in contracts to bind one party to performance at a specified time in order to bind the other party to performance.

Q: What is Time-Sharing?

A concept of ownership. The purchase of an undivided interest (usually in a resort area) for a fixed or variable time period.

Q: What is Title?

The evidence one has to right of ownership of land.

Q: What is Title Insurance?

Comprehensive indemnity contract to warrant against loss through certain defects in title to real estate or encumbrances or liens thereon.

Q: What is a Title Search?

A review of all recorded documents affecting a specific piece of property to determine the present condition of title.

Q: What is a Townhouse?

Originally a house in a city as opposed to a country estate. More recently, the term is applied to certain types of row houses, whether planned unit developments or condominiums.

Q: What is a Tract?

A parcel of land. In some states, synonymous with a subdivision.

Q: What is a Tract House?

A house built using the plan of the builder. Generally, the term refers to a large parcel being divided into many smaller lots upon which the builder/developer will construct several of the dwellings at one time, often duplicating a few of the dwellings.

Q: What are Trade Fixtures?

Personal property used in a business that is attached to the property, but removable on sale or termination of a lease as part of the business and not the real estate.

Q: What is Transfer Tax?

State tax on the transfer of real property.

Q: What is Treble Damages?

Three times the amount of actual damages. Awarded, when allowed by law, as a penalty.

Q: What is a Trust?

A fiduciary relationship under which one holds property (real or personal) for the benefit of another.

Q: What is a Trustee?

(1) One who holds title to real property under the terms of a deed of trust. (2) One who holds title to real or personal property pursuant to a written trust agreement (family trusts).

Q: What is a Trustee's Sale?

A sale at auction by a trustee under a deed of trust, pursuant to foreclosure proceedings.

Q: What is an Unconscionable Contract?

A contract so unfair to one of the parties to the agreement that a court will not allow it to be enforced.

Q: What is Unencumbered?

Free of liens and other encumbrances.

Q: What is Unimproved Land?

Most commonly land without buildings.

Q: What is Unincorporated Area?

An area that has not formed a municipal government (city).

Q: What is Unit Cost?

In relation to real estate, a cost per square foot.

Q: What is Unlawful Detainer?

The unjustifiable possession of property by one whose original entry was lawful but whose right to possession has terminated.

Q: What is an Unrecorded Instrument?

A document that may affect title to real property that is not recorded in the recorder's office. Therefore, the holder of it is not afforded protection under recording statutes. The document remains valid between the parties.

Q: What is Urban Renewal?

Razing and rebuilding of economically obsolete sections of cities through financing by federal, state, and local governments.

Q: What is Use Density?

The relationship of the number of buildings to a given land area.

Q: What is Usury?

Charging an illegal rate or amount of interest. Penalties for usury are criminal and civil in many states.

Q: What is a VA Escape Clause?

A clause stating that the buyer (borrower) shall not be obligated to buy, nor shall any deposit be lost if the appraisal is less than the agreed purchase price.

Q: What is a Variable Interest Rate?

An interest rate that fluctuates as the prevailing rate moves up or down. Also called "flexible interest rates."

Q: What is a Variance?

Excusing compliance with a portion of zoning requirements without permanently changing the zoning.

Q: What is Vested?

Present ownership rights, absolute and fixed.

Q: What are the Veteran's Administration (VA) Loans?

Housing loans to veterans by banks, savings and loans, and other lenders that are insured by the Veteran's Administration.

Q: What is a Voluntary Lien?

A lien placed against real property by the voluntary act of the owner. Most commonly, a mortgage, mechanic's lien or deed of trust.

Q: What is Warehousing?

The depositing of loans by a lender such as a mortgage company, in a bank, for sale at a later date. The mortgage company then borrows against these loans.

Q: What is a Warranty?

A legal, binding, promise given at the time of a sale, whereby the seller gives the buyer certain assurances as to the condition of the property being sold.

Q: What is a Warranty Deed?

A deed used in many states to convey free title to real property.

Q: What is "Wear and Tear?"

The deterioration or loss in value caused by the normal and reasonable use of the property. In leases, the tenant is not usually responsible for "normal wear and tear."

Q: What is Without Recourse?

A finance term. A mortgage or deed of trust securing a note without recourse allows the lender to look only to the security (property) for repayment in the event of default, and not personally to the borrower. Some states do not allow secured purchase money obligations to be enforced personally against the borrower (anti-deficiency legislation).

Q: What is a Wrap-Around Mortgage?

A second (or junior) mortgage with a face value including both the amount it secures and the balance due under the first mortgage. The mortgagee under the wrap-around collects a payment based on its face value and then pays the first mortgagee. It is most effective when the first mortgage has a lower interest rate than the second, since under the wrap-around the mortgagor may obtain a lower rate than if refinancing.

Q: What is a Zero Lot Line?

The construction of a structure on any of the boundary lines of a lot.

Q: What is a Zero Side Yard?

The building of a subdivision with each house built on a side boundary line. This gives more usable yard space on narrow lots. An easement for maintenance is given over a portion of the lot adjoining each house.

Q: What is a Zone?

An area in which the use of the land is restricted by law (zoning ordinance).

Q: What is Zoning?

The division of a city or county by legislative regulations into areas (zones), specifying the uses allowable for the real property in those areas.

Q: What is a Zoning Map?

A map of the community showing the zones of permitted use under zoning ordinances.

Q: What is a Zoning Variance?

See Variance.

8

Pitfalls—How to Avoid Them

Buying real estate can involve more pitfalls than purchasing a brand name CD player from a streetcorner vendor. It can also lead to legal and IRS problems, as well.

Q: What guidelines must investors follow when executing a commercial real estate exchange?

Commercial real estate exchanges enable investors to defer paying taxes on the gains from the sale. Investors, however, must be sure to follow specific guidelines when utilizing the exchange. Those guidelines were established in a landmark decision (and case) called "The Starker Case."

The Starker family had owned property in the northwestern part of the United States, and over a long period of time they had purchased and consolidated some of the finest timber land in the country. The land had been in the family for years, but one day a prominent lumber company made an offer the Starkers could not refuse. They agreed to sell, but knowing they would face a heavy tax burden they negotiated an unusual transaction that they believed would help them defer their tax liability to the IRS.

Instead of taking cash for the land, the lumber company agreed to find equivalent valued properties—that met the Starker's specifications—acquire them, and then transfer the land to the Starker's estate. No cash involved. Instead, a nice simple exchange, and an excellent way to defer taxes—at least the Starkers and the lumber company thought so.

The Starkers agreed to the arrangement, conveyed their land to the lumber company, and during the next five years the Starkers searched, found equivalent properties, had the lumber company purchase them, and the company then transferred the land to the family. It did not take long before the IRS found out about the deal and entered the case. Not to everyone's surprise, the IRS maintained taxes were due on the transfer of the Starker's land to the lumber company, because it was not a simultaneous exchange. In other words, the sale and exchange did not take place at the same time. In fact, argued the IRS, five years was anything but simultaneous.

The case was argued in court and eventually the Starkers prevailed on all but one segment of the transaction. The ruling in favor of the family was based on one fact: the Starkers never received or had access to cash from the transfer of their property to the lumber company. That was the key. The ruling was important to real estate investors for several reasons. Aside from the no cash aspect, the concept of "delayed exchange" was recognized. In other words, a buyer and seller did not have to simultaneously exchange properties to defer taxation. There could be a delay between the exchanges. However, the IRS has subsequently modified its code to permit a delayed exchange of the Starker type.

Q: How long can an investor take to make the exchange to defer capital gains taxes in a commercial real estate transaction?

Today, investors have 45 calendar days from the transfer of title on the property they have disposed of in which to locate and identify the replacement property, and a total of six months in which to acquire title to the replacement property from the transfer of title on the property of which they have disposed. One day more and the transaction will fail to qualify as an exchange and, of course, the gain becomes taxable.

Q: To whom should investors go for advice on commercial real estate exchanges?

Real estate can be a complex issue, and when buyers are dealing with potential legal and tax problems they should consult a real estate attorney and/or certified public accountant.

Q: Should investors consult a real estate broker or a sales associate in determining the rules on commercial exchanges?

It is possible, but not advisable. There are many brokers and sales associates who are very familiar with the so-called "1031 exchange," but the wise investor plays it safe and goes to the proper professional before entering into an agreement to exchange properties. In other words, seek the advice of a real estate attorney or certified public accountant.

Q: What investment rules should investors keep in mind when evaluating real estate?

Do not let greed and trust enter the transaction. First, do not be greedy; nobody gives you something for nothing. And, second, do not trust anyone. Make sure everything is in writing and you read it—at least twice, and understand what you have read. The ultimate objective is to achieve a profit—not a loss.

Q: What clues should investors look for when trying to find the best "deal" possible?

The best deals are not always the most obvious. Sound investments do not always come out of nowhere and hit you on the head. Most of the time, you have to look. Residential investors should always be watching for "distress" sales. The astute investor investigates the seller's financial situation. Do they need to sell? Is the clothes closet half-empty—an indication that one spouse has left the home and the other must sell.

Experienced investors do not buy the first property that looks good. They do "comparative shopping." They check the price and compare it with others in the area. They investigate the market. Have properties been moving? What is appreciation like? If properties have not been moving and appreciation is insignificant, why is the seller trying to sell the property? Is the seller under pressure to sell quickly? Divorced? Has there been a death in the family and the surviving spouse does not want to live in the house any longer? Is there a job transfer involved? Do they have to travel more than an hour to work at the new position? Has the seller (or seller's spouse) lost a job by firing or discharge?

If the seller falls into one of these categories, there is a good chance the property can be purchased at below market price, especially in a slow market. But if the investor does not fall into one of those classifications, ask some questions. More than one investor has run into a situation in which a nearby, vacant piece of land is about to be developed into a garbage dump, state prison, or something equally undesirable.

Q: How should investors act when shopping and negotiating?

Do not get emotionally involved. In other words, never show emotions over the property or price. Be sure—if you take a partner along—to settle your differences before (or after) the inspection of the property with the owner—never during.

Do not argue over or praise the property. Buyers are more adroit at purchasing a $15,000 automobile than they are at buying a $250,000 property. They reveal less to the used car salesman than they do to the IRS. But put them next to an agent who is taking them through a property, and for some reason many will reveal even the most intimate details about their resources. That is a definite mistake. A salesperson who knows what you have and where it is coming from is in a position to maneuver for the sale.

Second, if the salesperson discovers a buyer is enthused about a property, it puts the agent in the driver's seat for negotiating. One of the best policies to follow if there are two buyers is establish groundrules and do not make positive comments about the property in front of the agent or if that is not possible, have only one buyer (the silent member) go through the property. The more buyers talk, the more they reveal, and the weaker their position. Good negotiators never have all their cards face up.

Q: What is the true goal of the real estate salesperson?

Good real estate salespeople get the investor in an answering mode. They ask questions. Where did you go to school? Did you graduate from college? Have you taken any other courses? Are you married? How many children? Before long the agent knows everything there is to know, including how much cash is available and what the investors think of the property. Your objective should be to get the real estate agent talking. When they do the talking, you learn.

Q: What are the advantages of being honest with a real estate salesperson?

If you expect agents to be able to assist you, you cannot mislead them by responding untruthfully to their inquiries. Either answer truthfully or decline to answer. You want to supply them with accurate information regarding the size and price of the investment you are interested in acquiring.

This does not mean you should reveal personal feelings, etc., which give the salesperson a clue as to your "soft spots," or weaknesses. Overall, the agents want to do their best for you because they want recommendations from you as to friends and associates. They also want you to have pleasant memories of the purchasing experience so that you will think of them when it comes time to list and sell the property.

Q: Which property is usually the best investment—the sharpest, mid-range, or "bottom of the line"?

Obviously, every investor wants to purchase the best looking property in an area at the cheapest price. In most cases, buyers are able to purchase the most attractive property, but they find they have to pay fair market value for it. The sharpest property usually carries the highest price tag. Investors do not have to purchase the top property to generate a solid return on their investment. The best approach is to stay away from the sharpest property. (There are, of course, exceptions, but, for the most part the best looking property is going to cost the most.) Instead, stay in the mid-range; pick a property in the area that is between the top and bottom of the line. An investor who stays in the mid-range will find that the property will appreciate (from a percentage standpoint) just as much—if not more—than the high-priced property.

At the same time, stay away from the rock bottom priced properties. They are usually priced lower for a reason, and usually the cause of the lower price will not go away. A corner property, one on a busier street, or with a shorter driveway is worth less because of the inconvenience. Buying that property will take less capital, but it will appreciate less. The key is to carefully investigate an area, tract, or development before you buy. If you can, rent first and become familiar with the area in which you intend to invest.

Q: Can properties be evaluated by square footage (in other words, the bigger the more costly)?

Do not buy strictly on the basis of square footage, either. Some investors divide the price by the square footage and determine exactly how much they are paying per square foot. They compare the next house the same way. To compare houses in adjacent areas (or even in the same tract) by evaluating square footage can be a mistake. There are too many other factors to consider—location within the tract (i.e., cul-de-sac or busy corner) and proximity to good schools—that are much more important.

Q: Do auctions really offer good values?

Rarely. Every buyer, of course, is always looking for a bargain and some have mistaken certain economic signals as the basis for one. For example, toward the end of 1989, real estate began slowing in almost every area of the country. Numerous builders were caught with unsold homes and mounting interest payments. In an effort to move these properties, so-called auctions were developed. To most, these auctions appeared to be the perfect way to invest and get the property at a below-market cost. In theory, that sounds nice, but in reality it does not always happen.

You can get a good buy at an auction if you are willing to work. You must thoroughly investigate the conditions which existed prior to the property being offered at an auction. Compare the subject property with comparable properties in the community. Determine the value of the property being auctioned and do not bid over that amount. Do not get caught in a bidding war.

Auctions have simply become a marketing tool for builders. The use of the term auction suggests to many investors that they will be offered a bargain. That does not usually happen because of the way the auction has been designed. Usually, there is a floor or bottom bid on a property that will be accepted. That bottom bid may be exactly the price the builder has been asking all along. Investigate, be informed.

In other words, a builder may have constructed a tract of 25 homes valued at $250,000 to $275,000. Sales open and five of the properties are sold. Suddenly, a plant in the area lays off 1,000 workers and buyers become cautious. The builder is paying interest on a construction loan to the bank. The builder may have borrowed 80 to 90% of the fair market value of the property and interest payments are mounting daily. If the homes are held too long the builder may go bankrupt. The marketing tool: an auction.

The builder calls in a professional real estate auction firm. (In fact, during the slowdown that started in 1989, many real estate companies formed "auction subsidiaries" to handle these problem tracts.) The builder and auctioneer decide on a minimum acceptable bid per property. That minimum for the $250,000 home may actually be $250,000. For the $275,000, it may be $275,000. On the other hand, the property may be offered at the auction for several thousand dollars below the builder's original prices. Is this a bargain? Only your comparison shopping will reveal whether the builder had the property overpriced or if the auction price is a bargain.

If no one bids the minimum, the property will not be sold. A week before the auction, there is an advertising blitz sponsored by the builder. The idea is to generate a good crowd because it takes a crowd to create excitement and enthusiasm—two ingredients needed for a successful auction. If the auctioneer is able to generate the minimum bids, the properties are sold. Under few circumstances, however, are the properties sold for less than the minimum that has been established.

Q: Where might buyers find potential bargains aside from fixer-uppers?

There are often bargains in new tracts. Some builders pressed by lenders reduce prices, offer extras at no cost, or a buydown. The buydown refers to a fee that could amount to hundreds or thousands of dollars that the developer/builder will pay to the lender to provide a lower interest rate loan, which, of course, is going to result in lower monthly payments for the buyer. Usually, the buydown is for the first five years of the loan, then the interest rate increases—as does the monthly payment. It has become another marketing tool for those in the industry to utilize.

Q: What physical attributes reveal what a property is really worth?

It is important to compare the condition of residential areas, especially if there are price differentials in adjacent tracts with similar homes. Buyers should study the maintenance of each area. Are the streets, parks, driveways, and front yards well-groomed or are they deteriorating? Do the properties need paint, or do the owners keep the exteriors in good shape. Properties down the street and in an adjacent tract will impact the value of anything nearby.

Q: Why is it advisable to get to know an area when it comes to real estate investment?

Wherever you decide to buy, get to know the area. Aside from touring the area and checking schools and ratings, real estate brokers can be a significant help in answering questions about the area. Check with brokers outside the area as well. Although many do not market properties in the community, they may know something about it and, often, can be more objective than a broker or salesperson who is trying to market a property within the area. When you know the area, you know the pitfalls.

Q: What is a "bad front door" and how does it impact an invest-ment?

This is where a tract or gated community is adjacent to a rundown area. To get to the community, you must go through this section. Although the adjacent housing may be separated by a gate and wall from the complex, it will still impact the value of the homes. Builders know this and they often try to conceal bad front doors by constructing another street or entrance into the community. Investors should not just examine the primary entrance. They should examine all access routes to the property, and travel around the development and study the surrounding properties. If there is an undesirable area or access they will discover it.

Q: What are some of the drawbacks of gated communities?

Gated communities are frequently sold to investors because buyers believe they offer prestige and protection from outside intruders. Although this may be true in some instances, buyers should remember the drawbacks of these gated developments. Property owners own—and must maintain—a variety of things within the enclosed community such as streets, recreation areas, pools, tennis courts, or any other amenities within the gates. The fees to maintain these facilities are generated through home-owner association dues, assessments, and fees that can be signifi-cant. A $100 a month fee may be affordable for a buyer today, but what if it were raised or doubled in 10 years? With a higher fee would the property be that appealing to other investors if you wanted to sell it?

Q: What is the problem with all-electric homes?

The utility bill in the winter may exceed the mortgage pay-ment. All-electric homes, which were a fad a number of years back because of electrical cleanliness, can turn into a black hole for an investor's money. And as energy costs increase, the cost of electricity is rising faster than the cost of gas and remains expensive in most areas.

Q: What risks do buyers run when they purchase homes that are in the 15- to 20-year-old age bracket?

Homes that are somewhere between 15 and 20 years old may be in need of new pipes, especially if the old ones are galvanized. Watch out for properties with water softeners and galvanized pipes. That is a deadly combination and, after 15–20 years, re-plumbing is usually required.

Flush toilets, turn on all the taps, put plugs in sockets, open the windows, and turn on the lights. A window that will not open may be the signal of a more significant problem such as a wall that has shifted. Examine the utility bills for insight into what heating and air conditioning costs you may expect.

Q: What is the main problem with home warranties?

Most of the time the exclusions are designed to cover the things about which you are most concerned. A buyer who is interested in the warranty should check the exclusions, which are usually in small print.

Q: What should be kept in mind when evaluating a time share?

The restrictions on when you can use it, and the difficulty of selling these properties may outweigh the ownership advantages. Time shares are popular, but they are atypical real estate investments.

Q: Is real estate a long- or short-term investment?

Investors should not consider property as a short-term (less than five year) commitment. Be aware of the cycles and the fact that real estate is not the kind of venture that always offers a quick, six or seven month turnaround. Plan to hold the property. That is when the payoff starts to become significant.

Q: What protection is there for the commercial property buyer?

Although residential properties can have numerous pitfalls for the buyer, commercial/investment properties have even more. In most states, there is little legislation to protect the investor and disclosure laws frequently do not apply. For the commercial/investment buyer, it remains "caveat emptor," or buyer beware.

Q: What are some of the problems that limited partnerships can pose for investors?

With projects that have 35 or more investors (a partnership or association of investors), the department of corporations (in most states), department of real estate, or some other government agency dictates what can and must be disclosed to investors. Investors should carefully examine the prospectus, and look for some of the key words. For example, the regulating agency normally requires a number of "red flag" or precautionary statements to be included in the prospectus.

Unfortunately, many investors fail to read and appreciate these statements, although they may be printed in red. For instance, investors should watch for statements such as "this project is being developed on expansive soil" or "investors should be apprised that this project may require additional capital." Either of those statements is a warning that is really saying to investors "check this project out carefully before you put your money into it." But many investors fail to heed these "red" printed warnings because of their trust, enthusiasm for the project, and, of course, greed.

Q: What is the importance of excess capital when it comes to investing in a commercial venture?

Capitalization is extremely important. Buying on a shoestring leaves the door open for problems. If every dime has been sunk into a building, what happens if a plumbing or electrical problem develops? With residential purchases, a buyer can live with a broken light fixture or other needed repair. But when you own commercial property, tenants will not tolerate below par maintenance. Repairing damage or fixing problems immediately determines how viable an investment can be. Delays lead to people withholding rents, breaking leases and moving, or potential tenants leasing in another property. Additionally, they also spread the "word" about the building and can kill any pending leases. That is why excess capital is critical. Investment groups should keep several thousand dollars in a fund for maintenance and/or other contingencies.

Q: What clues do maintenance records give buyers?

Maintenance records give buyers an excellent idea as to the possible condition of the building. For example, are needed repairs being put off? If so, the problem is only going to grow and what might have been a minor expenditure can turn into a major cost. Highly leveraged properties leave little room for mistakes. They are also difficult to finance and banks will charge premiums for loans of this type. The more money down the better interest rate and the easier the investors can breathe.

Q: How is the return on investment determined with commercial investments?

In commercial investments, it is based on how much actual cash you are investing and how much actual cash you are taking out. A building that requires a $50,000 down payment and returns $25,000 a year in spendable income provides an extraordinary return (50% on your cash investment). But a $1 million purchase that requires $300,000 in invested capital and returns a spendable income of $10,000 a year provides an extremely poor (3.3%) return on your cash investment. An investor may be better off putting funds in a certificate of deposit. Analyze the return.

Q: What are the riskiest and least risky commercial ventures and why?

There is a pyramid of risk when it comes to commercial investment. Generally, the riskiest can be the strip center, and the investment with the least risk is the industrial complex. The strip center may be frequented by under capitalized and inexperienced retailers who are here today and gone tomorrow. If an investor is purchasing a strip location, they should be aware of the problems pizza parlors and donut shops create. Certainly, they may be stable clients but once they move in the odors they create may remain in the center forever.

Parking within the center can be a massive problem. The center that has just enough spaces to accommodate three or four automobiles per store will have definite problems if one of the businesses is a pizza parlor, restaurant, beauty shop, or other retail outlet where consumers may use the parking facilities for an hour or more.

The industrial center, on the other hand, usually requires only four walls and a roof until a lease is signed and tenant improvements are agreed on. These centers have the advantage of being leased to manufacturers and other long-term, more stable tenants. Improvements should be amortized and built into the cost of the initial term of the lease for each tenant.

Q: What role does image play in commercial investment?

Industrial centers—like strip centers—have images. Is the industrial complex automotive or high tech? Grease or computer chips? The image not only shapes the tenants but the future of the development. Investors should be wary of the office complex image, too. The complex that houses a well-known branch of a bank, group of attorneys, or accountants normally will continue to attract that type of clientele. By not planning the tenant mixture, investors make a grave mistake. The complex should be targeted at a specific group. For example, doctors tend to locate where other physicians are grouped. The same is true of other professions.

Q: What are "as is" plans and why are they important?

Plumbing and electrical wiring may not be where the original plans indicate; however, "as is" plans show any variations from the original approved blueprints. Without the "as is" plans in hand, investors and their partners may find themselves spending countless dollars to repair walls and replace other structural elements that were removed, but would not have been if accurate plans were available. For example, a water line shown in the original plans to be located six feet from the floor in a wall might be shown in the "as built" plans as being located six inches from the ceiling, because the plans were modified to allow for a future door to be cut through the wall.

Q: What disadvantage does a limited partner have in an investment?

The limited partners are much like shareholders of a corporation and have little or no say in the operation or management of the project. The general partners are in control.

Q: What precautions should an investor who is thinking about getting involved in a limited partnership take?

If the partnership is going to purchase an existing building, investors should scrutinize the past performance of the general partners, check the location, and inspect the leases. If, however, the partnership is planning to develop its own commercial development, the investor should ask the following key questions: Who is going to build it? What is their track record? Are there tenants slated for the center? Have they agreed to move in? Have they signed leases? How well capitalized is the partnership? How strong are the potential tenants? Who is the lender? How flexible are they? Has the partnership dealt with the lender before? Is there, in fact, a need for the development?

Q: Is there a problem with leases that are executed by potential tenants before a center or development is built?

Many times a lender will request that the partnership present duly executed leases for a portion of the building before the lender will make the construction loan. It is not uncommon to find partnerships obtaining the required leases but, all too frequently, the prospective tenants have no intention of fulfilling their obligation to move in. These tenants are simply "doing the developer a favor" in executing the leases, thereby enabling the developer to obtain the necessary construction loan.

At other times, the prospective tenant will sign a "letter of intent" expressing serious intention of becoming a tenant on completion of the project. This, obviously, is not a binding agreement to lease and is of little or no value.

Q: What guidance does a market study provide for the investor when it comes to commercial investment?

The marketing study is normally requested by the bank to verify that there is in fact "need" for the proposed development. Smart builders do not start constructing a project until there is a need. For instance, if a builder is going to construct an office complex, the actual building should not start until there is evidence that a shortage in office space is developing. Although vacancy rates will vary from area to area, building cycles are generally not triggered until there is approximately a 10% vacancy rate. Another indicator is the number of "for rent" signs. When it becomes obvious that "for rent" signs are rapidly disappearing, it is an indicator that additional space may soon be needed. All this takes investigation and research.

Q: What is the building cycle, why should it be tracked, and what implications does it have for investment?

The building cycle is easily tracked and highly predictable. At the beginning of a recession, there is usually construction; however, as soon as the builders see the economic slowdown, they cease new construction. It is not until builders see the community coming out of the downcycle that they start construction again. Prospective investors should not just take the word of a general partner or a market study. They should tour the area and talk to real estate licensees. They should also be talking to bankers in the community. It is the bankers who ultimately have to lend the funds for construction, and often they have an excellent view of the market, the demand, and vacancy rate.

Q: How do property usage and location tie in when it comes to investment?

Obviously, the viability of any real estate investment depends on location, and every location can be analyzed and judged based on its projected usage. A strip center needs foot traffic. An office that is aimed at attorneys needs proximity to a courthouse. A medical office center should be close to a hospital.

An industrial complex should be near freeways, expressways, rail, or other transportation. In addition, an available supply of labor is a key requirement. Every development should have a reason for being built and there should be evidence that it will be economically viable.

Q: What is meant by "spreading the risk" in real estate?

Investors should divide resources into various investments. In other words, instead of putting everything into one apartment house or office complex, why not invest in five different properties in five different geographic areas.

For example, instead of investing $50,000 of your available funds into one apartment building, invest in five single residences in five different geographic areas that might require $10,000 apiece. Spreading the investment affords some protection. For instance, if investors put all their money into an apartment and rent control is suddenly approved, they may have impaired future incomes. But, if they invest in five different properties in five different areas, rent control in one of those communities will not impact the others. Eighty percent of the total investment is still protected.

Q: What problems are there for investors when it comes to legal agreements?

Real estate agreements are designed to avoid court conflicts, however, many investors sign contracts without realizing their actual commitment. For instance, even simple clauses in contracts can cause problems. Astute investors always consult a real estate attorney before signing any agreement. They do not take anything on face value.

Q: How can investors save money when it comes to a bond or assessment that is on the property that they are thinking of buying?

When investors purchase property they should examine the property tax bill to see if there is a lien—in the form of a bond or assessment—placed on it. Most bonds and assessments are assumable, but buyers may be able to save considerable money in future monthly/annual payments if they can persuade the seller to pay off the bond when negotiating the purchase and sale agreement.

Q: What are property rights, and what are some of the misconceptions about them?

Property rights are the right of one or more persons to possess and use property. This right may extend to an individual, partnership, corporation, or other association of persons. One can own a "property right" without owning the property. For example, the lease. A leasee does not own the property, but does have the right to occupy the property, which is a "property right."

Q: What misconceptions are there about holding title?

Two of the major misconceptions about holding title to real property involve married couples. Usually, married couples select joint tenancy as the form of ownership. Simply stated, joint tenancy provides for two or more people to create a right of survivorship by holding title to property as joint tenants. Interests must be equal among the co-owners and may be sold, gifted, or deeded during an individual owner's lifetime. However, an owner may not dispose of a joint tenancy interest by a written Will because the survivor(s) automatically acquires the decedent's interest at the moment of death. The bequest contained in the Will will be of no effect.

Community property, in community property states, applies to all property acquired by a husband and/or wife during marriage, unless the acquired property was a gift or inheritance. (When received by gift or inheritance, the property remains the separate property of the recipient.)

Although joint and community sound similar, they have radically different tax ramifications on the death of a spouse. Today, there is no reason for married couples to vest title in property in anything other than community property. It offers similar advantages as joint tenancy, however, when it comes to tax issues the community property has significant advantages. This is the reason all investors, particularly those who are married, should consult an attorney or CPA prior to deciding how they intend to hold title to their purchase.

Q: What is the family or living trust?

This is another vesting vehicle that is becoming popular. The object of the family trust is to avoid lengthy probate, court costs, and legal fees should one of the property owners die. It can also be an effective tax avoidance planning tool.

Typically, when an owner dies the owner's estate, including real property, passes through a probate procedure to the heirs, unless the property is held in joint tenancy and, in many states, if it is held as community property. This usually requires a minimum of six months and it can take up to several years depending on the complexity of the estate. The costs of the probate process can be considerable, since the attorney's fees are normally calculated as a percentage of the total estate that is being distributed through the probate process.

With the family trust, the property owners transfer title to themselves as trustees of the family trust. They can place a great majority of the assets they own in the trust, ranging from personal property and rental properties to their own residence. The "successor" trustee (or trustees) is normally empowered to act on behalf of the trust should one (or both) of the property owners die. The owners, however, do not lose control of their property during their lifetime by putting it into the family trust because the owners usually appoint themselves as the original trustees. If, however, the owners who formed the trust fail to transfer title of a particular property to the trustees of the trust, it could be necessary to put those properties excluded through probate. Obviously, the creation of the family trust should be handled by an attorney. Avoid the "do it yourself" method. An improperly prepared and implemented family trust can have disastrous consequences, increase tax liability and probate costs, and create extensive delays. In the area of family trusts and estate planning the quote 'he who acts as his own attorney has a fool for a client' is particularly applicable.

Q: What does it cost to create the family trust?

The cost for creating the family trust and requisite wills will be somewhere between $600 and $2,500, depending on the complexity and how much the standard agreements are altered to fit the needs of the client. Shop around and get quotes. This expense may seem high, but without a family trust, on death, the probate of a $200,000 estate will run into significant expense.

Q: Whenever possible, what type of guarantee should commercial property owners seek from those who are leasing?

Owners should demand the personal guarantees of the principal owners or partners on leases whenever possible. Even though the business entity you intend to lease your property to has been around for some time and appears to be well managed, if the entity is not financially sound it can go bankrupt and your lease is worthless. From a property owner's standpoint, one unfortunate consequence of a default on a lease is the property may have been altered or customized to meet the defaulting leasee's needs, and it may be difficult to rent the modified property without further significant alterations. More than one owner has remodeled a property for a tenant with unusual needs and found that once the tenant vacates, the building as remodeled is virtually useless to another tenant.

Q: What impact does a personal guarantee have on a lease?

Obtaining personal guarantees from tenants (versus having the entities guarantee it) is additional assurance the rent will be paid. The value of a personal guarantee of a principal is obviously limited by that person's financial net worth. Of course, in a difficult economic environment, where there is an abundance of space available, owners may have difficulty obtaining personal guarantees.

Q: What important role does the accommodator and/or facilitator play in an exchange?

The financial strength of these individuals and their companies should be thoroughly investigated since the facilitator actually holds title to the property and the proceeds of the sale of the property that is being exchanged. The replacement property is transferred from the seller to the facilitator and is then transferred to the owner. A facilitator with poor financial strength can cause untold problems for a buyer during an exchange. Make sure the facilitator deposits all funds from the property being exchanged in an interest-bearing trust account for your benefit.

Q: How can investors protect themselves from environmentally unsafe properties, or lawsuits stemming from these problems?

Investors should make sure they are not purchasing a parcel of land or a building that is going to require toxic cleanup. If, for instance, you own property onto which someone dumped toxic materials five years ago, the law may require you to clean it up because of your ownership interest—even though you did not own the property at that time.

Another way to protect yourself is to check the chain of title of the property you are considering purchasing. See who owned the property in the past. ABC, Inc. may not reveal much, but Standard Oil or Union 76 appearing as a prior owner may indicate the property use may have involved petroleum or petroleum-distilled (gas station) products that may have leaked into the ground, and were concealed by the subsequent construction of a building. The fact the building is now in place does not alter the environmental concerns and legal problems that could emerge should you invest in the property.

Q: What is meant by "joint and several" liability in real estate?

Collective and individual liability. This means that someone who was only 1% responsible for a problem can be 100% responsible for the liability. For example, if XX and XYZ company engaged in an activity that caused a toxic waste problem on a piece of property that XYZ owned, the court could hold both responsible for the cleanup. If XX owned only 1% of the property and XYZ owned the other 99% it would not make any difference, they would both be liable for the cleanup. Naturally, XX and XYZ would argue as to who would have to clean up what. Normally, you would expect the company that owned 99% of the land (and was 99% responsible) to pay for 99% of the cleanup. But suppose XYZ company goes bankrupt and is without funds. Who pays then? In the court's view, there is no question—it is XX, the major Fortune 500 company. Although they were only 1% responsible and 1% owner, liability is "joint and several." They are liable for the entire bill.

Under the theory of strict liability, there is no requirement to prove how the soil contamination occurred. All the government need prove is that you owned the property at the time the incident took place, or are now the owner. Once contamination is found, the owner is liable for the cleanup. The owner may have the right to bring a suit against the person who actually contaminated the soil to recover all or a portion of the cost of the cleanup. This does not release the owner of the duty to clean the property up—now. On the other hand, the lawsuit the owner files against a previous owner may take years to be concluded. That is one reason owners should be particularly careful, especially when it comes to industrial property, about who is leasing it and what does their use (or the prior use) entail.

Q: How can the law impact lenders when it comes to environmental real estate issues?

The long arm of the law extends to lenders. Take, for instance, the investor who purchases a $1 million property and obtains a $700,000 loan. The investor's interest is actually only $300,000, the amount of the cash down payment that was made at the time of purchase. Now, suppose toxic waste is found on the property. The cleanup will cost $2 million, or $1 million more than the property is worth. The investor may throw up his hands and say "I give up . . . take the property back. I'm not about to spend another $2 million to clean it up. I can't afford it."

If the lender forecloses, it may suddenly find itself (and all assets) at risk. The government can say "clean it up." Lenders are familiar with these new legal interpretations, and they have become cautious about supplying funds for properties because of them. A lender may require the investor and title company to go back 50 years (or more) to determine who owned the land in an attempt to discover the historical use of the property. They want to avoid toxic problems at all cost. In some states, the lender can foreclose on the property through the judicial system and obtain a judgment against the owner/borrower for any loss they sustain. In these states, the owner/borrower's risk of loss can actually exceed the initial investment. Know the laws of the state where you purchase real property.

Q: Can real estate be a "get-rich-quick" scheme?

Real estate is not a get-rich-quick scheme. Despite what some of the "no money downers" and other similar marketers proclaim, real estate is like any other business—it takes work, study, concentration, and the exercise of good sound judgment to be successful. Few buy a property one day and sell it the next for a profit. Those are tales for fiction novels and motion pictures. It has and can happen (just as winning the lottery is a possibility), but not with the frequency one would like to believe. It is the exception, rather than the rule.

To many, however, real estate ownership can be the fulfillment of the great American Dream. And, for those who remember the rules and guidelines and how to play the game, real estate investment will not only be the answer to their dreams, but the opportunity for true financial independence.

Index

Grantee, 218
Grantor, 218
Gross income, 218
Gross income multiplier, 218
Growing Equity Mortgage (G.E.M.), 219
 See also Mortgage

Hard money mortgage, 219 *See also* Mortgage
Heat pump, 12
High-risk returns, 61
Home inspector, 144
Homeowners' association, 219
Home protection plans, 173
Homes, all electric, 20, 262; electric, 24
Homestead, 219; declaration of, 211
Home warranties, 144–145
Home warranty insurance, 220
Hypothecate, 220

Idem sonans, 220
Implied contract, 220
Impound account, 220
Income approach, 220
Incumbrance, 220–221 *See also* Encumbrance
Indexing, 221
In perpetuity, 221
Installment, contract, 221; sale, 221
Insurance, private mortgage, 235
Insured mortgage, 221 *See also* Mortgage
Interest, extra note, 221; included note, 222; only, 222; rate cap, 222 *See also* Mortgage
Internal Revenue Service (IRS), 163, 181, 253–254, 257
Interpleader, 222
Investment, "forcing the," 103; potential, 10; return on, 73–74, 265; "working backward," 98
Involuntary Lien, 222 *See also* Lien

Joint protection policy, 223; tenancy, 223; tenants, 223
Judicial foreclosure, 223; nonjudicial, 230
Jumbo VA loan, 223 *See also* Loan
Junior mortgage, 223 *See also* Mortgage

K-Mart, 8, 56

Land, contract, 223–224; "land's best use," 69; vacant, 18

Landlocked parcel, 224
Land patent, 224 *See also* Patent
Late charge, 224
Latent defect, 224
Lease, length of, 11; option to purchase, 224–225; short-term, 11
Leasehold, improvements, 224; interest, 224
Legal description, 225
Leverage, 132
Liability, 53; collective and individual, 275; joint and several, 275
Liber, 225
Lien, 225; federal tax, 215; involuntary, 222; mechanics, 24, 59
Limited partnerships, 53, 59, 61, 63–65; precautions of, 268; problems of, 264 *See also* Partnerships
Liquidated damages, 174–177
"Lis pendens," 59, 225
Listing agent, 225
Loan, accelerating, 196; accepting, 147; appel, 196; assuming, 147; construction, 87; G.I., 217; jumbo va, 223; origination fee, 225; package, 226; personal property, 233; Piggyback, 233; veteran's administration, 218
Location, 80; selection, 88
Los Angeles, 28

McDonald's, 3
Maintenance fee, 226
Malls, auto, 4; fast-food, 5; (mini) ingress, 7; (mini) egress, 7
Management, 13; certified property (cpm), 210; fee, 56; professional, 76–77; property, 106–107
Market, price, 226; value approach, 226
Marshall Fields, 8
Massachusetts, 38
Master plan, 81, 226
Materials, exterior, 15
Mechanics lien, 24, 59, 226–227 *See also* Lien
Mets and bounds, 227
Midwest, property, 35
Misrepresentation, 227
Mission Viejo, 83
Month-to-month tenancy, 227
Mortgage, 227; adjustable, 193; blanket, 202; certificate backed, 207; chattel, 207; fixed-rate, 39; growing equity, 219; hard